EZRA POUND

The portrait of Ezra Pound as a young man
is reproduced by gracious permission of Mrs. Drusilla Lodge,
of Madison, Indiana.

EZRA POUND

Poet as Sculptor

DONALD DAVIE

OXFORD UNIVERSITY PRESS

New-York

Copyright © 1964 by Donald Davie
Library of Congress Catalogue Card Number: 64-24860
First published by Oxford University Press, New York, 1964
First issued as an Oxford University Press paperback, 1968
Printed in the United States of America

ACKNOWLEDGMENTS

It is dispiriting to have to admit that the study of Ezra Pound's writings, if it has moved out of the pioneering stage, has only just done so. At any rate anyone who now offers to write about Pound cannot but be aware of how much he is indebted to previous students who have broken the ground. I have attempted in footnotes to acknowledge my debts to these pioneers, but I am under a more particular obligation to one of them, Hugh Kenner, for *The Poetry of Ezra Pound*. To George Dekker, the author of *Sailing After Knowledge*, I am indebted not only for information collected in that book, and discussions therein, but also for conversations about Pound which have taken place intermittently over the last six or seven years. Some of the material of Chapter VII first appeared in rather different form in *The Twentieth Century*, and I am obliged to the editor of that journal, as also to Mr. Adrian Stokes for information by which I was able to check and confirm the findings of the argument there conducted. I am grateful in a similar way to the editor of *Irish Writing* for printing much of what now appears as Chapter XII. Some pages of Chapter VI derive immediately from conversations with J.H. Prynne. And much of what appears in Chapters III, VII, IX, and X was delivered as part of the George Elliston lectures at the University of Cincinnati in 1963.

CONTENTS

EZRA POUND

The Classic Anthology Defined by Confucius

Ezra Pound was sixty-nine years old, and he had been a patient for nine years in St. Elizabeth's Mental Hospital in Washington, D.C., when in 1955 he published a volume under the title, *The Classic Anthology Defined by Confucius*. This was the culmination of nearly half a century's dedication by Pound to the art of verse translation: 305 poems translated from a notoriously difficult language, and from that language at an archaic stage. Moreover, the poetic strategies and conventions were as much in dispute among scholars as were the social matrix from which the poems sprang and the social function they were meant to serve, and the reasons for their preservation were hardly less a mystery than the reasons and the validity of the arrangement in which they survived. And yet these poems represented, according to Confucius himself, the core of the Confucian ethics for which

Pound had been campaigning, in pamphlet and polemic, in prose translation and in his own poems, for some three decades. Thus these translations sum up more of Pound, in more compact and accessible form, than any other single volume; and there is perhaps no better place for the reader to strike into the bewilderingly various and dauntingly voluminous corpus of Pound's writings.

The volume is elaborately and elegantly, but also confusingly, arranged. The list of contents gives no page numbers but instead places the poems under four heads: Part I Folk Songs; Part II Elegantiae, or Smaller Odes; Part III The Greater Odes; and Part IV Odes of the Temple and Altar. Each of the four sections is further subdivided, Part I into no less than fifteen categories, each with a title which, so far from illuminating the reader, seems on the contrary to insist on how remote from him is the world from which these poems come and to which they refer. And truly their world is remote, not just in time and space but also in spirit.[1] Accordingly this is not a volume to be read solidly through from first page to last. The section which promises most, if only because it is articulated less elaborately than the others, comprising as it does only three categories, is Part III, The Greater Odes. With this the reader might start, reading to begin with only rapidly and skimmingly.

The Greater Odes start with poem number 235. The version runs to forty-nine lines of verse, arranged in seven strophes, varying between six and nine lines in length with irregular rhyme. The poem is prefixed by a brief headnote in bold type and, in the same type, an irregular quatrain as epigraph. It has to do, apparently, with the triumph of one dynasty over another through the virtue of a hero called King Wen; it counsels the new regime, or the heirs of that dispensation, to be clement toward the dispossessed and to learn humility from

[1] For an invaluable explanation of how the arrangement of the Anthology makes good sense in the tradition of Confucian thought in China, see L.S. Dembo, *The Confucian Odes of Ezra Pound* (Berkeley and London, 1963), pp. 11-13.

4

the overweening by which those others fell. We pick up, too, a chain of words that bind the poem together in references to light: "bright," "glitteringly," "sun's fountainhead," "sun's turn," "of light a fountainhead," "radiant," "gleaming," "white," and

> Wen, like a field of grain beneath the sun
> when all the white wheat moves in unison,
> coherent, splendid in severity,
> Sought out the norm and scope of Heaven's Decree.

"Splendid," we may realize, and (in the poem's last line) "candour," are words that by association with the imagery of light regain some of the pristine metaphorical sharpness that in common literary usage they have normally lost; but there are other words and expressions that at first sight strike as literary in a different sense, words that have not been in the spoken language of English for a long time: "supernal," "gat new decree," "brought under fealty," "clad in their antient splendid broideries." In the last case archaic spelling underlines the archaism of vocabulary. Pound is a translator, it seems, who puts an archaic text into archaic English, for whom the archaic and exotic character of what he is translating is something not to be overcome in translation, but on the contrary reproduced there. If he wants to familiarize and make accessible, he will not do so without making his reader aware of the gulf which reader and poet together are trying to span.

Poem 236 following, forty lines long in eight strophes of various length, continues to talk of King Wen and his victory over his adversaries, though it celebrates also some women of his line and his heir who completed his conquests. A cursory reading notes this as a more forbidding poem, with more Chinese names in it, the sparse rhyming more strained, extremely crabbed in expression at certain points (for instance in "blood-might to harm"), and in diction more obtrusively archaic ("from inwit to his act," "laudable in his stance") and odd in other ways too, as in the line "layed out so towering Yin."

Poem 237 is of about the same length, in nine strophes; but the measure has shortened, with four or fewer stresses to the line, more singable and accordingly rhyming much more frequently and insistently. The poem speaks of "Old Duke T'an Fu," apparently a subordinate officer of King Wen, whose achievement was in reconstruction and civilized settlement.[2] The diction here for the first time permits modern colloquialisms like "after you" and "at any rate," but the archaic flavor is preserved resourcefully and pleasingly ("a proctor of prentices"), and one notes the striking word "chthonian," its strikingness neither colloquial on the one hand nor archaic on the other. Rather plainly, as the diction thus swings over a wider arc of the English language, so presumably does the feeling of the poem range over more various experience. The question will be whether the poem can harmonize these potentially disparate elements; cursory reading suggests that it does, reports it as attractive and exhilarating and worth returning to.

Poems 238 and 239 go together, partly because they are shorter; more importantly because they both, the second more notably, break with the narrative impulse into a more nakedly didactic style, gnomic or aphoristic; and most importantly because they have a common imagery of growing timber. The archaism here cannot easily be located in details of diction but is rather in the unabashed didacticism of the gnomic style; a word that, like "chthonian," draws attention to itself is "tensile" from 238.

Number 240 is unattractive. Pound gives in the margin an alternative version of the third of its five stanzas, differing so widely from the first version that we are bewildered; there is a footnote to the poem which calls for a knowledge of Chinese ancient history such as we didn't know we needed; and the rhythms lurch disjointedly. The headnote is a piece of jaunty slang "Three generations to make a gent"; and the jauntiness rings stridently, as if trying to force on the poem a modern parallel which does not fit the poem and which, if it did, could

[2] In fact, the old Duke was Wen's grandfather.

6

only vulgarize it. The long poem 241 is more interesting. It is once again narrative in structure arranged in eight strophes varying between eleven lines and fifteen. It begins with a strophe of two-stress lines tightly rhyming in couplets—a fresh meter and apt to the subject matter, which seems to demand the effect of chanted chronicle. This strict and primitive form is thus firmly asserted only so that later strophes may depart from it; but through much of the poem, and perhaps through all of it, the departures take the form of variations on a norm that is never lost sight of altogether. Though the rhyme, for instance, can quickly become sparse, it at the same time becomes more intricate, a matter of internal chimings and partial echoes. The diction is insistently archaic, in expressions like "Kingstead," "the Welkin," "suzerain," "fiefs," "carrochs," "arbalasts." On the other hand there are colloquial or conversational expressions like "take . . . in his stride" and "a decor without great noise." The phrase "in jactancy" joins "tensile" and "chthonian": all seem to belong in the same idiosyncratic jargon. The poem ends on an exquisite cadence.

A novel feature in this poem is a wholly opaque expression put between quotation marks as if to acknowledge its opacity—"the 'string tribes.'" There is an identical effect in each of the two poems following (242 and 243), and, since each of these is shorter—a ceremonial chant rather lyrical than narrative—this nugget of unexplained foreign matter in the poem is in both cases more disconcerting. Number 244, the last of the "Decade of King Wen," praises Wen through eight stanzas of three or four lines apiece, with a refrain to each stanza on the pattern "Wen! avatar, how!"—where the "how," we must take it, is the Redskin ceremonial greeting familiar from Western movies. Such are the risks, and perhaps the liberties, that this translator will take!

The reader has now scanned in a deliberately unfocussed way ten poems, and has found himself no doubt intrigued, arrested, and offended by turns. In any case he has the right to begin to be restive, to ask for some more solid connection than any he has yet found between the conventions of this poetry and those familiar to him from other poems in English. This he finds with poem 246. The preceding poem 245 recounts a creation myth in which, by a transition that will not seem grotesque to anthropologists, the imagery of a supernatural Nativity is crossed with imagery of the planting, nourishing, and harvesting of grain. Pound helpfully points up both elements by, in the one case, a marginal note about the lamb and the burning babe, and, in the second case, headnote references to "John Barleycorn," in British folk-usage a sort of demigod of the cornfield and the whisky-still. Since the Chinese wines are made from grain, this prepares us for poem 246, headed "Festal":

> Tough grow the rushes, oh!
> No passing kine break down
> their clumpy wads, and blades so glossy growin'.
> Our brothers will be here at call
> assembled as to rule
> wherefore lay down the mat, the mat
> and bring the old man his stool.

> 2
>
> Put a soft straw mat on a bamboo mat
> let lackeys bring in the stools,
> toast against toast, wine against wine
> observant of all the rules,
> Then rinse the cups and bring catsups
> with pickles, roast and grill,
> trype and mince-meat and while drums beat
> let singers show their skill.

> 3
>
> The trusty bows are tough, my lads,
> each arrow-point true to weight

and every shot hits plumb the spot
as our archer lines stand straight.
They shoot again and four points go in
as if they were planting trees,
For a tough wood bow and the archers row
attest the gentilities.

4

An heir to his line is lord of this wine
and the wine rich on the tongue.
But by the great peck-measure, pray in your leisure
that when you're no longer young
Your back retain strength to susteyne
and aid you kin and clan.
Luck to your age! and, by this presage,
joy in a long life-span.

Rather plainly, this poem is in itself less ambitious, and to that
extent less interesting, than many that have preceded it. But
it has the merit of being familiar—familiar in its type, in the
conventions it uses, in the social occasions it is designed to register and celebrate. Indeed, Pound so deftly plucks, in phrase
after phrase, cadence after cadence, the strings of the English
folk-verse tradition, that there can be no question of hunting
out and identifying all the echoes that give the piece its reso-
nance. The very first line, for instance, echoes a folk-composi-
tion reworked memorably by Burns. Of the many traditional
poems in English that this version depends upon our half-
remembering, what may come to mind first is the famous
"Back and side go bare, go bare":

I can not eate, but lytle meate
    my stomacke is not good;
But sure I thinke, that I can drynke
    with him that weares a hood.
Thoughe I go bare, take ye no care,
    I am nothinge a cold:

I stuff my skyn so full within
  of ioly good Ale and olde
    Backe and syde go bare, go bare,
      booth foote and hand go colde;
    But Bellye god send the good ale inoughe,
      whether it be new or olde.

I love no rost, but a nut browne toste,
  and a crab layde in the fyre;
A lytle bread shall do me stead
  much breade I not desyre:
No froste nor snow, no winde, I trowe,
  can hurte mee if I wolde;
I am so wrapt, and throwly lapt
  of ioly good ale and old
    Backe and syde go bare, &c.

And Tyb my wyfe, that as her lyfe
  loveth well good ale to seeke,
Full ofte drynkes shee, tyll ye may see
  the teares run downe her cheekes:
Then dooth she trowle, to mee the bowle
  even as a mault worme shuld,
And, sayth sweethart, I tooke my part
  of this ioly good ale and olde
    Backe and syde go bare, &c.

Now let them drynke, tyll they nod and winke,
  even as good felowes shoulde doe;
They shall not mysse, to have the blisse
  good ale doth bringe men to;
And all poore soules that have scowred boules
  or have them lustely trolde,
God save the lyves, of them and theyr wyves
  whether they be yonge or olde.
    Backe and syde go bare, go bare,
      booth foote and hande go colde:
    But Bellye god sende thee good ale inoughe,
      whether it be new or olde.

The point of our making this comparison, and of the poet's inviting it, is not just that we may see what tradition the poem is in, and what conventions it observes; but also that we may see where it diverges from that tradition. For, in proportion as the traditional norm is established firmly, to just that extent do the departures from it stand out as intentional and significant.

The first way in which the sixteenth-century poem is instructive, when set beside Pound's, is that it shows how in traditional songs of this kind the rhythms are less regular than later, more streamlined, examples might lead us to suppose. Just because the swinging rhythm is so strong and insistent, it can accommodate and ride over the roughness of extra syllables crammed and jostling in some of the lines. In "Back and side go bare," though it is in the meter of the fourteener (which Pound admired when it was used by Arthur Golding, the Elizabethan translator of Ovid), there are several examples of extra syllables thus hurried and stumbled over; Pound contrives the same rough-hewn effect in his line about "the great peck-measure" where the weight of the rhythm emphasized by the heavy rhymes it is slung between ("measure"/"leisure") can easily and profitably carry a clutter of additional light syllables. At such a point the accomplished professional displays his accomplishment, as well as his taste, by contriving an unsophisticated effect.

Not all of Pound's metrical variations, however, are of this kind. In the third stanza the reader's expectations, which have been roused so confidently by the insistent simple rhythms, are dashed all the more painfully by the second line. Every reader's ear demands "each arrow-point weighs true," and on each new reading there is a shock when we stumble instead into "each arrow-point true to weight." And yet it would be a very naïve reader who supposed that Pound did not find "weighs true" for himself. Why did he reject it? Not, I think, for any "primitive" effect, but rather so as to jar the reader into attending to what is said. For, if the traditional meter is established so insistently only to be rudely disrupted at crucial points, so the traditional sentiments are invoked only to throw into relief the places where the Chinese sentiments go beyond the tradition. These are the places where the feeling is exotic, no longer to be paralleled from Old English but, on the contrary, strange and stubbornly Chinese. And since the object of translation, presumably, is to bring over into English modes of feeling not already extant, these points where the poem refuses to be acclimatized into the extant traditions are the most important of all, the nub of the whole enterprise. To look again at the sixteenth-century poem is to see very clearly where in the Chinese this stubborn novelty is. In a sense it is pervasive throughout, but it comes to a head in "attest the gentilities"; what is novel and non-Western and therefore especially valuable about this drinking-chorus is that in it drinking, and the rural sports which go with drinking, are seen in a peculiarly strict and insistent way as decorous, even ceremonial. "Assembled as to rule," "observant of all the rules"—these are the lines, seeming unimportant at first, which are taken up in "attest the gentilities," and are then seen to be the backbone of the poem. As the word "decorous" will have suggested to students of Elizabethan poetry, it is in Elizabethan poems that the English tradition comes nearest to expressing this Chinese perception or range of perceptions, and so it is appropriate that, down to details like his spelling of "susteyne," Pound should challenge comparison with sixteenth-century poets.[3]

Thus we conceive the possibility that there is more to Pound's archaism than meets the eye. In some cases at least the principle is not just to match archaic Chinese with archaic English; we seem required or invited to distinguish just what degree of

[3] See especially Ben Jonson; in many of Jonson's epistles the ceremonious character of unforced social encounter is brought out in almost Oriental fashion. Pound acknowledges the affinity, but very obliquely, when he gives as epigraph to Ode 57 the phrase "Sidney's sister" from Jonson's "To Penshurst."

archaism is being practised, precisely what period out of the long past of English poetry is being alluded to—and this so as to suggest that in just that period English approximated most nearly to such and such a Chinese perception, or cluster of perceptions. If we return to The Greater Odes, we find something similar only four poems further on from "Festal":

> Duke Liu, the frank,
> unhoused, unhapped,
> from bound to bourne
> put all barned corn in sacks
> and ration bags
> for glorious use, stretched bow
> showed shield, lance, dagger-axe
> and squared to the open road.

To my ear there is an echo in this, too loud to be accidental, from Robert Browning's "Marching Along," the first of three "Cavalier Tunes" from Browning's Dramatic Lyrics of 1842:

> Kentish Sir Byng stood for his King.
> Bidding the crop-headed Parliament swing:
> And, pressing a troop unable to stoop
> And see the rogues flourish and honest folk droop,
> Marched them along, fifty-score strong,
> Great-hearted gentlemen, singing this song.
>
> God for King Charles! . . .

This appears to be a different case from "Back and side go bare, go bare." That seemed to provide an illuminating commentary on the translation "Festal"; but there was no reason to suppose that Pound had it specifically in mind, only that he had in mind poems of roughly that period and specifically that type. One may believe, on the other hand, that Pound had "Kentish Sir Byng," if not in mind, at least echoing in his ear. What strengthens this supposition is Ode 36, which is headed "(King Charles)"; here the reference directly to Browning's

13

"Cavalier Tunes" cannot be doubted, though it may have more to do with the second of them:

> King Charles, and who'll do him right now? [4]

If the parallel was thus close and conscious, it is instructive to see how Browning's ringing internal rhymes—"Byng" and "King," "troop" and "stoop," "along" and "strong"—dissolve into the intricately delightful chimings of "bound" and "bourne" with "barned" and "corn," of "unhoused" with "bound," of "bow" with "showed." As was seen with some of the other Odes, Pound is often rhyming most richly and elaborately when he seems to be rhyming hardly at all. To put it more exactly, by such verse as this we are made to realize that terminal rhyme is only one arbitrarily codified aspect of the multifarious orchestration by sound that should be going on all the time. And Pound appears to have trained his ear in these matters, above all through the translations he made in his youth from the intricately musical poems of mediaeval Provence. In any case, if we catch a submerged allusion to Browning's poem in Ode 250, we are invited to understand its hero Duke Liu by regarding him as at least in part analogous to the faithful Royalists of the English Civil War in the seventeenth century.

Having got as far as this with the *Classic Anthology*, we can begin to profit from the brief introduction to the volume, by Achilles Fang. Fang there remarks of Pound's translations:

> the choice of the ballad meter is a happy one, as it not only makes the translation readable but accurately brings out the original rhythm of the Odes. For the Odes are essentially ballads; they were all sung, and some of them were probably dance-songs as well.

Well! "Festal" and the poem about Duke Liu are undoubtedly in ballad meters; they observe, though with variations, that

---

[4] L.S. Dembo, however, in *The Confucian Odes of Ezra Pound*, pp. 65-6, very justly and acutely defines the verse-form of Ode 36 as "Skeltonics."

metrical convention as well as other non-metrical conventions familiar from what we normally think of as ballads. On the other hand, this was not true of any of the poems we scanned more rapidly; several of these, in their stately ceremoniousness if in nothing else, seemed nearer to what is normally understood by "ode." In fact, if these poems are ballads, how can they be odes also? For in normal parlance these two kinds of poem are poles apart. Mr. Fang declares:

> the term "odes" applied to the 305 poems in this volume is to be understood in its etymological sense of songs meant to be sung.

And it is quite true that if we stretch our minds into ancient times, far behind any English precedents, we can just envisage, and find scholarly reasons for envisaging, a form of poetry written for singing or chanting, in which the ceremonious solemnity of what later became the ode is married indistinguishably to the artless vigor and grace of the folk poem sung to commemorate rural life and accompany rural sports. What Achilles Fang is saying, it appears, is that, because the ancient Chinese poems in the anthology are poems of this sort, the translator is under the necessity of creating, in order to be faithful to his originals, a form of poem for which no precedent exists in English. If so, this explains much of the difficulty we have with these translations; at least it should make us reluctant to jump to conclusions about them. Pound, as has been seen, can find English precedents for certain passages, certain turns of thought and feeling, and in these cases he will invoke the English precedents or analogues so as to ease the way for the English-speaking reader. But the Chinese poems as wholes, the kind of poem all of them exemplify, the body of conventions governing them as wholes, have no English precedents.

One was compelled to realize, moreover, in the case of "Festal," which seemed to rest on an English precedent in the wassail or festive ballad, that in the end the Chinese poem in Pound's translation strained away from that English kind of poem. And what went outside the English ballad-convention was "attest the gentilities," a sort of formal and ceremonious civility which goes rather with what we conceive of as "ode." Thus what seemed the exception in fact proves a rule.

It is from this same emphasis on "gentilities" that we can understand Achilles Fang's insistence on how, in Confucius's teaching, the singing of the Odes is intricately bound up with observance of "the rites." At the end of the Introduction, Achilles Fang glosses the word *li*, which is sometimes translated as "rites," by saying that in other contexts the English equivalent may be "tact" and in still others "character." More generally,

> The word *li*, essentially a code of behavior, is generally rendered as "rites" when that behavior is directed toward the supernatural or the manes, and as "etiquette" when it concerns man's relation with his fellow men.

Plainly, the creation of a kind of poem that is neither wholly "ode" as understood in the English tradition, nor wholly "ballad" as so understood, that partakes of both kinds in a way for which there is no English precedent—this represents not only a fusion of the artless and spontaneous with the ceremonious and fixed, but equally a fusion of piety toward the superhuman with common courtesy among humans. We are being asked to perceive how a proper attitude toward God might be no more than just good manners toward Him, and conversely how no manners can be truly "good" that do not introduce into human intercourse a sort of humility toward the more than human.

With these perceptions, or rather the possibility of these perceptions, held in mind, a reader is well equipped to embark upon the *Classic Anthology* as a whole. And a reader who understands by this argument how a question of poetic genre, and of the marrying of genres, is necessarily a question of entertaining certain ranges of perceptions rather than others, and of combining some perceptions with others in unprecedented

16

ways—such a reader has the central clue to Pound's works as a whole, to the entire labyrinth. He will realize, for example—what has baffled and continues to baffle many readers—why Pound's thoughts about style and styles of poetry cannot help but spill out beyond poetry into politics, ethics, economics. For on this showing certain kinds of human behavior, for instance certain kinds of economic behavior, conform to or comport with certain kinds of poetry, whereas others cannot do so. And thus the poet who takes with real seriousness matters of his own vocation, such as genre and style, must by that very token pass judgment on human affairs in general.

I

The Early Collections · "The Seafarer" · *The Spirit of Romance* · Canto I · *Ripostes* · Imagism

Ezra Pound set out in life by preparing himself for a career in literary scholarship. He spent his childhood in a suburb of Philadelphia and enrolled in the University of Pennsylvania in 1901, when he was not quite sixteen. In 1903 he transferred to Hamilton College in Clinton, New York, but returned to the University of Pennsylvania in 1905. "Belangal Alba" or "Alba Belingalis," a translation from Provençal which was to survive into *Personae* in 1909, first appeared in the *Hamilton Literary Magazine* for May 1905. Returning to Philadelphia as a graduate student now specializing in the Romance languages, Pound by 1906 was a Graduate Fellow in that field, working under Felix E. Schelling, to whom in later years he addressed some of his most interesting letters. When he used his fellowship to visit Europe, he seems to have taken the advice of another

Philadelphia scholar, Dr. Hugo Rennert, who is introduced respectfully into Pound's book of essays *The Spirit of Romance* (1910) and also into Canto 20.

There is nothing in this pattern to disturb the picture of an enterprising young scholar preparing himself for an academic career in his chosen field; and when in 1907 Pound accepted the offer of a teaching post at Wabash College in Crawfordsville, Indiana, it must have seemed that he was embarked upon an arrangement which has become more familiar in later generations than his, a way of life by which, for some years, the young poet combines without too much trouble the writing of poems with the teaching of literature and the pursuit of research.

The story has often been told of how provincial Mrs. Grundyism in Indiana deprived Pound of his teaching post; as Charles Norman acutely implies,[1] his dismissal from Wabash College probably rankled with Pound less bitterly than the failure of the University of Pennsylvania to stand by him by offering an alternative position. At all events, when Pound in the winter of 1908-9 lectured at the Regent Street Polytechnic in London on "Developments of Literature in Southern Europe," and again in 1909-10 on "Mediaeval Literature," his was not the impudent initiative of an amusing charlatan; he was thoroughly qualified to offer instruction in these fields, and *The Spirit of Romance*, which gives the substance of these lecture courses, is a piece of intelligent popularizing which suggests that his audiences got value for their money. One of Pound's hearers was Dorothy Shakespear, whose mother Mrs. Olivia Shakespear was a friend of Yeats and of other writers; Ezra Pound and Dorothy Shakespear were married in 1914.

By that time, however, Pound at 29 had already published, apart from *The Spirit of Romance* and a translation, *The Sonnets and Ballate of Guido Cavalcanti* (1912), six books of original poems: *A Lume Spento*, published in Venice in June 1908; *A Quinzaine for This Yule*, published in London in December

[1] Charles Norman, *Ezra Pound*, New York (1960), p. 24.

of that year; *Personae* and *Exultations*, both published in London in 1909; *Canzoni* (1911); and *Ripostes* (1912). *Ripostes* marks a new departure, but the other volumes were enough to make Pound's name in London. Of *Personae*, *The Bookman* said, "No new book of poems for years past has had such a freshness of inspiration, such a strongly individual note"; and in *The English Review* a British poet of comparable seriousness, Edward Thomas, declared admiringly, "He cannot be usefully compared with any living writers, though he has read Yeats." Pound was to declare that indeed Yeats (the Yeats of *The Wind Among the Reeds*, not the greater poet who was to emerge later) was the magnet which drew him to London in the first place. But if Yeats was the only *living* poet whose voice sounded in Pound's early volumes (for instance in "La Fraisne" from *Personae*, with its direct reference to "The Madness of King Goll" from *The Wind Among the Reeds*), the voices of dead poets echoed there as they always must in the first volumes of young poets, and in this case more loudly than usual. Swinburne speaks in "Anima Sola" from *A Lume Spento* and in "Ballad for Gloom" from *Personae*, as well as in a poem from *A Lume Spento* which is patently and admiringly addressed to him, "Salve Pontifex"; and his "Madonna Mia" has something to do with a poem from *Exultations*, "Sestina for Isolt." William Morris speaks in the ballads "Oltre la Torre: Rolando" and "Ballad Rosalind," both from *A Lume Spento*, and in "The House of Splendour" from *Canzoni*. There is Rossetti (though there is Browning also) in "Fair Helena, by Rackham" from *Exultations;* and Rossetti's love sonnets contribute something to "Camaraderie" from *Personae*.[2] Pound, by refusing to reprint these early poems in later, more definitive, collections, seems to concede that in them these influences were not properly assimilated.

These styles and models were not fashionable in Edwardian London. For British poets of that period the styles of Swin-

[2] See N. Christoph de Nagy, *The Poetry of Ezra Pound: The Pre-Imagist Stage* (Bern, 1960).

burne, of Rossetti, of Morris were available for serious use only as they had been muted and modified by the writers of the 'nineties; and for these mutings and modifications, except as they are practised in a special way by Yeats, Pound seems from the first to have had little sympathy. "Piccadilly" from *Personae* is the only poem approaching the "impressionism," as it was called, that inspired John Davidson and Arthur Symons, under the influence of Baudelaire, to write poems about the metropolis; and "In Tempore Senectutis" from *A Lume Spento* advertises by its subtitle, "An Anti-Stave for Dowson," that it is tilting polemically against another of the characteristic styles of the 'nineties. In "The Flame" from *Canzoni*, an early poem which Pound has consented to retain in later collections, there is an allusion to Arthur Symons's *Days and Nights*, "the first representative collection of impressionistic verse in England" (de Nagy, p. 41), which seems to single this out as treading in a wrong path, as against the path trodden by Yeats, who is present in allusions to *Countess Cathleen*.

Pound's reaching back over a poetic generation to echo directly some Victorian poets must have seemed a symptom of provincialism, something possible to an American, but not to a British poet. And Pound himself was thoroughly aware of this possibility and of himself as indelibly American. Though it is British voices which sound, he knows that they sound differently in his American ear, and that just for that reason they may be fruitful for him as they could not be for his British contemporaries. He hints at this in a touchingly boyish essay of 1909, "What I Feel About Walt Whitman," which was first published only in 1955:

> It seems to me I should like to drive Whitman into the old world. I sledge, he drill—and to scourge America with all the old beauty. (For Beauty *is* an accusation) and with a thousand thongs from Homer to Yeats, from Theocritus to Marcel Schwob. This desire is because I am young and impatient, were I old and wise I should content myself in seeing and saying that these things will come. But now,

since I am by no means sure it would be true prophecy, I am fain set my own hand to the labour.

It is a great thing, reading a man to know, not "His Tricks are not as yet my Tricks, but I can easily make them mine" but "His message is my message. We will see that men hear it." [3]

It was not until another four years had passed that Pound trusted himself to employ Whitman's "tricks" and to print Whitmanesque poems. But he knew already that he must be nearer to Whitman than he could ever be to those British poets whom, just by reason of that saving distance between them, he could afford for the moment to imitate. Later he was to look for support to some of his countrymen who had been expatriates as he was himself—to James McNeill Whistler and Henry James.

It is surprising, and it is to the credit of the British reviewers of 1909, that in the author of *Personae* they recognized this American-ness, and relished it. But it is true that they had before them poems more powerful than any so far mentioned. These were the poems written under the influence of yet another British Victorian, Robert Browning: in *Exultations*, "Piere Vidal Old" and "Sestina: Altaforte"; and in *Personae*, "Cino," "Na Audiart," and "Marvoil." There is no denying the influence on these poems of Browning's experiments with the dramatic monologue. Pound has acknowledged his debt generously, and in *Personae*, quite apart from the amusingly affectionate homage to Browning in "Mesmerism," there is, for instance, the Browningesque writing of "Famam Librosque Cano" and of the important poem "In Durance" with its specific allusion to Browning's "Pictor Ignotus." Moreover, Browning was to exert a powerful influence for many years yet—up to and into the first of the Cantos. But Browning could be a more fruitful influence than William Morris, for instance,

[3] Herbert Bergman, "Ezra Pound and Walt Whitman," in *American Literature*, 27 (March 1955), 56-61.

chiefly because his influence was always combined with some other. The poems just cited can draw fruitfully on Browning's previous experience in the dramatic monologue only because they are modifying that poetic form into something that Browning hardly dreamed of. On the one hand, under pressure from Pound's study of mediaeval Provence, the dramatic monologue becomes in his hands something much closer to translation or at least paraphrase; on the other hand, because of Yeats's ideas of the "mask," Pound's Provençal personae are less *dramatis* personae than they are embodied aspects of his own situation and his own personality (though this is truer of some of these poems than of others).

The most impressive is "Sestina: Altaforte." Though this can be read, as undoubtedly and properly it most often is read, as a successful and stirring dramatic lyric or dramatic monologue (not that these, in Browning's use of the terms, are the same thing), Pound's poem has, in fact, another dimension of interest available only to the erudite: it is only the instructed reader who can appreciate how close the poem is to a translation of Bertran de Born's "Praise of War," and how the sestina is a form invented not by Bertran but by Arnaut Daniel, and how Pound switches the conventional *envoi*, the address to a named auditor (Papiols), from the end of the poem to the beginning (de Nagy, p. 125). These aspects of the poem are not merely formalistic, part of the scaffolding that can be torn down once the building is erected; it was probably these considerations which, by giving the poet other things to aim at than Browning had aimed at, permitted him to draw on Browning's precedent without being overwhelmed by it. (Similarly, though in a less complicated way, Villon's French counterbalances translations of him by Rossetti and Swinburne, in "Villonaud for This Yule" and "A Villonaud: Ballad of the Gibbet," two near-translations in *Personae*.) What gives pre-eminence to "Sestina: Altaforte" over a poem no less affecting and memorable, such as "Piere Vidal Old," or over a straight translation from Bertran de Born, the "Planh for the Young English King," is what Edward Thomas noticed: a verse-movement that breaks away from Tennysonian mellifluousness so as to replace it by something positive. The opening of "Sestina: Altaforte" is very arresting indeed, with a quality of assured "attack." But the metrical effect, if one may isolate it, is more remarkable because it is harder to parallel. The verse-lines are true units, rhythmically and in meaning; and yet each of them is broken near the center much more forcibly than by a caesura in traditional accentual-syllabic meters. The break in "I have no life/save when the swords clash" depends upon a rising beat before the break, crammed against the emphatically falling rhythm of the trochee "save when." But this is not true of other lines where the break apart is just as pronounced. In any case, this breaking of the line near mid-point (which Pound at this stage cannot maintain through a whole poem) was to be the hallmark of his writing in verse. It can be found elsewhere in *Personae;* strategically placed, and to plangent rather than forcible effect, the dismembered line appears in "Praise of Ysolt," for example, and to scornful effect in "Au Salon."

The rhythms which thus reappear in modern English were common enough before English meters were settled at the end of the sixteenth century as accentual-syllabic in principle. From this point of view, Pound's translation of the Old English poem, "The Seafarer," does not come as a surprise; from every other point of view it is very surprising indeed, coming as it did in *Ripostes* (1912) from the poet who had seemed wedded to the Romance languages of Southern Europe.

The Anglo-Saxon poem, however, appealed to Pound for other than metrical reasons. A few years later, after Pound had begun translating and adapting from Chinese, he was to find much in common between the Anglo-Saxon poet and the Chinese poet whom he most admired, Li Po (A.D. 701-762). Later still, in his prose tract *The A.B.C. of Reading* (1934), he related:

I once got a man to start translating the *Seafarer* into Chinese. It came out almost directly into Chinese verse, with two solid ideograms in each half-line. Apart from the *Seafarer* I know no other European poems of the period that you can hang up with the "Exile's Letter" of Li Po, displaying the West on a par with the Orient.

Pound's interest in meter, in the Anglo-Saxon verse-line with its heave in the middle between two alliteratively combined rhythms, is what makes him speak of the half-line rather than the line. Yet his comment shows that for him "The Seafarer" and the Chinese poem have more than this in common, and more than is involved in their being roughly of the same date. For "Exile's Letter" is, of all the poems which Pound was to translate, that one which presents Li Po as legendary anecdote preserves him through tradition: a drunkard, an idler, disreputable, undependable, without self-respect. The author of "Exile's Letter" is recognizably the man of whose poems Po Chu-i complained that "not one in ten contains any moral reflection or deeper meaning"; of whom Wang An-shih declared that "his intellectual outlook was low and sordid." [4] But we can thus recognize this poet in his poem only because he speaks in it very directly, reveals himself with such unhesitant nakedness. And this he has in common with the poet of "The Seafarer" as Pound gives him through translation: in "The Seafarer" too we are struck by the directness of address, the completeness of the self-exposure.

Pound's version of the Old English poem is very inaccurate. And yet not all his howlers are on a par. For instance:

Disease or oldness or sword-hate
Beats out the breath from doom-gripped body.
And for this, every earl whatever, for those speaking after—
Laud of the living, boasteth some last word,

[4] Po Chu-i, writing about A.D. 816; Wang An-shih (1021-86). I take these quotations from Arthur Waley's paper to the China Society at the School of Oriental Studies, London, delivered on 21 November 1918. Mr. Waley endorses these strictures. See Waley, *The Poet Li Po*, A.D. 701-762 (London, 1919).

That he will work ere he pass onward,
Frame on the fair earth 'gainst foes his malice,
Daring ado,...
So that all men shall honour him after
And his laud beyond them remain 'mid the English,...

These verses, in which the mid-line heave or thump comes with ultimately monotonous impact, correspond to those in which the Anglo-Saxon poet exhorts men to combat the malice of devils so that their good fame may live for ever with angels. Pound, wittingly or not, uses in "remain 'mid the English" the Augustinian pun on "Angles" and "angels" so as to shut out the Christian reference. This can hardly be on a par with his misunderstandings elsewhere: of *stearn* (a seabird) for the stern of a ship; of *byrig* ("towns") for berries; of *thurh* ("through," "in") for *thruh* ("tomb").[5] In the original the genuflections toward Christianity are so conspicuous that they could not escape the hastiest reading; and Pound consistently eliminates them. Many a scholar has also wished them away, since perfunctory genuflections is all that they seem to be, and their presence has led many readers to rate "The Seafarer" below its companion piece, "The Wanderer," which one suspects that Pound has never read. Pound had to eliminate these references if he was to give us a poet who would expose himself with the same unconcern for received opinion as Li Po exhibits in "Exile's Letter."

Pound does not merely eliminate the Christian values, he replaces them by something positive, not just pagan but barbaric. Kenneth Sisam says that he "makes malice the source of everlasting renown among the English." So he does. And he might well be impenitent about it, for one may detect in Kenneth Sisam's protest (perhaps unfairly) the same note of outraged respectability as in Wang An-shih's objection to Li Po, that his outlook was "low and sordid." *Épater le bourgeois* has never

[5] See Kenneth Sisam's letter to the *Times Literary Supplement* for 25 June 1954. I am greatly indebted to Mr. Sisam's letter throughout this discussion.

been beneath Pound's dignity, and there is a comically anachronistic zest about his references in "The Seafarer" to the "burghers" who are "wealthy and wine-flushed." As Li Po shocked the respectable Chinese of his day by his wine-bibbing and interest in concubines, so Pound makes the Anglo-Saxon poet shock the mores of his society by putting a high value on "malice."

Épater le bourgeois in the Anglo-Saxon kingdoms of the Dark Ages! Obviously this is to romanticize. In Pound the youthful author of *The Spirit of Romance* it could hardly be anything else. And yet some pages in that first of Pound's prose works ought to shield him from any facile gibes at his anachronisms. There is, for instance, an essay on Villon:

> thief, murderer, pandar, bully to a whore, he is honoured for a few score pages of unimaginative sincerity; he sings of things as they are. He dares to show himself.

But Pound goes on to protect Villon against the romanticizing of taverns and harlots which had made the old French poet a favorite in the generations of Swinburne and R.L. Stevenson. For Pound's romanticizing has to do, not with *romanticism*, but with *romance* in the strict sense in which one speaks of "Romance languages." And thus his romanticizing of a mediaeval writer like Villon is not anachronistic at all; on the contrary, it is scholarly and historical, faithful to the romance sensibility and tradition which as a fact of chronology lay behind such a writer:

> Villon's verse is real, because he lived it; as Bertran de Born, as Arnaut Marvoil, as that mad poseur Vidal, he lived it. For these men life is in the press. No brew of books, no distillation of sources will match the tang of them.

Romantic is what Villon is, in a stricter, more disconcerting way than romanticists of the nineteenth century realized.

As Pound here compares Villon with three Provençal poets (each of whom had had a fine poem to himself in *Personae*), so elsewhere in *The Spirit of Romance* he compares him with a poet of Spain:

> His poems are gaunt as the *Poema del Cid* is gaunt; they treat of actualities, they are untainted with fancy; in the *Cid* death is death, war is war. In Villon filth is filth, crime is crime; neither crime nor filth is gilded. They are not considered as strange delights and forbidden luxuries, accessible only to adventurous spirits.

And what Pound has to say of the *Poema del Cid* strikes the by now familiar note, very excitedly:

> it is the unquenchable spirit of that very glorious bandit, Ruy Diaz, which gives life to the verse and the apparently crude rhythm.

Ruy Diaz, *el Cid* (who is to appear in Canto 3), takes his place beside Li Po and the poet of Pound's "Seafarer" and, more somberly, François Villon, as an engaging, because uncompromising, ruffian—"that very glorious bandit." This is a refreshingly unsophisticated way of responding to poetry.

But it raises questions that reach rather far if we look ahead a few years and find Pound using his "Seafarer" measure for translating Homer.[6] For Homer, every one knows, is an epic poet; and Pound's translation from Homer's *Odyssey* inaugurates that poem, *The Cantos*, which he himself has offered as a modern epic. The *Poema del Cid*, moreover, so far as it is a *geste*, is epic no less. And yet, not only was the style of "The Seafarer" evolved for a poem not epic at all but elegiac, but also the element Pound most values in the *Cid* as in "The Sea-

---

[6] *The Letters of Ezra Pound, 1907-1941*, ed. D.D. Paige (London, 1951), p. 137: "I don't know that one can read any trans. of the *Odyssey*. Perhaps you could read book XI. I have tried an adaptation in the 'Seafarer' metre, or something like it, but I don't expect anyone to recognize the source very quickly" (to Iris Barry, 1916).

All subsequent references to this volume will describe it as *Letters*.

farer" and the poems of Li Po, the robust fullness of self-exposure in narrator or protagonist, is a fundamentally non-epic quality. This appears very clearly in Chapter IV of *The Spirit of Romance* where Pound strenuously maintains the superiority of the *Poema del Cid* to that other epical *geste*, the *Chanson de Roland*. As might be predicted, what Pound objects to in the French *épopée* is precisely a cherished characteristic of epic writing—its impersonality:

> The personality of the author is said to be "suppressed," although it might be more exact to say that it has been worn away by continuous oral transmission.

And, of the death of Roland, Pound observes:

> Perfect chivalric pose, perfect piety! The hero goes out of this chançon of gesture, and one feels that perhaps he and the rest of the characters are not wooden figures, that they are simply "latin." Heroic, his hands joined, in death he forgets not etiquette. He is the perfect hero of pre-realist literature.
>
> But ... one is grateful for the refreshment of the Spanish *Poema*, and for the bandit Ruy Diaz.

Moreover, the antipathy that Pound expresses thus temperately toward one of the received masterpieces of European epic is in line with his indifference to Spenser and Tasso, his lukewarmness about Camoens,[7] and is as nothing beside his violent dislike of Virgil[8] and of Milton.[9] Unless the *Divine Comedy* is to be called an epic, Pound has pronounced an anathema upon the whole epic tradition since Homer, with the solitary eccentric exception of the *Poema del Cid*. In the only modern poet

---

[7] *The Spirit of Romance* (London and New York, 1910), ch. X.
[8] E.g. *Letters*, p. 138 (1916): "Virgil is a second-rater, a Tennysonianized version of Homer."
[9] E.g. "Notes on Elizabethan Classicists," in *The Egoist*, IV, 120-22, 135-6, 154-6, 168; V, 8-9 (Sept. 1917 to Jan. 1918); reprinted in *Pavannes and Divisions* (New York, 1918) and in *Make It New* (London, 1934; New Haven, 1935).

who has essayed epic in the English-speaking world, this is noteworthy.

It is proper to anticipate the Cantos this early in an account of Pound's career. For, though his readers in 1912 could not know of his epic ambitions, Pound had been setting his course toward that objective for several years. In a recent interview he has declared, "I began the Cantos about 1904, I suppose. I had various schemes, starting in 1904 or 1905." [10] Certainly his friend William Carlos Williams knew that he was working on an epic as early as 1908.[11] And Pound says, "In the first sketches, a draft of the present first *Canto* was the third." In that Canto Homer is invoked through translation to preside over the epic pretensions of the poem thus inaugurated. But it is the Homer of the *Odyssey*. The Homer who is the father of the European epic is the poet of the *Iliad*; and in the *Iliad* Pound has consistently shown comparatively little interest.[12] Yet ever since ancient times it has been realized that the *Odyssey* is hardly epic at all:

> in the *Odyssey* one might liken Homer to a setting sun; the intensity is gone, but there remains the greatness. Here the tone of those great lays of Ilium is no longer maintained—the passages on one level of sublimity with no sinking anywhere, the same stream of passion poured upon passion, the readiness of turn, the closeness to life, the throng of images all drawn from the truth: as when Ocean retires into himself, and is left lonely around his proper bounds, only the ebbings of his greatness are left to our view, and a wandering among the shallows of the fabulous and the incredible. While I say this, I have not forgotten the storms in the *Odyssey*, nor the story of the Cyclops,

[10] *The Paris Review*, 28 (Summer-Fall, 1962), p. 23.
[11] *Selected Essays of William Carlos Williams* (New York, 1954), p. 105.
[12] Though see "Translators of Greek" in *The Egoist V*, 95-7, 106-8, 120-21, 130-31; *VI*, 6-9, 24-6 (Aug. 1918 to April 1919), reprinted in *Make It New* (1934).

nor certain other passages; I am describing an old age, but the old age of Homer. Still in all these, as they follow one another, fable prevails over action.[13]

One need not follow the ancient critic in thinking the *Odyssey* inferior to the *Iliad*. But one must agree with him in thinking them profoundly different, with a difference that puts the *Odyssey* apart from the epic as traditionally conceived. The *Odyssey* is nearer to the novel than it is to the epic; as Longinus goes on to imply:

> You may recognize how the decline of passion in great writers and poets passes away into character-drawing: the sketches of the life in the household of Ulysses much resemble a comedy of character.

Indeed Pound would concur, for in his later prose polemics he would repeatedly cite the *Odyssey* as a model for the novelist.[14] What he seems not to have realized is that the nearer the *Odyssey* is to a novel, the further it is from an epic—or at any rate, that this might be argued.

It is something more than a quibble. We may well feel that a novel can speak to our modern condition as no epic can, and that one reason why the *Odyssey* may speak to us as the *Iliad* nowadays cannot is that its protagonist can be re-created by James Joyce in the figure of Leopold Bloom, and by Joyce's friend Pound as something between Li Po and the author of "The Seafarer": "Born un po' misero, don't want to go to war, little runt who finally has to do all the hard work, gets all Don Juan's chances with the ladies and can't really enjoy 'em."[15] But when Pound defines epic as "a poem including history,"[16] we have the right to ask *how* Pound's epic will do

[13] Longinus, *On the Sublime*, tr. A.O. Prickard (Oxford, 1916), sect. IX.
[14] Cf. *Guide to Kulchur* (London, 1938), p. 146 in the New Directions (New York) reprint.
[15] *Letters*, p. 362 (to W.H.D. Rouse, 1935). All the letters to Rouse on his translation of the *Odyssey* are relevant.
[16] "Date Line" in *Make It New*.

31

this: in what spirit will history be included? And we may legitimately think that a poem which begins in the style and measure of "The Seafarer" will "include history" in a spirit not epical but elegiac.

The use of the "Seafarer" meter in Canto I has been explained in another way, as a matter of chronological propriety. For this most ancient of Greek poems (Pound believes the *nekuia* episode which he translates in Canto I to be more archaic than the rest of the *Odyssey*—Letters, p. 363), it was appropriate—so the argument runs—to use the most ancient of poetic styles extant in English. This argument seems too schematic to be convincing, especially if it is extended, as in logic it has to be, to explain why Pound took Homer's Greek through the medium of a translation into Renaissance Latin.[17] Similarly, the usual way of explaining Pound's choice of the *Odyssey* as his standard of poetic reference, rather than the *Iliad*, is to insist, as Pound invites us to do, on Odysseus as "the voyager," like Hanno the Carthaginian and other navigators who are to appear in the *Cantos*, as the man who knows his world experimentally in coastlines followed and landfalls aimed at, not as configurations on a map. But this is to make of Pound's Odysseus the Odysseus of Tennyson, not the Odysseus of Homer (or of Du Bellay). For Homer's Odysseus is voyaging *home*. Thus, in the strictest sense of nostalgia,[18] Homer's Odysseus is a nostalgic hero. And nostalgia, once again, comports with elegy better than with epic. Certainly one may read quite a long way into the *Cantos* in the spirit of "Lordly men are to earth o'er given" from "The Seafarer."

Apart from "The Seafarer," *Ripostes*, the collection of 1912, is insubstantial, as if Pound had scraped his bottom drawer

[17] The Latin source, together with Pound's translation, is in "Translators of Greek," reprinted in *Make It New*.
[18] See D.W. Harding, "A Note on Nostalgia," in *Determinations*, ed. F.R. Leavis (London, 1934).

to find enough for a volume. For instance "Salve Pontifex," the elaborate tribute to Swinburne, is salvaged from *A Lume Spento*. In some ways, indeed, *Ripostes* represents, not a marking time since *Personae*, but a losing of ground there gained. This is particularly true of meter: "Portrait d'une Femme" is an interesting, even a distinguished poem (on a subject to be more characteristic of Eliot's work than of Pound's) which fails to realize its full potential because it is in blank verse; Pound had appealed and attracted attention because he was singing to other tunes than those of the iambic pentameter, yet it is those old tunes sounding here again. "Silet," with its opening echo of a famous sonnet by Keats; "In Exitus Cuiusdam" and "Phasellus Ille," which admirably incorporate the modern world of letters; the appealingly vulnerable love-poems, "The Needle" and "A Virginal"—though in different ways each of these is distinguished and memorable, in none of them is the voice that speaks a new and unmistakable voice, the voice of "Sestina: Altaforte." For in all of these the measure, though it is varied more in some than in others, is still the iambic pentameter.

There are, however, two pieces of which this is not true: "Apparuit" and "The Return." And they are very important because in them Pound experiments metrically not with the line but with the strophe. "Apparuit" is in Sapphic stanzas and seems to be a reworking of "The House of Splendour" from *Canzoni*. Pound draws from Sapphics a melody altogether more haunting and enervated than the urgent rapidity of earlier English Sapphics like Isaac Watts's "Day of Judgment" or Cowper's "Stanzas Written in a Period of Insanity." It is this melody, once discovered, by which Pound attains a sort of unearthliness that he seems to have tried for also in "The House of Splendour." He was balked on that occasion by the incongruous materiality of heraldic or pageant-like imagery he seems to have taken over from Morris; all trace of Morris's influence has been purged from "Apparuit," and whatever happens in the poem (we cannot give a name to it) is clearly happening in a dimension beyond time and space. The same is true of "The Return," where the Sapphic stanza has a sort of phantasmal presence in or behind the first four lines, but only as a sort of musical theme which is at once thereafter developed and elaborated not quite beyond recognition but certainly beyond analysis:

> See, they return; ah, see the tentative
> Movements, and the slow feet,
> The trouble in the pace and the uncertain
> Wavering!
>
> See, they return, one, and by one,
> With fear, as half-awakened;
> As if the snow should hesitate
> And murmur in the wind,
>   and half turn back;
> These were the "Wing'd-with-Awe,"
>   Inviolable.
>
> Gods of the wingèd shoe!
> With them the silver hounds,
>   sniffing the trace of air!
>
> Haie! Haie!
>   These were the swift to harry;
> These the keen-scented;
> These were the souls of blood.
>
> Slow on the leash,
>   pallid the leash-men!

The decay of classical studies? The etiolation of Hellenism as an intellectual and artistic stimulus? The virtual extinction of any sense of retributive justice in the frame of things, such as the ancients figured by the avenging furies? Even the etiolation of the Sapphic stanza, considered as the classic vehicle for expression of sexual passion? These ideas or some of them (and certainly others) are part of the "complicated sort of significance" Pound was to claim for the poem; one might think that the poem has the sort of meaning that music normally has, but Pound found analogies for it in another art, in sculpture.[19]

It is surprising that a poet who had scored his most brilliant successes with Browningesque poems, dense with the tangible presences of men recorded in history and occupying a very particular time and space, should have wanted to write a poem like this—let alone, that he should have brought it off. But, in fact, he had tried for this effect many times without success. Among the earlier poems, "Threnos" is like "The Return" in its tone, though nowhere near it in accomplishment. "In Durance" is a discursive poem arguing for a Platonic understanding of poetry, on the authority of Coleridge's essay "On the Principles of Genial Criticism." There is Platonism also in "Paracelsus in Excelsis" and in the fine "Blandula, tenulla, vagula." And a poem from *Canzoni*, "The Flame," is quite explicit:

> There *is* the subtler music, the clear light
> Where time burns back about th'eternal embers.
> We are not shut from all the thousand heavens:
> Lo, there are many gods whom we have seen,
> Folk of unearthly fashion, places splendid,
> Bulwarks of beryl and of chrysophrase.
>
> Sapphire Benacus, in thy mists and thee
> Nature herself's turned metaphysical,
> Who can look on that blue and not believe?

In fact, throughout the earlier collections, Pound is to be heard more often asking for a Platonic poetry of the metaphysical, transcending place and time, than for a poetry dense with the particulars of history. Over Pound's career as a whole

[19] *Gaudier-Brzeska* (London, 1916), p. 98: "poems like 'The Return', which is an objective reality and has a complicated sort of significance, like Mr. Epstein's 'Sun God' or Mr. Brzeska's 'Boy with a Coney.'" Such poems, Pound says, "are Imagisme, and insofar as they are Imagisme, they fall in with the new pictures and the new sculpture." ("The Return" appeared originally in *The English Review* in June 1912.)

the wish to transcend history is more powerful than the wish to act in history, but the Cantos seem governed by the conviction that the poet has to earn the right to such transcendence, that history can be transcended only after it has been understood.

The last pages of *Ripostes* are taken up by "The Complete Poetical Works of T.E. Hulme" (five poems), and Pound's introductory note to these, oddly evasive as it is, gives the first uncertain notice of his involvement with the programmatic movement, imagism. The history of imagism has been told several times, first by Glenn Hughes thirty years ago [20] and most recently and entertainingly by Charles Norman in his biography of Pound. With the movement thus chronicled, which began with T.E. Hulme and F.S. Flint in 1908/9 and persisted into the 'twenties under the able sponsorship of Amy Lowell, Pound's association was, though spectacular, brief and tangential. Pound's poetic path intersected at one stage with those of Flint, of John Gould Fletcher, Richard Aldington, and H.D. (Hilda Doolittle, an old acquaintance of Pound's from his college days with William Carlos Willams), but he was set on a different course and in a short time was distinguishing his "imagisme" from the "Amygisme" of the others. Whereas Flint, for instance, had taken his bearings from the ideas of T.E. Hulme, Pound had been set on his course by conversations with Yeats and Ford Madox Ford. It is Ford (or Hueffer, as he then called himself) who is more important than Hulme in this connection, for whereas Hulme's *Speculations* have been given deservedly close and respectful attention by students of twentieth-century poetry, Ford's contributions to that theory have been overlooked—naturally enough, since he made them in conversation, or else by implication in his own poems, now little read, or else (most significantly of all) in his brief but brilliant tenure of the editorial chair of *The Eng-*

[20] Glenn Hughes, *Imagism and the Imagists* (Stanford, 1931).

lish Review. Ford's half-serious claim to be the father of imagism,[21] though it does not at all supplant the claim of Hulme, is certainly just insofar as it refers to the poems that Pound wrote in his imagist phase and, indeed, later. Pound has been at pains to acknowledge this. Ford, far more a novelist than he was a poet, insisted that the modern poet was in competition not only with great poets of the past but also with great novelists, with Turgenev, Flaubert, Stendhal, James. This conviction, the necessity for this emulation of the realistic novel, had a permanent effect on Pound's poetry. It lies behind, for instance, Pound's admiration for the poetry of Crabbe [22] and also, I suspect, behind Eliot's declaration, in relation to the poems of Samuel Johnson, that "poetry must be at least as well written as good prose." [23]

[21] Ford Madox Ford, "A Jubilee," in *Outlook* (London), 10 July 1915, reviewing *Some Imagist Poets* (1915). See also Ford's preface to *Imagist Anthology* (New York and London, 1930).
[22] See "The Rev. G. Crabbe, LL.B.," in *Future*, I, 4 (February 1917), reprinted in *Literary Essays of Ezra Pound*, ed. T.S. Eliot (London, 1954).
[23] T.S. Eliot, Introduction to *"London" and "The Vanity of Human Wishes,"* ed. McAdam and Nichol Smith (London, 1930). See *Guide to Kulchur*, ch. 28.

II

C*athay* · Arnaut Daniel · The Noh

Ode 167 from the *Classic Anthology* is a doing over of a translation, under the title "Song of the Bowmen of Shu," that stands first in Pound's collection of 1915, *Cathay*. A comparison of the later version with the earlier one is startling and instructive. The poem in *Cathay* is called "Song." But in fact it nowhere recalls any of the forms of English verse for singing—not either of the forms of English ode, nor any of the many forms of English ballad, nor the "air," nor the hymn. Ode 167, on the other hand, *is* cast very conspicuously in the form of a ballad, in this case of a modern ballad like "The Quartermaster's Stores," such as British or American troops even today can make up for themselves to express, just as the Chinese poem does, the tribulations of campaigning.

Two consequences follow. First, Ode 167 is necessarily far

more colloquial than "Song." What in 1915 was "Here we are because we have the Ken-nin for our foemen" becomes in 1955 "We are here because of these huns." The second consequence is more dismaying: because Ode 167 is an English poem for singing, it is incomplete without a musical setting; it is deliberately and conscientiously left incomplete, in order that the musician, when he comes to set the poem, shall have something to do. On the other hand the earlier version, "Song of the Bowmen of Shu," aspires to be, and is, complete in itself, with a verbal music of its own wholly composed by the poet-translator so as to leave no margin for a musician to work with. Thus "Song of the Bowmen of Shu" will inevitably and rightly please many more readers than Ode 167. For we have to go back to the seventeenth century to find English readers to whom it comes naturally to think of a poem as incomplete until it is set to music. We expect our poems to bring their music along with them, as the *Cathay* poems do but the *Classic Anthology* poems do not. Thus the seventeen translations offered as *Cathay* have for long been among the most popular of Pound's works; and there are good reasons for thinking they will continue to be liked much more than the more ambitious, but less appealing, translations of the Odes.

Cathay was published in April 1915 in London. It represents Pound's first venture into understanding Chinese culture, and it is tempting to say that it came about by accident. But this would be an injustice to Mrs. Ernest Fenollosa [1] who, since the death of her husband in 1908, had been looking out for a writer who would make the most of what Fenollosa had left behind him: fragmentary translations from Chinese and Japanese, with notes on these and the draft of a momentous essay on the su-

[1] Fenollosa's second wife, born Mary McNeil of Mobile, Alabama, had lived in Tokyo with her first husband and lived there again with Fenollosa from 1897 to 1900. Japan is the setting of novels she later wrote under the name Sidney McCall. See Van Wyck Brooks, *Fenollosa and His Circle* (New York, 1962).

perficially recondite subject of the Chinese written character as a medium for poetry. It was no accident, but the sure and independent taste of Mrs. Fenollosa, that made her choice light upon Pound on the strength of a group of his poems in the Chicago magazine *Poetry* for April 1913. Pound, when in 1916 he had worked over Fenollosa's translations of the Japanese "Noh" plays, introduced them by declaring that "the life of Ernest Fenollosa was the romance par excellence of modern scholarship." [2] Not only is this true of Fenollosa, Salem-born and Harvard-educated, who became Commissioner of Arts for the Imperial Japanese government; it is also revealing about Pound. Some of Pound's incautious defenders may have confused scholarship, and especially literary scholarship, with dry-as-dust pedantry; Pound himself, in his fiercest polemics against pedantry and the inertia of institutionalized learning, has always honored true scholarship and has been excited by the romance as well as the dignity of the life of learning. Every one of his translations is in intention a scholarly translation; and if it is true that his scholarship has not kept pace with his zeal and enthusiasm, this is because he has not observed a rule that the scholar may groan under even as he is governed by it— the rule of specialization. Pound has been interested in too many things, in particular in too many languages, for his learning to be adequate in all of them. But he has conspicuously refused to take the position that his expertise as a poet absolves him, in translating, from the scruples and responsibilities of the scholar. By a mournful paradox the scholars would have treated him less harshly if, with the arrogance of a Bohemian, he had thought that his talents permitted him to bypass the necessity for a scholar's accuracy.

Thus, when Mrs. Fenollosa suggested to Pound that he "finish" Ernest Fenollosa's translations, she had found a man

[2] *"Noh," or Accomplishment, A Study of the Classical Stage of Japan* (London, 1916; New York, 1917); and *Certain Noble Plays of Japan,* from the manuscripts of Ernest Fenollosa, chosen and finished by Ezra Pound, with an introduction by William Butler Yeats (Dublin: Cuala Press, September 16, 1916).

with a scholar's conscience as well as a poet's talent. Perhaps she had been shrewd enough to discover this and check on it for herself. For, although he had in the meantime made his name in London as an original poet and a man of letters, Pound had also published a scholarly translation deriving immediately from his academic training in Romance philology, his first version of *The Sonnets and Ballate of Guido Cavalcanti* (London and Boston, 1912). All the same, Pound of course was quite inadequately equipped to apply his scholarship to Oriental texts; and *Cathay* includes one memorable howler: "The River Song" is a conglomeration of two distinct poems by Li Po, the title of the second being versified and submerged in the four lines beginning "And I have moped in the Emperor's garden."

The melody of the translations in *Cathay*, wholly a poet's melody leaving no room for collaboration with a musician, is less a matter of meter than of syntax. What is most immediately striking about these poems is the frequency with which a line of verse comprises one full sentence:

South-Folk in Cold Country

The Dai horse neighs against the bleak wind of Etsu,
The birds of Etsu have no love for En, in the north,
Emotion is born out of habit.
Yesterday we went out of the Wild-Goose gate,
Today from the Dragon-Pen.
Surprised. Desert turmoil. Sea sun.
Flying snow bewilders the barbarian heaven.
Lice swarm like ants over our accoutrements.
Mind and spirit drive on the feathery banners.
Hard fight gets no reward.
Loyalty is hard to explain.
Who will be sorry for General Rishogu,
      the swift moving,
Whose white head is lost for this province?

The first three sentences, each with a line to itself, are separated only by commas, whereas later sentences, again one to a line, are closed off by full stops; this is important, for it takes us with a rush into a poem which then seems to get slower. But this is to plot the movement only generally, over the whole poem. Where the expectation of the complete sentence has been built up so strongly, the three pieces of stabbing telegraphese in the sixth line have the effect of speeding it up almost uncontrollably; but the slow pace is then reasserted. In the last three lines the break into a limp and liquid elegiac cadence is chiefly a matter of one question about General Rishogu being plangently trailed across three lines (or two and a half), whereas the measure which the poem has established is of one sentence to a line. More important, however, is the way in which we are persuaded to see or hear such a line as "Loyalty is hard to explain" as of equal fullness, occupying as much of time as "Flying snow bewilders the barbarian heaven" (which has the beauty of Racine), or, in a significantly dissonant tone, "Lice swarm like ants over our accoutrements." The poem establishes a convention by which the gauge of a poetic line is not the number of syllables or of stressed syllables or of metrical feet, but the fulfillment of the simple grammatical unit, the sentence; and, the convention thus established, we conspire in giving to naïvely abstract sentences like "Hard fight gets no reward" and "Loyalty is hard to explain" as much weight as to the longer sentences which make vivid images about lice on armor, and flying snow in the skies. This seems to be a wholly original and brilliant way of embodying abstractions in English poetry.

It is not clear whether, at the time of making the *Cathay* translations, Pound had already studied Fenollosa's essay on the Chinese written character, which he was to edit later. It is reasonable to suppose that he had read it through at least. Although other and more questionable parts of Fenollosa's argument have attracted more attention, one finds in this little treatise just what might have led Pound to this way of writing, an impassioned plea by Fenollosa for the sentence, in its naked anatomy of subject/verb/object, as the natural unit of poetic perception, in Chinese but also (so Fenollosa suggests) in other languages.[3] And, in fact, other languages than Chinese could bring the same lesson home to the English-speaking reader. Bishop Lowth and Christopher Smart in the eighteenth century had recognized in Hebrew poetry what Gerard Manley Hopkins in the nineteenth was to call "the Figure of Grammar," the way in which the structural units of, for instance, the Psalms of David are not metrical but syntactical. And occasionally, as in "Song of the Bowmen of Shu," when Pound establishes the norm of not one but two sentences to the line, his lines for the moment echo the antiphonal structure of the Psalms or the Song of Solomon, where the grammar of the second half of the verse parallels the grammar of the first half:

> We have no rest, three battles a month.
> By heaven, his horses are tired.
> The generals are on them, the soldiers are by them.
> The horses are well trained, the generals have ivory
>   arrows and quivers ornamented with fish-skin.
> The enemy is swift, we must be careful.

The same principle operates: though the ear necessarily registers "the generals have ivory arrows and quivers ornamented with fish-skin" as longer than "the soldiers are by them," yet the ear takes pleasure in being persuaded by the mind that since these units are grammatically equal (being both complete sentences), the sentence about ivory arrows and fish-skin quivers takes up no more time than "the soldiers are by them," or "we must be careful." All sorts of changes can be rung; for instance, in "The River Merchant's Wife: A Letter," in which the norm is one sentence to a line but there are also many sentences strung over two lines, there is an exceptional poign-

[3] See Donald Davie, *Articulate Energy: An Enquiry into the Syntax of English Verse* (London, 1955), ch. 4.

43

ancy about the one short line which comprehends two complete sentences:

> They hurt me. I grow older.

Vers libre on these or similar principles has been written in French by Claudel and St.-John Perse and in English by Eliot in his translation of Perse's *Anabase*.

This is not to say that the discovery or re-discovery of this principle absolves the poet from listening to what his verse sounds like; as if the reader's ear were always ready to be persuaded by his mind into taking as metrically equal two cadences of very unequal length. On the contrary, the ear permits itself to be thus persuaded only in specially favorable circumstances. And Pound goes to great pains to arrange the circumstances. Years later he was to say (Canto 81), "To break the pentameter, that was the first heave." And *Cathay* shows the pentameter already "broken."

It is important to understand what is involved. From Edmund Spenser onwards in English verse the finest art was employed in running over the verse line so as to build up larger units of movement such as the strophe, the Miltonic verse paragraph, or, in Shakespearean and other theatrical poetry, the sustained dramatic speech. This too is more an effect of syntax than of anything else: the grammatical unit, the sentence, is draped over the metrical unit, the line, so as to play off the pauses of different weight demanded by the grammar against the pauses demanded at line-endings (and sometimes within the line) by meter. This is not to "break" the pentameter (or more generally the verse-line of whatever length), but rather to submerge it, by incorporating the line into the building of larger and more intricate rhythmical units. Even the masters of the heroic couplet, Samuel Johnson no less than Pope or Dryden, frequently incorporated their couplets into verse-paragraphs conceived as rhythmical and rhetorical wholes; and even when they do not do this, their unit rhythmically is in any case the couplet, the pair of lines, rather than the line. It was only when the line was considered as the unit of composition, as it was by Pound in *Cathay*, that there emerged the possibility of "breaking" the line, of disrupting it from within, by throwing weight upon smaller units within the line. "South-Folk in Cold Country" is an exceptionally simple case, but even there the ear registers in the second line the phrase "in the north," as a rhythmical unit: isolated between commas, it is breaking free from the line of which it is a member, in a way which would be impossible for any comparable phrase in poetry that rode over line-endings as Pound's does not. Only when the line was isolated as a rhythmical unit did it become possible for the line to be rhythmically disrupted or dismembered from within. The phrase "the swift moving," left hanging between the penultimate and the last lines of "South-Folk in Cold Country" is not heard by the ear as itself an extra line, but rather as the rhythmical member of some vanished line, torn free and standing free on its own account. And in a piece as elaborately composed as "Song of the Bowmen of Shu," there are lines such as:

Sorrowful minds, sorrow is strong, we are hungry and thirsty.

or:

Horses, his horses even, are tired.   They were strong.

where the line breaks up into its rhythmical members, three in the first case and four in the second, between grammatical pauses which assert themselves as rhythmical pauses—which assert themselves thus more disruptively than would be possible in verse composed paragraph by paragraph, or strophe by strophe.

This procedure was not unprecedented, to be sure. Quite apart from the model of Hebrew poetry, which enforces similar effects in, for instance, Smart's *Rejoice in the Lamb*, the pentameter had thus been analyzed into its component rhythmical members by Thomas Campion [4] and in practice by other

4 See M.M. Kastendieck, *England's Musical Poet: Thomas Campion* (New York, 1938).

45

English poets of the seventeenth century who wrote for musical setting. Before many years were out, Pound would esteem very highly musicians and composers who at that period thus collaborated, such men as Henry Lawes and Edmund Waller; and he would see that, in their ways of writing, these seventeenth-century artists were the legitimate heirs of those Provençal poets to whom he had admiringly devoted himself ever since his student days.

In the translations he made from the Provençal at this time, Pound nevertheless overlooked this English precedent. William McNaughton has declared, for example, comparing Campion's poem "Since She, ev'n She" with Arnaut Daniel's "L'aura amara":

> Campion's music fits the Daniel poem perfectly, with the repetition of Campion's last two lines as indicated by the score:
>
> > Since she, ev'n she, for whom I liv'd,
> > Sweet she by Fate from me is torne
> > Why am not I of sence depriv'd,
> > Forgetting I was ever borne?
> > Why should I languish, hating light?
> > Better to sleepe an endlesse night.[5]

Campion's lines are very ready to dismember themselves, as the music may prompt:

> > Since she
> > ev'n she
> > for whom I liv'd . . .

and so on.

But Pound, when he worked at translations from the Provençal

[5] William McNaughton, "Ezra Pound's Meters and Rhythms," *PMLA*, LXXVIII (March 1963), 136-46.

(he meant to publish them as a book, "Arnaut Daniel," dedicated to William Pierce Shepard, his old teacher at Hamilton), was looking for the musicality of poetry in such comparatively freakish or primitive features as onomatopoeia and intricately regular full rhyme. Thus of "L'aura amara" he says: "we have the chatter of birds in autumn, the onomatopoeia obviously depends upon the '-utz, -etz, -ences and -ortz' of the rhyme scheme." And Pound's version of the seventeen short lines of each of Daniel's strophes is painstakingly in keeping with this conception of the poem, matching off each Provençal sound against an English sound in the precisely corresponding place. The result is not happy. It is difficult to believe that the poet who wrote *Cathay* was at much the same time writing the "Five Canzoni of Arnaut Daniel" that appear in his volume of 1920, *Umbra*.[6] What first strikes the reader is the extraordinarily indiscriminate diction of these versions: in order to get onomatopoeic and rhyming words, Pound has to let his diction veer crazily from colloquial slang to bizarre archaisms like "raik" and "wriblis"; the syntax is often crabbed, and word-order obscurely inverted, for the same reason. But more important, in view of the principles behind the distinctive melodies of *Cathay*, is the way in which the verse-line is no longer the unit; syntax is jerked and heaved around line-endings by violently disconcerting enjambements: "What folly hath infected/Thee?" or "Disburse/Can she, and wake/Such firm delights, that I/Am hers, froth, lees,/Bigod! from toe to earring." The last example recalls Browning at his worst.

The work that Pound did on Fenollosa's manuscripts about Chinese literature introduced him to what was to be an abiding interest of his life, and one of the causes he was to serve most

[6] There are other translations from Daniel in an essay on him to be found in Pound's *Instigations* (New York, 1920), and these are gathered together with the five from *Umbra* in *The Translations of Ezra Pound*, ed. by Hugh Kenner (London, 1953).

zealously—the Chinese, more particularly the Confucian, system of ethics. The far more voluminous material which Fenollosa left bearing on Japanese poetry served Pound's purposes less well. If we look back down the perspective of Pound's career as a whole at the work he did, following Fenollosa, on the Japanese Noh plays, we see that this bore fruit in the later writings, not of Pound himself, but of an older poet who was his close associate when he was working on this material, W.B. Yeats. It was Yeats who, in "At the Hawk's Well," "The Dreaming of the Bones," and others of his *Plays for Dancers*, adapted into the English and the Irish theaters the dramatic form that the Noh plays represent, finding in these Japanese works the alternative he had long been looking for to the naturalistic theater of Ibsen and Shaw. Pound, on the other hand, seems seldom to have been attracted toward writing for the theater—a feature of his temperament that helps to explain, for instance, the small place Shakespeare has in his scheme of things, and the striking way in which Pound hardly ever, whatever style he is writing in, recalls Shakespearean ways of writing.

His versions of the Noh plays [7] are not for this reason to be overlooked or given scant attention. On the contrary, these translations show better than anything else the catholicity of Pound's taste and how capable he was of responding to ways and structures of feeling that were remote from his own. It is true that at the time Pound did not see his own course clearly enough to realize that the Noh plays represented for him a blind alley. Noting that "the plays have . . . a very severe construction of their own, a sort of musical construction," and that where their language seems vague and pale it is because the unity of emotion the Noh seeks is to be completed in dance, he then finds in them also, more questionably, "what we may call Unity of Image":

[7] In 'Noh' or Accomplishment, Pound incorporated plays previously published in *Certain Noble Plays of Japan* and in *Poetry* (Chicago), *Drama, The Quarterly Note-Book,* and *The Quarterly Review.*

At least, the better plays are all built into the intensification of a single Image: the red maple leaves and the snow flurry in Nishikigi, the pines in Takasago, the blue-grey waves and wave pattern in Suma Genji, the mantle of feathers in the play of that name, Hagoromo.

Pound in a footnote tries to make a connection on this basis with the poetic program of "imagisme," which at this early stage he was campaigning for and substantiating in his own poems. But the connection is a strained one, as is another he makes in a later footnote between a Provençal poem and a Japanese dance-lyric or *Saibara* quoted by Fenollosa. More convincing, in its frank avowal of temperamental impatience and hostility which has had to be overcome, is one of several passages in which Pound alludes explicitly to Yeats:

> I dare say the play, Suma Genji, will seem undramatic to some people the first time they read it. The suspense is the suspense of waiting for a supernatural manifestation—which comes. Some will be annoyed at a form of psychology which is, in the West, relegated to spiritualistic seances. There is, however, no doubt that such psychology exists. All through the winter of 1914-15 I watched Mr. Yeats correlating folk-lore (which Lady Gregory had collected in Irish cottages) and data of the occult writers, with the habits of charlatans of Bond Street. If the Japanese authors had not combined the psychology of such matters with what is to me a very fine sort of poetry, I would not bother about it.

And in the next paragraph he talks of how the Noh requires a sympathy that is not "easily acquired," that requires "conscious effort" in order to "get over the feeling of hostility." He concludes, "I have found it well worth the trial." It does not occur to Pound that some readers' sympathies will go out to the swimming colors and fluctuating outlines of the Noh more readily than to the hard distinctness of the poems in *Cathay*. Since Pound, however, has sometimes given the impression of one who will always give instruction but never take it, it is worth emphasizing this case in which rather plainly Pound allowed himself to be persuaded by Yeats.

Sometimes he was over-persuaded, as in the first play, "Sotoba Komachi," in which he gives to a Japanese woman prose that has too clearly felt the impress of Synge-song or Kiltartanese, the version of Irish folk-speech that Yeats, or his collaborators J.M. Synge and Lady Gregory, devised for Dublin's Abbey Theatre: "And I had a high head, maybe, that time." On the other hand, Pound's prose is in many pieces extremely moving. Many of the translations are wholly in prose; so that, when Pound speaks of "a very fine sort of poetry" in these plays, he must be taken to mean the poetry that is peculiar and proper to drama, a poetry of action and confrontation to which language (whether prose or verse) is only an adjunct and ultimately, when drama becomes dance as it does here, expendable altogether. As Yeats reveals his realization of this in the imitations he made of the Noh, so Pound shows it in these translations; and doubtless the two poets must be thought of as working toward this together, with Fenollosa's manuscripts to help them. Certainly "Tsunemasa," for instance, which is entirely in prose except for a last couplet, is full of a wonderful poetry throughout, as Pound points out in a brief foreword where he compares the Japanese poet with Dante:

Spirit   A flute's voice has moved the clouds of Shushinrei. And the phoenix came out from the cloud; they descend with their playing. Pitiful, marvellous music! I have come down to the world. I have resumed my own playing. And I was happy here. All that is soon over.

Priest   Now I can see him again, the figure I saw here; can it be Tsunemasa?

Spirit   It's a sorry face that I make here. Put down the lights if you see me.

Chorus   The sorrow of the heart is a spreading around of quick fires. The flames are turned to thick rain. He slew by the sword and was slain. The red wave of blood rose in fire, and now he burns with that flame. He bade us put out the lights; he flew as a summer moth.

"It's a sorry face that I make here" marks the momentary reappearance of the "Oirish" cadence. But the passage as a whole manifests what was to be seen in *Cathay* also, the stabbing pathos which comes with using, as Fenollosa had enjoined in his essay on the Chinese written character, that rapid and compact grammatical form, the simple sentence.[8]

In the verse, too, Pound sometimes seems still in *Cathay:*

> How sad a ruin is this:
> Komachi was in her day a bright flower;
> She had the blue brows of Katsura;
> She used no powder at all;
> She walked in beautiful raiment in palaces.
> Many attended her verse in our speech
> And in the speech of the foreign court.

But more typically the verse wanders into quite other areas; this is especially true of the most haunting and beautiful of the plays, such as "Kinuta" or "Nishikigi":

> At last they forget, they forget.
> The wands are no longer offered,
> The custom is faded away.
> The narrow cloth of Kefu
> Will not meet over the breast.
> 'Tis the story of Hosonuno,
> This is the tale:
> These bodies, having no weft,
> Even now are not come together.
> Truly a shameful story,

[8] Fenollosa's essay in Pound's redaction first appeared in *The Little Review*, VI (Sept., Oct., Nov., Dec. 1919). It was reprinted in *Instigations* and, along with translations from Confucius, in Washington, D.C., in 1951.

A tale to bring shame on the gods.
Names of love,
Now for a little spell,
For a faint charm only,
For a charm as slight as the binding together
Of pine-flakes in Iwashiro,
And for saying a wish over them about sunset,
We return, and return to our lodging.
The evening sun leaves a shadow.

It is hard to believe that there is in the Japanese an equivalent
to the submerged pun by which this speech floats onward—
"Now for a little spell"—where the spell is registered first as a
spell of time but then, as the references to "a charm" accumulate, transformed into the spell of a necromancer. Moreover,
the sentence in which this phrase occurs is only by courtesy
to be called a sentence at all: grammatical analysis cannot reveal its structure—and no wonder, for a firm and orderly structure would be out of place when the progression is, as it is
here, oblique and dreamlike, through the irrational associations
of pun. Pound was to use puns in his own poetry, but stridently, to draw attention to themselves, not as here. And,
though he sometimes writes visionary poems, one can see in
the perspective of his career as a whole that this poetry of the
swimming contour, and the states of mind that produce such
poetry and respond to it, are alien to his temperament. Within
a year or so after making these Noh translations, he was to
redefine his own "imagisme" more stringently, so as to set it
over against the "symboliste" poetry which seeks out the in-
definite. It is the more remarkable that, when challenged by
works such as the Noh which called for symboliste treatment,
Pound could write in the symboliste way very tenderly and
evocatively indeed. In any case one feature of this poetry appealed to him very strongly—its tact, its good manners:

> Our own art is so much an art of emphasis, and even of
> over-emphasis, that it is difficult to consider the possibili-
> ties of an absolutely unemphasized art, an art where the

author trusts so implicitly that his auditor will know what things are profound and important.

Others had worked at the Noh before Pound,[9] and new information was to impugn Fenollosa's scholarship. Arthur Waley's versions [10] were to make the Fenollosa-Pound versions out of date as scholarship, though not as English poetry. Meanwhile Pound had served Mrs. Fenollosa well, very deftly and beguilingly interweaving commentary of his own, the admirably vigorous reflections of Fenollosa himself, and the plays. But as early as 1918, Pound declared:

> I don't think Yeats' *Silentia Lunae* hangs together. At least, I don't think it in the same street with his Memoirs as writing. And I find *Noh* unsatisfactory. I daresay it's all that could be done with the material. I don't believe anyone else will come along to do a better book on Noh, save for encyclopaedizing the subject. And I admit there are beautiful bits in it. But it's all too damn soft. Like Pater, Fiona Macleod and James Matthew Barrie, not good enough.
>
> I think I am justified in having spent the time I did on it, but not much more than that. (*Letters*, p. 197.)

There is no evidence that he changed his mind later.

[9] See e.g. Marie Stopes, *Plays of Old Japan. The No* (London, 1912).
[10] Arthur Waley, in an Introduction (1960) to a new edition (London, 1962) of his *One Hundred and Seventy Chinese Poems*, declares interestingly that "in translating the lyric parts of Japanese Nō plays...I was as regards diction a good deal influenced by Hopkins." When Pound made his versions he had not read Gerard Manley Hopkins.

III

*G*audier-Brzeska · Vorticism · *Lustra*

Pound's most explicit attempt to distinguish his poetry, which he calls "imagiste," from symboliste poetry is to be found in what is unfortunately the most incoherent though also one of the most important of his prose works, his memoir of the French sculptor Gaudier-Brzeska, who was killed in the trenches in 1915 at the age of twenty-three. Pound had been associated with Gaudier-Brzeska, and with the painters Percy Wyndham Lewis and Edward Waddington, in a movement that christened itself "vorticism" and ran its own polemical magazine, the once notorious *Blast*. The vorticist movement is interesting as a deliberate attempt to embrace all the arts under one rubric and to help an artist in any one medium by inviting him to find analogies with what his colleagues were doing in the others. Because of this manifesto-program element, Pound in the memoir more than once invokes approvingly Pater's dictum, "All the arts aspire to the condition of music." But, in fact, the vorticist group did not include any musicians, and so the analogy with music, so important to symbolisme, is little explored by Pound; because Gaudier-Brzeska was a sculptor, it is the analogy between poetry and sculpture with which Pound is principally concerned. So he defines his own "imagiste" poetry as "a sort of poetry where painting or sculpture seems as it were 'just coming over into speech.'" [1] Since sculpture, or at least one aspect of sculpture, can be expressed in terms of a relationship between plane surfaces, Pound speaks in these terms of images in a poem:

> The pine-tree in mist upon the far hill looks like a fragment of Japanese armour.
>
> The beauty of this pine-tree in the mist is not caused by its resemblance to the plates of the armour.
>
> The armour, if it be beautiful at all, is not beautiful *because* of its resemblance to the pine in the mist.
>
> In either case the beauty, in so far as it is beauty of form, is the result of 'planes in relation.'
>
> The tree and the armour are beautiful because their diverse planes overlie in a certain manner. (pp. 146-7)

This way of talking about poetry is not so useless as it seems: no other vocabulary can render the method and the effect of Pound's late cantos, which significantly are entitled *Rock-Drill* after a sculpture by Epstein. Similarly, more than juggling with words is involved when Pound defines the poetic image in specifically vorticist terms:

> The image is not an idea. It is a radiant node or cluster; it is what I can, and must perforce, call a VORTEX, from which, and through which, and into which, ideas are constantly rushing. In decency one can only call it a VORTEX. And from this necessity came the name "vorticism."

[1] *Gaudier-Brzeska* (London, 1916), p. 95.

> *Nomina sunt consequentia rerum*, and never was that state-
> ment of Aquinas more true than in the case of the vorticist
> movement. (p. 106)

Nomina sunt consequentia rerum—"names are the consequences
of things." But in symboliste poetry the logic works all the
other way—things are the consequences of names; for we find
in such a case as Eliot's "penny world," from "A Cooking
Egg," that we cannot find a referent for this collocation, nothing of which "penny world" is the name. Rather we agree (as,
surprisingly, we find we can) that in the universe created by
the poem, the two words thus forced into conjunction call up
a thing, a "penny world," to which they refer, which they
name. Words, then, *can* create things—and do so continually in
symboliste poetry. But Pound, as his appeal to Aquinas shows,
is in this matter (as in surprisingly many others when one
comes to look) content to be a traditionalist. For "penny" and
"world" are not, in Pound's understanding nor, surely, in ours,
images; and Eliot's cramming of them together does not, therefore, create images whose "diverse planes overlie in a certain
manner." It is words that are put together, not images; and
while it seems to be true that the right words put together at
the right moment in the right way can create by fiat a thing of
which they are thenceforward the name, this is a capacity of
language which Pound is content to leave to symbolisme—
symbolisme which has, so far as he is concerned, "degraded the
symbol to the status of a word."

Particularly revealing of Pound's constant tendency to see
the objective world as indeed objectively there is his comment,
again in *Gaudier-Brzeska*, on a famous poem of his own, the
two-line poem like a Japanese *hokku* called "In a Station of
the Metro":

> The apparition of these faces in the crowd;
> Petals, on a wet, black bough.

Pound comments: "I dare say it is meaningless unless one has
drifted into a certain vein of thought. In a poem of this sort

one is trying to record the precise instant when a thing outward and objective transforms itself, or darts into a thing inward and subjective." [2] Here once again one sees the traffic being run all the other way from the symbolistes. For to Pound it is the outward that transforms itself into the inward, whereas to the devotee of the objective correlative it is always the inward (the poet's state of mind or state of feeling) that seeks in the outward world something to correspond to itself. Pound's poem answers to what he gives as his intention in writing it. The syntactical dislocation between the two lines permits two comparisons at once: the first, a simple register of the outward, by which the white faces against the gloom of the underground station are like white petals against a black bough; the second, a register of the inward state evoked as a response in the perceiver's mind, by which not the faces but the apparition of them stands out against the gloom of the observer's mind as petals stand out against the bough. It is surely untrue, therefore, that the poem "is meaningless unless one has drifted into a certain vein of thought." Its compactness is not superficial, but real and masterly.

Part of the trouble with *Gaudier-Brzeska* is that Pound is fighting on too many fronts at once. His quarrel with symbolisme, for instance, is blurred because Pound, insisting on how his poetry, unlike symboliste poetry, hews close to the contours of the perceivable world, is forced to insist that on the other hand the art he is promoting is not simply representational. Some progress is made, however sluggishly and lopsidedly, and it is surely no longer necessary to insist:

> We have again arrived at an age when men can consider a statue as a statue. The hard stone is not the live coney. Its beauty cannot be the same beauty. (p. 127)

[2] *Gaudier-Brzeska*, p. 103. See, on this poem and more generally on Pound's debt to *hokku* or *haiku* (alternative names for one verse-form), Earl Miner, "Pound, *Haiku*, and the Image," *The Hudson Review*, IX (Winter, 1956-57), 570-84.

And yet one cannot be sure: it is still easy to find critics for whom an imagiste poem such as "In a Station of the Metro" is a simple register of sense appearances, all outwardness, never darting "into a thing inward and subjective." In these circumstances one can only baldly assert that no retreat to representationalism is involved when Pound borrows from Whistler for his *profession de foi*:

> "Nature contains the elements." It is to be noted that one is not forbidden any element, any key because it is geological rather than vegetable, or because it belongs to the realm of magnetic currents or to the binding of steel girders and not to the flopping of grass or the contours of the parochial churchyard.
>
> The artist is born to pick and choose, and *group with science*, these elements, that the result may be beautiful.... (p. 153; italics as in the original)

On the other hand, the emphasis must certainly fall upon the worthiness of the external world to be imitated—and imitated not in the recondite sense by which Aristotle called music the most mimetic of the arts, but in the straightforward sense that recalls what Yeats, in an untypical moment, claimed for Bishop Berkeley: "Berkeley has brought back to us the world that only exists because it shines and sounds." It is this shining and sounding world for the recovery of which, in all its various glory, Pound is finally grateful to Gaudier-Brzeska and Epstein, to Wyndham Lewis and the other vorticists:

> These new men have made me see form, have made me more conscious of the appearance of the sky where it juts down between houses, of the bright pattern of sunlight which the bath water throws up on the ceiling, of the great "V's" of light that dart through the chinks over the curtain rings, all these are new chords, new keys of design. (pp. 155/6)

58

It is this shining and sounding world, this system of keys, not to an unapparent world of essence and Idea, but to design, which is carried over on to page after page of Pound's *Cantos*, as it could not be carried on to the page of Eliot, which arranges only objective correlatives, nor to the page of Yeats, the poet for whom the realm of the senses was so often only "this pragmatical, preposterous pig of a world." Silk purses have been made out of that sow's ear.

In *Lustra*, the collection belonging to the same period as the Gaudier memoir,[3] the poem that most clearly illustrates the memoir is "The Game of Chess," an exciting and attractive bravura piece. But a profounder treatment, though a more oblique one, is "A Song of the Degrees," a poem which looks forward over twenty years to the Usura cantos 45 and 51, which similarly explore the morality implicit in the painter's use of hue.

Pound's development since *Ripostes* had been so rapid, and he had advanced on so many fronts, that *Lustra*, though a very distinguished collection, is also very heterogeneous. It contains, for instance, all but one of the twelve poems published in *Poetry*, II, in April 1913 under the title "Contemporania," and within this group there are elements so different as markedly Whitmanesque pieces ("Salutation," "Salutation the Second," "Commission," "A Pact") and "In a Station of the Metro" which one would have sworn came later, out of vorticist theory and the reading of Fenollosa. "Further Instructions," "Dum Capitolium Scandet," and "Coda" are other Whitmanesque poems in *Lustra* [4] that consort oddly with the

---

[3] *Lustra*, trade edition, London, 1916; private edition, London, 1916; trade edition, New York, 1917; private edition, New York, 1917. Each of these editions differs slightly from all the others.

[4] See C.B. Willard, "Ezra Pound's Debt to Walt Whitman," in *Studies in Philology*, LIV (Oct. 1957), 573-81.

terse obliquities of Chinese pieces such as "After Ch'u Yuan," "Liu Ch'e," and "Fan-Piece, for Her Imperial Lord." [5]

"Ancora," "Surgit Fama," "April," "Gentildonna," and "Les Millwin" are other poems which were in print as early as 1913, and some of these are important and beautiful. By contrast the poems from *Lustra* which appeared first in magazines of the next year, 1914, are mostly slight and often unsatisfactory: the four epigrams headed "Ladies," [6] for instance, seem to have no point beyond the assertion of a very precarious urbanity, flawed and precarious because it is always toppling over into calculated insolence or a mere wish to shock. Some of these are idle squibs or lampoons which may once have had some topical or polemical point but now are only irritating—for instance, "The New Cake of Soap" or "L'Art, 1910," both from the first issue of *Blast*. Some, however, have interest of another, technical kind in the perspective of Pound's efforts to "break the pentameter." A case in point is the second of the pieces called "Amitiés" which ends on a carefully calculated and interesting free-verse cadence. Another such five-finger-exercise is " 'Ione, Dead the Long Year.' " And as early as 1917 Pound was warning a reviewer against supposing that because *Cathay* preceded *Lustra* the poems in the latter showed him applying to his original work lessons learned from his Chinese translations (*Letters*, p. 154); so much of *Lustra* had appeared in magazines two or three years earlier that this could not be the case.

In particular Pound observes, "I think you will find all the verbal constructions of *Cathay* already tried in 'Provincia Deserta.' " "Provincia Deserta" is one of the most masterly poems to be found not just in *Lustra* but in the whole body of Pound's

---

[5] See Achilles Fang, "Fenollosa and Pound," in *Harvard Journal of Asiatic Studies*, 20 (1957), 213-38. The Chinese poems in *Lustra* are derived not from Fenollosa but from Giles's *History of Chinese Literature* (1901) or else his *Chinese Poetry in English Verse* (1884).

[6] First printed in *Poetry*, IV, 5 (1914).

work; and its "verbal constructions" and rhythmical arrangements are, if not identical with those of *Cathay*, without doubt very closely related and even more elaborate:

> At Chalais
>   is a pleached arbour;
> Old pensioners and old protected women
> Have the right there—
>   it is charity.
> I have crept over old rafters,
>   peering down
> Over the Dronne,
>   over a stream full of lilies.
> Eastward the road lies,
>   Aubeterre is eastward,
> With a garrulous old man at the inn.
> I know the roads in that place:
> Mareuil to the north-east,
>   La Tour,
> There are three keeps near Mareuil,
> And an old woman,
>   glad to hear Arnaut,
> Glad to lend one dry clothing.

If "Old pensioners and old protected women" were allowed to set an iambic tune for the rest, there might emerge something like this, in regular though varied blank verse:

> Old pensioners and old protected women
> Have the right there, out of charity.
> I have crept along old rafters, peering down
> Over the Dronne, a stream there full of lilies.
> Eastward lies the road to Aubeterre,
> Where a garrulous old man is at the inn.
> I know the roads in that place; know Mareuil
> To the north-east, La Tour, the three keeps near,
> And an old woman glad to hear Arnaut...

But everything is lost by such a rearrangement. The information about "charity" is now delivered with a blank poker-face, whereas in Pound's poem it is spoken of haltingly and the speaker is as if wide-eyed. In the next lines the sense conveyed, the image presented, is completely changed, for the pentameter makes the creeping and the peering happen together, whereas in Pound's poem the man is seen first to creep, and then to peer. Moreover, in Pound's arrangement the reading eye as it moves over the page *discovers* that the Dronne is a stream full of lilies, just as the speaker may have known beforehand that the Dronne was what he was going to see, but not that it had lilies in it. In the blank verse we are told that the Dronne has lilies in it; we do not discover it for ourselves as the speaker did. In Pound's poem the speaker sees the road wind eastwards, and then reflects that Aubeterre is where it leads to; or else he reflects first on where the road is, then on where it is going. In the blank verse Aubeterre and the road are parts of a single act, in such a way that the road is swallowed up in "Aubeterre" and has no physical presence of its own. Pound's poem enacts the process of remembering about Mareuil, naming "La Tour" but then eddying back as the speaker reminds himself that there are three keeps in the vicinity (perhaps two more besides "La Tour"); in the blank verse the speaker does not remind himself of anything. And so on: Pound's lineation points up the distinctness of each image or action as it occurs, and thus insists on the sequence they occur in, whereas blank verse, by speeding up the sequence, blurs them together. As William Carlos Williams was writing at just this time:

> The virtue of strength lies not in the grossness of the fiber but in the fiber itself. Thus a poem is tough by no quality it borrows from a logical recital of events nor from the events themselves but solely from the attenuated power which draws perhaps many broken things into a dance by giving them thus a full being.[7]

[7] Prologue to "Kora in Hell," in *Selected Essays of William Carlos Williams* (New York, 1954), p. 14.

The pentameter's interwoven strands of sisal rope are replaced by one wiry and flexible steel cable.

The impression *Lustra* gives, of a bewildering but by no means aimless eclecticism, is crowned by the inclusion in the volume, among so many innovations, of an ambitious piece in one of the manners Pound had made his own almost from the start, the manner of Browning. This is the poem "Near Perigord," which had appeared first in *Poetry* for December 1915. It deals, like "Sestina: Altaforte," with the figure of Bertran de Born, and like "Sestina: Altaforte" its way of dealing with the subject is Browning's way. However, this is another Browning from the poet of dramatic monologues and dramatic lyrics. The one who presides over "Near Perigord" is the Browning of *The Ring and the Book*. Pound's poem, like *The Ring and the Book*, dramatizes the processes of historical research, forcing the reader to confront the conflicting testimonies and mutually exclusive hypotheses which are all that often enough the scrupulous historian has to show after all his labors among sparse and contradictory and dubiously authentic documents. Was Bertran, when he praised the Lady Maent, expressing his love for her? Or was this a fiction designed to permit his jongleur to spy into the strongholds of Bertran's neighbors and rivals, and to set them by the ears so as to improve Bertran's precariously exposed position among them? "Is it a love poem? Did he sing of war?" Which? The poem, by trying and failing to answer this question, dramatizes the difficulty of ever knowing anything with certainty; thus it asserts how in history, as in natural history, the investigator is faced, sooner than we like to realize, with something irreducible and inscrutable—historical reality, like physical reality, resists us and can only to a limited extent be either manipulated or "seen through."

Looking back at this poem out of the *Cantos*, one sees how near this is to one central and governing concern of that later writing, in which the life and person of Sigismundo Malatesta, for instance, is to set just the same riddle as Bertran de Born sets in "Near Perigord," and the attempt to solve the riddle will proceed in the same way.

Though the investigation must break off inconclusively, the poem demands to be concluded, resolved. The resolution is in the last line, "A broken bundle of mirrors. . . ." Grammatically this refers to the lady herself, Maent; but, concluding as it does a poem that has restlessly moved from one hypothesis to the next, it has the effect of summing up, not just Maent, but the whole situation involving Bertran and her and others. Thus, "a broken bundle of mirrors" is what the whole of recorded history is. It should also describe, and in a sense it *does* describe, the nature of a poem which, like "Near Perigord" and later the *Cantos*, stays close to historical record. And yet the very line that acknowledges this, because it is felt to be a satisfying resolution, denies what it states. One bundle differs from the next; and there is a poet's way of tying up the bundle of mirrors (for instance, Dante's way in lines on Bertran that Pound's poem incorporates) that somehow clarifies and harmonizes. "Near Perigord" acknowledges this and trusts the poet's harmonizing vision; it is doubtful whether that acknowledgment and that trust govern the writing of the *Cantos*.

IV

Gourmont

In the earliest of his comments on translating Greek drama, Pound considers the "Agamemnon" of Browning:

> His weakness in this work is where it essentially lay in all of his expression, it rests in the term 'ideas.'—'Thought' as Browning understood it—'ideas' as the term is current, are poor two-dimensional stuff, a scant, scratch covering. 'Damn ideas, anyhow.' An idea is only an imperfect induction from fact.[1]

This is just the criticism of Victorian poetry in general that W.B. Yeats had been voicing ever since the 1890's.[2] But Pound

[1] "Translators of Greek," *The Egoist*, V and VI (Aug. 1918 to April 1919); reprinted in *Make It New* (London, 1934; New Haven, 1935), p. 147.
[2] W.B. Yeats, *Ideas of Good and Evil* (London, 1900).

almost certainly took it not from Yeats but from *Le Problème du style* by the French poet, novelist, and critic, Rémy de Gourmont:

> Une idée n'est qu'une sensation défraîchie, une image effacée.

It was similarly from Gourmont that T.S. Eliot took his famous debating point about "the dissociation of sensibility." [3] And Frank Kermode is doubtless right to see behind the theory, in Gourmont and Eliot alike, "the historical effort of Symbolism ... to identify a period happily ignorant of the war between Image and discourse...." [4] Pound is by no means free of the historical nostalgia this involves. Yet, when he says that an idea is "only an imperfect induction from fact," this is not the same as calling it "une image effacée." And in the maddening hotchpotch that Pound presented in 1918 as an essay on Gourmont,[5] though he concedes that "in the symbolistes Gourmont had his beginning," he speaks also of "funny symboliste trappings, 'sin,' satanism, rosy cross, heavy lilies," and declares that the symboliste phase of the nineteenth century no less than earlier phases "had mislaid the light of the eighteenth century."

This is the point at which current explanations of Pound go astray; he is not (as T.S. Eliot perhaps is) a "post-symboliste" writer, except in the narrowest chronological sense; what he deserves on the contrary is the lame though honorific title "realist." This contention must rest in the first place upon the poems Pound has written; secondly on the theories of poetry he has peddled, particularly those which he called "imagism" and "vorticism"; and only in the third place on his choice of writers to applaud, through translation or otherwise. Among these last, however, Gourmont is a particularly important case, because if "the historical effort of Symbolism" did enlist

[3] See F.W. Bateson, in *Essays in Criticism* (Oxford), I, 3 (July 1951).
[4] Frank Kermode, *Romantic Image* (London, 1957), p. 150.
[5] "Rémy de Gourmont: A Distinction, Followed by Notes," *The Little Review,* V (Feb.-March 1919), [1]-19; reprinted in *Make It New,* p. 309.

Pound's energies (as is claimed), then it must have been through Gourmont that the meaning and motive of that effort were communicated to him..

Gourmont, however, though as editor of the *Mercure de France* he provided a platform for symboliste ideas among others, was at no time really close to the center of symboliste theory and practice, in Mallarmé's apartment in the rue de Rome. Even during the years from 1886 to 1895 when he wrote polemically as a self-avowed symboliste, the symboliste venture seems to have been for him more a matter of personal and professional friendships (with J.K. Huysmans, for instance) than it was a cause to which he was dedicated, And, indeed, his deliberately uncommitted stance, which often made his writings contradict themselves, unfitted him for the role of spokesman. Of his works that Pound cites most often, one, *Le Latin mystique* of 1892, a scholarly popularization of some Latin poetry of the mediaeval Church, is undoubtedly conceived in part as symboliste propaganda:

> Plus d'un trait de figure caractéristique des poètes latins du christianisme se retrouve en la présente poésie française,— et deux sont frappants: la quête d'un idéal différent des postulats officiels de la nation résumés en une vocifération vers un paganisme scientifique et confortable...; et, pour ce qui est des normes prosodiques, un grand dédain.[6]

Undoubtedly, however Pound regarded the first of these features of French symboliste poetry, the second, the matter of rhythm, interested him greatly. In the selections from French poets that Pound contributed, with commentary, to *The Little Review* for February 1918 (IV, 10), Gourmont is represented by his "Litanies de la rose," which Pound commends particularly for its intoxicating unmetrical rhythms. The intoxication is there certainly, as is the dismemberment of the poetic line in ways sometimes reminiscent of Scripture, for

[6] Rémy de Gourmont, *Le Latin mystique, les poètes de l'antiphonaire et la symbolique au Moyen Age*, 2nd ed. (Paris, 1892), Introduction.

instance, of the Song of Songs. But Gourmont, like Claudel and St.-John Perse later, has extended the line so far that it is a line no longer and can afford no model for Pound's efforts "to break the pentameter." Moreover, the substance of Gourmont's poem is far from novel, and it recalls in its excited eroticism some poems of that other intoxicating metrist, Swinburne, more than it recalls Mallarmé or Laforgue. Other features of Gourmont's symbolisme would be comfortably familiar to any reader of Dowson or other poets of the English 'nineties; for instance, an attitudinizing languor which is naïvely paraded in *Le Latin mystique*:

> Seule, que l'on soit croyant ou non, seule la littérature mystique convient à notre immense fatigue, et pour nous qui ne prévoyons qu'un au delà de misères de plus en plus surement, de plus en plus rapidement réalisé, nous voulons nous borner à la connaissance de nous-mêmes et des obscurs rêves, divins ou sataniques, qui se donnent rendez-vous en nos âmes de jadis. (Introduction)

And the "rêve . . . satanique" is indulged as early as the second chapter, in an excited meditation on the tortures peculiarly reserved for female martyrs. In all this there is more of what Pound very sensibly called "funny symboliste trappings" than there is of symbolisme as a serious poetic program.

One may suspect, in fact, that by 1918 Gourmont keeps his place beside Rimbaud and others, in Pound's reading of French poetry, chiefly out of the old loyalty that five years earlier had led Pound to invoke Gourmont's metrical practice when providing a skeletal analysis of the Bengali measures of Rabindranath Tagore's *Gitanjali*.[7] Moreover, in 1918, Pound had

[7] *The Fortnightly Review* XCIII (N.S.), 1913, p. 555: "This metre is . . . not quantitative as the Greek or Sanscrit measures, but the length of the syllables is considered, and the musical time of the bars is even. The measures are more interesting than any now being used in Europe, except those of certain of the most advanced French writers, as, for instance, the arrangements of sound in Rémy de Gourmont's 'Fleurs de Jadis' or his 'Litanies de la Rose.'"

probably not read *Le Latin mystique* at all recently or closely, for he declares of Gourmont that "influenced presumably by the mediaeval sequaires, and particularly by Goddeschalk's quoted in *Le Latin mystique*, he recreated the 'litanies.'" In fact, as the word would lead us to suppose, Gourmont's litanies owe much more to the mediaeval litanies (also discussed in *Le Latin mystique*) than they do to the *sequaires*. And Pound seems to remember the *sequaire* of Goddeschalk (which is always the case he cites from this book by Gourmont) for a reason which has nothing to do with form and rhythm— for what Goddeschalk says to Christ about Mary Magdalen, "*Amas ut pulchram facias.*" [8]

Gourmont built up a solid reputation in France on critical and philosophical essays published after 1900, in particular on *Le Problème du style* (1902).[9] This is one of Gourmont's writings that plainly influenced the early criticism of T.S. Eliot. Its importance for Pound is much less obvious and can easily be overestimated. Indeed, since it is a sustained sarcastic polemic against a textbook by Albalat written on the assumption that one may learn literary style by imitating the classic "stylists," much of Gourmont's book seems at odds with the position that Pound was later to take up in *How To Read*,[10] a work that could as well be entitled "How To Write," in which Pound seems near to proceeding on precisely Albalat's assumption. In fact, Pound could square his position with Gourmont's only by driving hard a distinction Gourmont makes between imitation of foreign writers (which may be fruitful) and the imitation of writers in one's own tongue. Another of Gourmont's emphases that must have been antipathetic to Pound is on impersonality. The impersonality that Gourmont argues for is of the peculiar kind that T.S. Eliot eagerly

[8] Gourmont, op. cit., 2nd ed., p. 115: "Tu l'aimes afin qu'elle soit belle,— 'Amas ut pulchram facias,'—ô noble cervelle si avancée en idéalisme!"
[9] See Karl-David Uitti, *La Passion littéraire de Rémy de Gourmont* (Paris, 1962).
[10] *How To Read* (London, 1931; Boston, 1932).

69

elaborated in his influential essay on "Tradition and the Individual Talent." [11] Both Gourmont and Eliot argue for an absolute discontinuity between the affective experience of the writer at all times when he is not writing, and the allegedly quite distinct sort of emotional experience that conditions his act of composition. Pound on the other hand admired Li Po and Villon just because the man who is personally present in the writing is recognizably the same who lived the dishevelled and turbulent life known from record, anecdote, and legend.

But what does most to bring Eliot to mind rather than Pound, in relation to *Le Problème du style*, is the tone and manner of Gourmont's procedure. In his dealings with the unfortunate Albalat, in his dealings with ideas, and in his dealings with the reader, the play of Gourmon't intelligence is very free indeed. *Le Problème du style* is a brilliant book, in every sense of "brilliant" including those that shade off into "superficial" and even "journalistic." It is continually arresting, it is not always judicious. F.W. Bateson remarks sourly, "Gourmont was never afraid to follow a bright idea to a nonsensical conclusion." And Gourmont himself admitted as much:

> ...il y a des nuances infinies; mais il faut toujours pousser une théorie a l'extrème, si l'on ne veut pas être tout à fait incompris.[12]

Pound has certainly driven to nonsensical conclusions himself, but unwittingly, seldom with this air of calculated insolence. It is this in Gourmont that accounted for the rather sudden extinction of his reputation soon after his death in 1915. After his death, as for some years before, Gourmont came under heavy attack on this score in the *Nouvelle Revue Française* at the hands of Gide, whom Gourmont had assisted and admired for many years beginning in 1891. Already in 1910 Gide, accusing Gourmont of "facilité intellectuelle," declared:

[11] "Tradition and the Individual Talent," *The Sacred Wood* (London, 1920).
[12] *Le Problème du style*, 13th ed. (Paris, 1924), p. 68.

> la pensée n'est point chez [Gourmont] le résultat d'une
> contention, d'un effort; comme d'autres à la paresse il
> s'abandonne à la pensée et c'est comme en se jouant qu'il
> écrit.[13]

As regards *Le Problème du style* at any rate, Gide's objection, though harsh, is no more than just. Indeed, Gourmont seems to have admitted its justice, regretting his own facility; and so in *Le Problème du style* he goes out of his way to give credit to honest inarticulate clumsiness in writing. Even so, his own facility may have been more damaging than he realized.

Pound certainly recognized this quality in Gourmont but he seems to have misinterpreted it in a way not uncommon among British and American Francophiles, who mistake this tone for the tone of Voltaire. Pound, in an obituary notice of Gourmont, explicitly made the connection:

> Voltaire called in a certain glitter to assist him. De Gour-
> mont's ultimate significance may not be less than Vol-
> taire's. He walked gently through the field of his mind.[14]

And Pound's "glitter" seems to mean that he is, if anything, readier to see meretricious brilliance in Voltaire. Elsewhere in the obituary Pound compares Gourmont with Anatole France, Henri de Regnier, Francis Jammes, and Laurent Tailhade, and decides

> from Rémy de Gourmont alone there proceeded a personal
> living force. "Force" is almost a misnomer; let us call it a
> personal light.

That note was struck again in the essay in *Make It New* ("the light of the eighteenth century"); it suggests that Pound saw Gourmont as a lineal successor of the French Enlightenment. And, sure enough, at the period when Pound was most con-cerned with Gourmont he was also reading admiringly some of

[13] Quoted by Uitti, op. cit., p. 47.
[14] *The Fortnightly Review*, XCVIII (N.S.), 1915, p. 588.

the *philosophes*, and Voltaire especially.[15] But in any case Pound's attachment to the French eighteenth century went deep and has remained strong. A product of it at this time was his translation of some of the dialogues of Fontenelle,[16] but it did not end with his youth. On the contrary perhaps the profoundest insight into Pound's later Confucianism was Yeats's brilliant *aperçu* about how Pound's Confucius "should have worn an Eighteenth Century wig and preached in St. Paul's." [17] For indeed, it could not be otherwise. When Pound discovered that the central insights of Confucian metaphysics were carried in images from the behavior of light, like those that were central also to Dante and Cavalcanti, he could not fail to take seriously the metaphor in the very words "age of enlightenment" or "age des lumières." It was this too which led him back into the historical experience of the American, for the America of the Founding Fathers, Jefferson and John Adams, was (or so he was to say) specifically an Enlightenment product, a transplanting to American soil of the noblest values of that French eighteenth century which had also, as a matter of historical record, first introduced Europe to the experience of Confucian and pre-Confucian China.[18] Pound's understanding of all European and American history is jeopardized, and his political miscalculations about the history of his own times are explained, as soon as we question whether the light that

[15] See the poem, "Impressions of François-Marie Arouet (de Voltaire)," originally in *To-Day*, I, 5 (1917), also "Genesis or The First Book in the Bible," and *Letters*, pp. 140, 150, 193-4.
[16] Originally in *The Egoist* III and IV (May 1916-June 1917).
[17] *The Letters of W. B. Yeats*, ed. Allan Wade (New York, 1955), p. 774.
[18] Cf. "Fenollosa on the Noh," *The Translations of Ezra Pound* (London, 1953), p. 269: "Bishop Percy, who afterwards revived our knowledge of the mediaeval ballad, published early in the 1760's the first appreciative English account of Chinese poetry; and Bishop Hood wrote an essay on the Chinese theatre, seriously comparing it with the Greek. A few years later Voltaire published his first Chinese tragedy, modified from a Jesuit translation; and an independent English version held the London stage till 1824." And cf. *Guide to Kulchur* (1938), p. 205, on "P. Lacharme ex soc. Jesu," who between 1733 and 1752 translated the Confucian odes into Latin.

shone in the Enlightenment on Voltaire and Jefferson was the same light that beamed on ancient China out of *The Unwobbling Pivot*, or on the Middle Ages out of Cavalcanti's "Donna mi prega" and Dante's *Paradiso*.

By the time he wrote *Le Problème du style*, Gourmont could have claimed kinship with figures of the Enlightenment in at least one important respect; no more than Voltaire or Fontenelle did he regard scientific discovery and theory as a world either closed to the man of letters or beneath his consideration. Gourmont seems to have entertained the delusory, and no doubt pointless, hope of making literary criticism into a science, and some of his allusions to scientific advances are tendentious coat-trailing, like T.S. Eliot's notoriously inexact analogy, in "Tradition and the Individual Talent," between the artistic sensibility in the act of creation and a bar of platinum acting as catalyst in a chemical solution. But Gourmont's interest in science went deeper than this, and *Le Problème du style*, no less than his *Physique de l'amour* of 1904, is an attempt to apply at least partially the theories of some biologists of his time, particularly the Lamarckian scholar De Vries (Uitti, p. 77). As Fenollosa writing of literature was guided by the scientific procedures of the biologist Agassiz, so Gourmont appealed not just to the classic French case of Buffon but also to the pioneering entomologist J.H. Fabre, and admired Taine as an earlier writer who had tried to apply scientific discipline to the writing of literary history. Out of Gourmont Fabre came to stand beside Agassiz and (later) Frobenius in Pound's gallery of admirable practitioners of scientific method, and it is certain that Gourmont won Pound's admiration at least in part for the same reason as Fenollosa.

It is this that makes Gourmont's campaigning for "the image" into something different from what symbolist or post-symbolist writers claimed for "the symbol." One cardinal case of "the image," for Gourmont as for Pound, is the carefully exact image the biologist constructs of the organisms he studies —an image created by nothing more recondite than scrupulously close and disciplined observation of the object as his senses apprehend it. It is not clear whether this is ever in T.S. Eliot's mind when he uses the word "image"; it is difficult to see how it can be, for "image," as Eliot used the word, seems to comprise also what he has called "the objective correlative." [19] And according to Eliot, the artist, in constructing his objective correlative out of phenomena offered to his senses, is not at all interested in these phenomena for themselves, in their objectivity, but only to the extent that they may *stand in for* the subjective phenomena (such as states of mind or of feeling) which can thus be objectified through them. The theory of the objective correlative seems much nearer to symboliste theory than Gourmont's or Pound's ideas of the image and, accordingly, much further from scientific method—so far indeed as to be quite incompatible with the assumptions on which a Fabre or an Agassiz proceeded. In fact, of course, the principle on which scientific empiricism proceeds, Locke's famous formulation *Nihil in intellectu quod non prius in sensu*, was called into question as soon as Coleridge (to cite only the principal English authority) pointed out that the processes of human perception are much less simple than Locke had supposed. Eliot's theories, like those of such symbolistes as Mallarmé and Valéry, have the merit of acknowledging the discoveries made by romanticism about the complexities of perception. Gourmont and Pound appear, by comparison, naïve, as nineteenth-century scientists seem naïve beside a twentieth-century physicist. Nevertheless, to get the record straight, it seems that they should be regarded not as post-symboliste theorists but rather as harking back to pre-symboliste and even pre-romantic convictions. In Pound's case, for instance, the element of sharp and exact observation that enters into his notion of the image relates him more closely to Ruskin than to

[19] T.S. Eliot, "Hamlet and His Problems," *The Sacred Wood*. When Graham Hough, on p. 16 of his *Image and Experience* (London, 1960), calls the theory of the objective correlative "one of the most celebrated offshoots of the Imagist idea," he is wrong unless he is using "imagism" in a sense too inclusive to be either serviceable or historically exact.

any of the symbolistes or to a thinker in the symboliste tradition such as Eliot.

Accordingly, it comes as no surprise that the work by Gourmont that Pound chose to translate, the *Physique de l'amour*,[20] is that in which Gourmont draws most directly and continually on the entomological observations of Fabre and others; nor that Gourmont in this work, as Pound translates him, should be heard echoing Ernest Fenollosa's strictures on "the old logic": "Far from wishing to impart human logic to nature, one attempts here to introduce a little natural logic into the old classic logic."

The translation is a careless performance. Occasionally Pound seems to achieve the charming Latinate elegance of an eighteenth-century naturalist like Gilbert White, as when he writes, "The salacity of certain birds is well known, and one does not see that the absence of an exterior penis diminishes their ardour, or attenuates the pleasure which they find in these succinct contacts." But alas! this is a delusion: the word "succinct" is an irresponsible Gallicism, for the French may speak of *un repas succint* to mean "a meager meal," and all that Gourmont means by the word is "brief" or "meager." Gourmont writes in his fourth chapter:

> Chez les insectes, la femelle est presque toujours l'individu supérieur. Ce n'est pas ce petit animal merveilleux, roi divergent et minuscule de la nature, qui donnerait le spectacle de cette douve, la bilhargie, dont la femelle, médiocre lame, vit, telle une épée au fourreau, dans le ventre creusé du mâle!

Here, by omitting to translate *cette douve*, Pound depends upon our recognizing in "the bilharzia" (though the word is not to be found in the Shorter Oxford English Dictionary) not an insect at all but a parasite-worm; otherwise we shall make

[20] *Physique de l'amour, Essai sur l'instinct sexuel* (Paris, 1904). Pound's translation, entitled *The Natural Philosophy of Love*, first appeared in New York in 1922.

the second half of Gourmont's sentence contradict the first half. And in Chapter 7 a similar heedlessness translates *en clôture* as "into cloisters."

All the same, *The Natural Philosophy of Love* is an amusing and instructive book. It has its sinister side, as when Gourmont's Lamarckian persuasion ("Instinct is merely a mode of intelligence") does not stop him arguing from the survival of the fittest to justify the enslavement of the black and brown races by the white. Darwinian arguments were used to the same end by jingo imperialists among Gourmont's British contemporaries, to the disgust of the Sussex squire Wilfrid Scawen Blunt, whom Pound admired. And when Gourmont goes on to prove from the behavior of bees that to neuter a part of a population is not unnatural, this casts forward a longer and even blacker shadow to the images of castration which were to run through Pound's mind at the height of his anti-Semitism. But there is an entertaining and admirably pointed wit to Gourmont's remark on polygamy among sticklebacks:

> When the stickleback world becomes reasonable, that is to say absurd, their philosophers will demand "Why should the father alone be charged with the education of his offspring?" Up to the present one knows nothing except that he educates them with joy and affection. Among sticklebacks and among men there is no answer to such a question save the answer given by facts. One might as well ask why humanity is not hermaphrodite like the snails, who strictly divide the pleasures and burdens of love, for all snails commit the male act, and all lay. Why has the female ovaries, and the male testicles; and this flower pistils, and that one stamens? One ends in baby-talk. The wish to correct nature is unnecessary. It is hard enough to understand her, even a little, as she is.

This too is a passage that would appeal to one who had read in manuscript Fenollosa's *Essay on the Chinese Written Character*, where there are passages informed by the same, perhaps naïve but certainly energetic, respect for natural processes.

76

V

Homage to Sextus Propertius •
Imaginary Letters • Hugh Selwyn Mauberley

By 1916, the work on or toward the *Cantos*, which had been in progress intermittently for ten years or more, had advanced to the stage where Pound was prepared to publish. *Three Cantos* appeared in the magazine *Poetry* in 1917.[1] These versions of Cantos I, II, and III were, as Yvor Winters was to remark, "awkward Browningesque affairs which bear little resemblance to the later *Cantos* or to their own later forms."[2] Nevertheless, they are worth taking note of, for this false start on the *Cantos* helps to get into focus the new start Pound made as soon as these were abandoned. For instance, it was of

[1] *Poetry*, X (June, July, and August 1917).
[2] Yvor Winters, *The Anatomy of Nonsense* (Norfolk, Conn., 1943); reprinted in *In Defense of Reason* (Denver, 1947), p. 495.

the new start (the first thirty Cantos) that Mr. Winters wrote in 1937:

> In the best *Cantos*, at least, Mr. Pound is successful, whether in fragments or on the whole, but he presents merely a psychological progression or flux, the convention being sometimes that of wandering reverie, sometimes that of wandering conversation. The range of such a convention is narrowly limited, not only as regards formulable content, but as regards feeling.[3]

And Mr. Winters may be right. But wandering reverie or wandering conversation is far more conspicuously the convention of the three cantos of the false start than of the received text—to such an extent, indeed, that Pound's reason for abandoning his first start appears to have been precisely what Mr. Winters goes on to observe:

> The feelings attendant upon reverie and amiable conversation tend to great similarity notwithstanding the subject matter, and they simply are not the most vigorous or important feelings of which the human being is capable.

If the convention of the *Cantos* is such as Mr. Winters says, at least this is unintentional on Pound's part; the abortive three cantos reveal that he had seen the damaging limitations of this convention, and when he started again was trying to avoid it.

The poems Pound wrote between 1917 and 1920 have been the subject of so many claims and counterclaims, so much vilification and approbation, that to get at the poems one has to fight through a cloud of witnesses. Certainly this is true of *Homage to Sextus Propertius* which, punctiliously dated by the poet as of 1917, was not printed until 1919 (in *New Age*, XXV). No poem by Pound has caused more offense. The pro-

[3] *Primitivism and Decadence* (1937), in *In Defense of Reason*, p. 145.

tests began when a part of the sequence in *Poetry*, XIII, 6 (March 1919), provoked Professor William Gardner Hale into attacking Pound for mistranslation. The attack, which was reproduced in part in the Chicago *Tribune*, was particularly awkward since Hale was a friend of Harriet Monroe, the editor of *Poetry* (*Letters*, p. 310); and it broke up the association between Pound and Miss Monroe that had made *Poetry* the principal organ by which "the new poetry" (of Pound, but also of others whom he campaigned for generously) had got into print.

And yet Pound's defense against Hale's charges was impregnable: there could be no mistranslation, since, as Pound wrote in 1919, "there was never any question of translation" (*Letters*, p. 211). Later, he elaborated this:

> No, I have not done a translation of Propertius. That fool in Chicago took the *Homage* for a translation, despite the mention of Wordsworth and the parodied line from Yeats (As if, had one wanted to pretend to more Latin than one knew, it wdn't have been perfectly easy to correct one's divergencies from a Bohn crib. Price 5 shillings.) (*Letters*, p. 245.)

The parody of Yeats is in Section IV:

Sadness hung over the house, and the desolated female attendants
Were desolated because she had told them her dreams.[4]

And Wordsworth is named in Section XII.

This should have been conclusive. That is was not so—that Robert Graves should to this day bring the charge of mistranslation, and Robert Conquest expatiate upon it in a truly scandalous article as late as 1963 [5]—this is partly Pound's fault, but more the fault of his apologists and admirers. T.S. Eliot in 1928, Hugh Kenner in 1951, John Espey in 1955, J.P. Sullivan

---

[4] Cf. Yeats: "I have spread my dreams under your feet;/Tread softly because you tread on my dreams." (*The Wind Among the Reeds*, 1899)
[5] *The London Magazine*, III, 1 (April 1963), 33-49.

in 1960 [6]—every one of them is determined to eat his cake and have it, to assert that *Homage to Sextus Propertius* is not a translation and yet that somehow it is. As soon as Espey, for example, observes that Pound's poem "requires, for its fullest savour, some knowledge of the text on which it is based," he opens the door to regarding the poem as translation; and Robert Conquest has the right to complain. And Espey is surely wrong, as are Eliot and Kenner and Sullivan also; so far from a knowledge of Propertius's Latin being a help to the understanding of Pound's poem, it is a perhaps insurmountable hindrance, as Conquest's essay proves. Pound's poem is *in no sense* a translation—not in the sense, for instance, in which Pope's "Imitations of Horace" are translations of Horace, or Johnson's "Vanity of Human Wishes" is a translation of Juvenal. Indeed, it appears that training as a Latinist tends to debar the reader from appreciating Pound's poem, and so one may commiserate with Robert Conquest on his deprivation. But of course he in turn is wrong to claim that "even 'homages' should have some connection with the spirit of their original." A "homage" means whatever Pound wants it to mean, since it is an *ad hoc* term he has invented. And again Conquest is wrong to say that Pound's poem "relies entirely on the kudos, and on the properties, of the original." How can this be true in the case of a reader who has not enough Latin to know the original? And whereas in 1919 perhaps two out of every three readers would be in this position, nowadays nine out of every ten will be thus fortunately insulated, debarred from making the comparison that spoils the poem for Conquest.

T.S. Eliot was in 1928 so far from agreeing that he declared, astonishingly, "If the uninstructed reader is not a classical scholar, he will make nothing of it." The readers the poem has

---

[6] T.S. Eliot, Introduction to *Ezra Pound: Selected Poems* (London, 1928); Hugh Kenner, *The Poetry of Ezra Pound* (London, 1951); J.J. Espey, *Ezra Pound's* Mauberley (London, 1955); J.P. Sullivan, "Pound's *Homage to Propertius:* The Structure of a Mask," in *Essays in Criticism* (Oxford), X, 3 (1960).

found in the years since 1928—years when "classical scholars" have become ever thinner on the ground—seem to disprove Eliot; but since Robert Conquest will maintain that these readers have been bullied by academically institutionalized literary criticism, it is worthwhile spelling out how a reader with no Latin (though with a sense of how much the Latin civilization has contributed to the English) may come at Pound's poem.

Two earlier poems by Pound, and one piece of prose, should prepare such a reader. One poem is "Prayer for His Lady's Life" from *Canzoni*, 1911, which is glossed "From Propertius, Elegiae, Lib. III, 26." It is an early attempt at what becomes the second part of Section IX of *Homage to Sextus Propertius*, and the very title given to the earlier version ("His Lady") indicates how in 1911 the best Pound could do was to convert Propertius into Villon's "Où sont les neiges d'antan?" as seen through the spectacles of Rossetti and Swinburne. As the uninstructed reader compares "Ye might let one remain above with us" (1911) with "There are enough women in hell" (1917), he will not care whether he is getting any nearer to Augustan Rome; he will know that he is moving from the nineteenth century into the twentieth.

The other poem that will help is "Au Salon":

> I suppose there are a few dozen verities
> That no shift of mood can shake from us:
>
> One place where we'd rather have tea
> (Thus far hath modernity brought us)
> "Tea" (Damn you!)
> Have tea, damn the Caesars,
> Talk of the latest success, give wing to some scandal,
> Garble a name we detest, and for prejudice?

Here the poet has the wish to speak in the accents of the present century, but not the capacity to do so. The most successful of his early poems had been those where we overhear him speaking to himself, privately; "Au Salon" is one where he tries for a public voice, one which we shall hear, not overhear. The only public voice that he can command, however, is the voice of Whitman; his dissatisfaction with that voice is presumably what prompts unsuccessful but praiseworthy attempts to find another voice, as here, where the "Damn you!" in its frustrated stridency betrays at once the desperation of the wish and the impossibility of fulfilling it. The epigrams of *Lustra*, their style painstakingly evolved out of Chinese and Japanese models, out of Latin models such as Martial, and out of the French model of Laforgue, represent another attempt to find a public voice, and a significant but still partial and precarious advance in that direction. Only with the style of *Homage to Sextus Propertius* does Pound find the public voice he has been looking and listening for.

This distinction between the public voice and the private, between (in the terms of John Stuart Mill) the poem that we hear and the poem that we overhear, was overlooked by Pound when he adumbrated his notion of the *persona*:

> In the "search for oneself," in the search for "sincere self-expression," one gropes...for some seeming verity. One says "I am" this, that or the other, and with the words scarcely uttered one ceases to be that thing....I began this search for the real in a book called *Personae*, casting off, as it were complete masks of the self in each poem. I continued in a long series of translations, which were but more elaborate masks.[7]

The word "mask" suggests here a direct influence from the conversation of Yeats; and commentators have eagerly fastened upon this theory precisely because it seems to provide common ground between Eliot, Yeats, and Pound. But the naturally histrionic talent of the Anglo-Irishman, Yeats, needs to speak

[7] *Gaudier-Brzeska: A Memoir*, p. 98; quoted by J.P. Sullivan, loc. cit.

through the masks of assumed characters in a different way from Pound and Eliot, and for different reasons. In the case of the American expatriates the need arises, one suspects, only when they want to use a public voice; it arises in fact from the awkwardness of the relation between the poet and the public in Britain and America, the inability of the British and the American publics, then as now, to determine what status to give to the poet and to poetic utterance. Certainly Pound sells the pass on his own translations when he calls them "but more elaborate masks." If *Cathay*, if "The Seafarer," if "Planh for the Young English King" were indeed nothing but masks for Pound, we should not value them so highly as we do. Their virtue as translations is precisely that they are so much more than masks for the translator. Sextus Propertius on the other hand is truly nothing but a mask; and this is why *Homage to Sextus Propertius* is not and cannot be in any sense a translation. When T.S. Eliot says that the *Homage* "is also a criticism of Propertius," and when Pound himself says that it "has scholastic value" (*Letters*, p. 245), they are surely wrong, because, for this to be true, Pound's poem would need to be far more of a translation than it is.

"Au Salon," though it is spoken in what aspires to be a public voice, is in fact an excited plea for the poet's right to be private, to eschew civic responsibilities in what he writes. And this is not paradoxical. When the poet announces his determination to speak about matters of the bedroom or the salon rather than the market place (and this is the substance of *Homage to Sextus Propertius*, as of "Au Salon"), it is in the market place that the announcement must be made; the poet announces at the top of his voice his right to speak *sotto voce*, he denies in a voice of thunder that he is in duty bound to speak thus always. Similarly Pound the publicist in prose is never so shrill and vehement as when he complains that his function as a publicist is a distraction from his main concerns, a distraction forced upon him by the heedlessness and stupidity of the public:

83

Time was when the poet lay in a green field with his head against a tree and played his diversion on a ha'penny whistle, and Caesar's predecessors conquered the earth, and the predecessors of golden Crassus embezzled, and fashions had their say, and let him alone....

Metastasio, and he should know if any one, assures us that this age endures—even though the modern poet is expected to holloa his verses down a speaking tube to the editors of cheap magazines—S.S. McClure, or some one of that sort— even though hordes of authors meet in dreariness and drink healths to the 'Copyright Bill'; even though these things be, the age of gold pertains. Imperceivably, if you like, but pertains.[8]

Metastasio figures in just this connection in one of the abortive cantos published in 1917:

> 'Non é fuggi.'
>> 'It is not gone.' Metastasio
> is right, we have that world about us.

And the ambitious work of that year, the *Homage to Sextus Propertius*, has no other theme than this, says nothing more devious or abstruse than had been said in the unconsidered prose of 1912. Nothing, indeed, is more striking and astonishing than the discrepancy between the straightforward obviousness of what *Homage to Sextus Propertius* has to say, and the intricacy of what commentators have to say about it. True, once Pound's poem is set beside the poems of Propertius from which it is quarried, there emerge all the baffling layers of irony which so delight some of the commentators; and it is just for this reason perhaps that they insist on bringing the Latin poet into consideration. But this is to regard the *Homage* as a translation. The *Homage*, considered apart from its Latin

---

[8] "Prolegomena," from *The Poetry Review* (edited by Harold Monro), 1912. Reprinted in "A Retrospect" (*Pavannes and Divisions*, New York, 1918; and *Literary Essays of Ezra Pound*, ed. T.S. Eliot, London, 1954, p. 8.)

sources, says something so simple that the question arises whether the poem is not too long for what it has to say. It is the easiest of Pound's poems, and it has been treated as one of the hardest.

To be sure, what could safely and inoffensively be said in 1912 had become, by 1917, something very offensive indeed. For an expatriate American to tell London, after the Flanders trenches had endured three years of hideous futility, that the poet had the right and sometimes the duty to turn his back on all affairs of state and national destiny, in order to celebrate his love affairs with witty cynicism—this was a very perilous enterprise. And it was doubtless this (though also, one may suppose, common decency of feeling) that caused Pound not to print the sequence until after the war was over. On the other hand, it was precisely because the thing to be said was much harder to say in 1917 than in 1912 that the poet at the later date found it worth saying—and in plangent and mordant verse, not journalist's prose. Because Pound had taken care to date the poem, he carried conviction when he declared of it in 1931:

> ... it presents certain emotions as vital to me in 1917, faced with the infinite and ineffable imbecility of the British Empire, as they were to Propertius some centuries earlier, when faced with the infinite and ineffable imbecility of the Roman Empire. These emotions are defined largely, but not entirely, in Propertius' own terms. If the reader does not find relation to life defined in the poem, he may conclude that I have been unsuccessful in my endeavour. (*Letters*, p. 310.)

The *Homage* is in the fullest sense an occasional poem. And it is only when we remember the occasion that we see it as written against imperialism and against war.

Yeats in 1936, introducing *The Oxford Book of Modern Verse*, said of Pound:

Even where the style is sustained thoughout one gets an impression, especially when he is writing in vers libre, that he has not got all the wine into the bowl, that he is a brilliant improvisator translating at sight from an unknown Greek masterpiece.

Of no poem is this more true than of *Homage to Sextus Propertius*, yet it is just as true of poems where no question of translation arises, of many of the *Lustra* epigrams for example. And Yeats's example (which explains why he makes the unknown masterpiece Greek) is a wholly original poem, "The Return."

Robert Conquest's way of making Yeats's point is to say (having noted that "the howlers are not mere accident: Pound could not have really thought that 'votas' meant 'votes' "):

Such mistakes lend colour to the notion of his just writing down how the thing appeared to him at first sight, without dictionary, and without taking much trouble either, and then simply not bothering.

Just so. And why not? There may be some rules about how to translate: but there are no rules about how to make poems, and if Pound chose to make his poem in this way, what follows? Conquest concludes with boyish petulance, "He is just seeing how much he can get away with." Yeats, who had found in Pound "at moments more style, more deliberate nobility and the means to convey it than in any contemporary poet known to me," limits himself to noting the effect, though it is clear that he was at a loss to see why the effect was worth attaining—as much at a loss as the less modest Conquest is. Yet it is not hard to see what point there might be. Why should a poet contrive the effect of translating carelessly when in fact he is doing something else? To begin with, Yeats's *desiderata* can be stood on their head: a poet might contrive this effect because he wants *not* to seem to have "got all the wine into the bowl," because "deliberate nobility" is the last thing he is after. If he is sure that there is more to his subject (more

86

perhaps to any subject) than he got out of it, or ever could get out of it, if he believes that all the wine never *can* be got into the bowl or into any bowl, then, like Michelangelo leaving some portion of stone unworked in his sculptures, the poet will deliberately seek an effect of improvisation, of haste and rough edges. For only in this way can he be true to his sense of the inexhaustibility of the human and non-human nature he is working with, a sense which makes him feel not noble but humble. And the same reason will make him use rhythms which seem, or are, uncontrollable, not to be measured—free verse measures which diverge from any measurable course or pattern—in order to compass the unforeseen which inexhaustible nature necessarily and continually provides.

The *Homage*, then, is written in "translatorese." In particular Pound makes the most of the grotesque and risible discrepancy between the vocabularies of poetry and of prose, a discrepancy which is known to any one who has made a rough working transliteration from a foreign poem into English prose:

> Me happy, night, night full of brightness;
> Oh couch made happy by my long delectations;
> How many words talked out with abundant candles;
> Struggles when the lights were taken away;
> Now with bared breasts she wrestled against me,
>   Tunic spread in delay;
> And she then opening my eyelids fallen in sleep,
> Her lips upon them; and it was her mouth saying:
>   Sluggard!

"Me happy" is an expression that has no home in English except in the schoolchild's painful transliteration in the classroom; similarly the whole of the second line recalls nothing but the stilted, partly comic and partly touching expressions that arrange themselves across the page of an exercise-book when foreign words are looked up one by one and their dictionary equivalents are written down. "Delectations" in particular is a word that exists in a dictionary, and nowhere else. It is typical of the Latinate polysyllables that trumpet mournfully and uncertainly on every page of the *Homage*. It is usual to say that the function of these is ironical, and that Pound learned the trick of them from Laforgue. There is little doubt that Laforgue's poems, still more perhaps the Laforguian English poems of the young T.S. Eliot, have contributed to the diction of the *Homage*. Yet, on this showing, the irony of the *Homage* is disconcertingly pervasive and undirected: the speaker is being ironical about civic and imperial affairs, certainly, and about the poetry that celebrates these affairs; but he is ironical no less about his young lady, about himself, even about his art. The irony begins to define something only when the pompously polysyllabic words are seen as the products of "translatorese," not of Jules Laforgue. It is true that Pound was later to claim that Propertius and Laforgue were two of a kind, and to define the kind as "logopoeic."[9] But this is unconvincing, and irrelevant to the *Homage*. In the *Homage* as a poem in English, the irony carried in the polysyllabic words is directed at the reader; the diction puts the reader in the position of one who has transliterated into his own pompous and civic English a poem that deserves to be read precisely because it derides and denies all pompous and civic pretensions.

Thus, *Homage to Sextus Propertius* is in verse, and yet its diction is that of verse translated into prose:

> The twisted rhombs ceased their clamour of accompaniment;
> The scorched laurel lay in the fire-dust;
> The moon still declined to descend out of heaven,
>
> But the black ominous owl hoot was audible.

In "declined to," and the absurdly stilted passive construction "was audible," the discrepancy between prose language and verse language, which is brought out by translatorese, is ex-

[9] "How To Read," *New York Herald Tribune Books*, V, Nos. 17, 18, and 19 (13, 20, and 27 Jan. 1929). In *Literary Essays of Ezra Pound*, pp. 25, 33.

ploited to ends that are no longer grotesque or awkwardly touching so much as comical.

But what happens to rhythm in verse like this where the diction persuades us that what we are reading is a clumsy translation of verse into prose? Something very similar to what happened in *Cathay*. Of the four lines just quoted, no one line is to the ear equal to any of the others; yet, as when reading *Cathay*, the ear allows itself to be persuaded by the mind into regarding the lines as metrically equal because they are equal syntactically. Moreover, in this poem, which is not a translation yet creates the illusion that it is, just as in the poems of *Cathay* that truly *are* translations, the ear is the readier to be persuaded in this way since we are persuaded to think that each line, thus heavily end-stopped, corresponds to a line of the real or fictitious original. The same is true of the first four lines of the passage beginning, "Me happy, night..."; these lines are unequal to the ear, yet the ear permits itself to regard them as equal because they are syntactically equal (being all syntactically imperfect in just the same way).

Where all these lines differ, however, from the characteristic lines of *Cathay* is that in none of them is there any sign of the verse-line being dismembered into smaller rhythmical components. True, there is

> Me happy, night, night full of brightness,

where the commas indicate pauses that make the line musically delightful, but that is their sole purpose: to be easy on the ear. We should be grateful. Nevertheless, this way of pausing is different from the pauses that dismember the lines of *Cathay* and of "Provincia Deserta"—different, and less serious, for those pauses enacted or sharpened or invigorated perceptions, as these do not. The difference becomes very clear when the lines begin to surge across their end-stoppings:

> Now with bared breasts she wrestled against me,
>   Tunic spread in delay;

> And she then opening my eyelids fallen in sleep,
>   Her lips upon them; and it was her mouth saying:
>   Sluggard!

There is no longer any wish "to break the pentameter." The pentameter, indeed, was broken for good and all long before; here the iambic rhythm makes not even a phantasmal appearance. But there is no longer any wish to break the verse-line, of whatever meter, into its rhythmical members; the intention is no longer to dismember the verse-line, but rather, in the traditional way, to submerge it by enjambement into the larger rhythmical unit of the strophe. And thus, in a very special and esoteric way, the rhythms of the *Homage* show Pound, even so early, making his peace with Milton.

To be sure, there are many more lines that are end-stopped than there are lines that are "run over." Pound husbands his resources so that only at long and calculated intervals does he permit composition by strophe to supervene upon the composition by verse-line that is still his staple procedure. One place where this happens is in Section V, where it permits the masterly and audacious pun on "volume":

> If she goes in a gleam of Cos, in a slither of dyed stuff,
>   There is a volume in the matter; . . .

The start of Section VI is another place where it happens, and the most beautiful example of all comes when Pound rehandles the passage he had translated in 1911—in the second part of Section IX, where the strophe comes to rest on the rocking rhythms of two lines that untypically *are* dismembered in the manner of *Cathay:*

> Beauty is not eternal, no man has perennial fortune,
>   Slow foot, or swift foot, death delays but for a season.

Here indeed, as Charles Norman says, "Pound's rhythms stride with giant steps, and there are great gulps of air instead of mere caesurae in the clash of syllables." [10]

[10] *Ezra Pound* (1960), p. 209.

90

Yet by and large, if "Provincia Deserta" represents one development from the vers libre of *Cathay*, the *Homage to Sextus Propertius* represents another, radically different. Both kinds of writing appear in the *Cantos*.

In 1918 Percy Wyndham Lewis went into the army, and Pound continued a series of "imaginary letters" that Lewis had been contributing to *The Little Review*. Though Pound's imaginary letters have been twice reprinted (in Paris in 1930, and in London in 1960), they are among the least known of his works, and yet they cast light on one of the best known and most often discussed, on *Hugh Selwyn Mauberley*.

The supposed author of the imaginary letters is one Walter Villerant, a man more interesting than likeable. He writes to "Mrs. Bland Burn," whom he addresses as "My dear Lydia." In the first letter he refuses to marry:

> I am, with qualifications, Malthusian. I should consent to breed under pressure, if I were convinced in any way of the reasonableness of reproducing the species. But my nerves and the nerves of any woman I could live with three months, would produce only a victim—beautiful perhaps, but a victim; expiring of aromatic pain from the jasmine, lacking in impulse, a mere bundle of discriminations.

This is very like a type of personality that appears in *Hugh Selwyn Mauberley*:

> Drifted ... drifted precipitate,
> Asking time to be rid of ...
> Of his bewilderment; to designate
> His new found orchid....
>
> To be certain ... certain ...
> (Amid ærial flowers) ... time for arrangements—
> Drifted on
> To the final estrangement;

Hugh Selwyn Mauberley exists as two intricately linked poem-sequences, one of thirteen poems dated 1919, and a further sequence of five poems dated 1920. In the piece just quoted, the second in the 1920 sequence, there is a phrase ("He had moved amid her phantasmagoria") which Kenner has noted as an allusion to *The Ambassadors* of Henry James.[11] But then Walter Villerant, who borrows from "The Author of 'Beltraffio'" in this very letter, is in an unsubtle way a very Jamesian person, at least as "Jamesian" is commonly understood; before the first letter is out we are wondering, for instance, if he is not an American expatriate—a haughty passage on Coney Island and the racial melting-pot seems to suggest as much.

His first allegiance is, in any case, in a very self-congratulating way, to "art":

> It may be fitting that men should enjoy equal "civic and political rights," these things are a matter of man's exterior acts, of exterior contacts. (Macchiavelli believed in democracy: it lay beyond his experience.) The arts have nothing to do with this. They are man's life within himself. The king's writ does not run there. The voice of the majority is powerless to make me enjoy, or disenjoy, the lines of Catullus. I dispense with a vote without inconvenience; Villon I would not dispense with.

And this attitude is echoed elsewhere in the 1920 sequence:

> The glow of porcelain
> Brought no reforming sense
> To his perception
> Of the social inconsequence.
>
> Thus, if her colour
> Came against his gaze,
> Tempered as if
> It were through a perfect glaze

[11] Cf. Lambert Strether in *The Ambassadors*: "Of course I moved among miracles. It was all phantasmagoric...."

He made no immediate application
Of this to relation of the state
To the individual, the month was more temperate
Because this beauty had been.

This, however, does not catch the supercilious tone of Villerant; nearer to it are some quatrains from the 1919 sequence:

Even the Christian beauty
Defects—after Samothrace;
We see τὸ καλὸν
Decreed in the market place.

Faun's flesh is not to us,
Nor the saint's vision.
We have the press for wafer;
Franchise for circumcision.

And yet there is energy in this, and anger behind it, which are foreign to Walter Villerant. Villerant, parading his detachment, fails to convince us of it; the speaker of the 1919 poem convinces us of his detachment, and earns our respect for it, precisely because anger is contained in it, controlled by it. The speaker of the 1920 poem ("The glow of porcelain...") has detachment of another kind again, diagnostic and therefore dispassionate, superior to Villerant's because it is in no way self-regarding; but he does not sustain this throughout his poem, which degenerates into precisely Villerant's dandified diction and cadence:

A Minoan undulation,
Seen, we admit, amid ambrosial circumstances...

From most points of view, in a poetry like this which maneuvers in the fluctuating and elusive medium of "tone," these differences in the tone of voice are precisely what matter, far more than the identity of what is said. On the other hand, the identity is striking and must be significant.

In his second letter Villerant takes on the lineaments of Ford

Madox Ford rather than Henry James, particularly in a passage where Dante is compared with French realists of the novel. And Ford is also thought to be in the background of *Hugh Selwyn Mauberley;* in particular Ford's situation in the first year after the Armistice seems to have suggested the tenth poem in the 1919 sequence, three quatrains about "the stylist" finding refuge in a country cottage.[12] There is a good deal in this letter about Swinburne, who fails to satisfy Villerant as he had not failed to satisfy the author of *Personae;* but the author of "Yeux Glauques," sixth in the 1919 sequence,[13] sees Swinburne and his Victorian contemporaries with something of Villerant's coolness. Something more striking emerges when Villerant refuses to be interested in the Russian writers with the solitary and significant exception of Turgenev—it was James's exception, and Ford's, and George Moore's, as well as Pound's. Villerant declares:

> I mistrust this liking for Russians; having passed years in one barbarous country I cannot be expected to take interest in another. All that is worth anything is the product of metropoles. Swill out these nationalist movements. Ireland is a suburb of Liverpool.

And Villerant's "barbarous country" seems to be the United States, as does the "half savage country" of the first poem in *Hugh Selwyn Mauberley:*

> Wrong from the start—
>
> No, hardly, but seeing he had been born
> In a half savage country, out of date;

The sneer at Ireland as a suburb of Liverpool also gets into *Hugh Selwyn Mauberley*, but thickly disguised. Through his

[12] The piece owes much to two poems by Gautier, "Fumée" and "La Mansarde."
[13] With "Yeux Glauques" cf. Gautier's "Caerulei Oculi." *Glauque* is a word to which Pound draws attention in "A Study of French Poets" (*Little Review*, 1918); for another unusual word, *maquero*, see Ford quoted in Douglas Goldring, *The Last Pre-Raphaelite* (London, 1948), p. 216.

association with Yeats presumably, but still more through his correspondence with the enlightened patron John Quinn in New York, Pound had come in touch with the Irish nationalists in London, and specifically with the intransigent revolutionary Maud Gonne, object of Yeats's hopeless passion until she married John MacBride, one of the leaders and martyrs of the Dublin rising in 1916. In January 1918 (*Letters*, pp. 189-90) Pound wrote to John Quinn reporting the result of an intervention he had made at the Home Office on Maud Gonne's behalf, and plainly feeling little sympathy with her. In November of that year he wrote to Quinn again, no longer concealing his annoyance and coupling Maud Gonne's fanaticism with Yeats's about psychic phenomena:

> The other point M.G. omits from her case is that she went to Ireland without permit and in disguise, in the first place, during war time.
> "Conservatrice des traditions Milésiennes," as de Gourmont calls them. There are people who have no sense of the value of "civilization" or public order.
> She is still full of admiration for Lenin. (I, on the other hand, have talked with Russians.) The sum of it being that I am glad she is out of gaol, and I hope no one will be ass enough to let her get to Ireland. (*Letters*, p. 201.)

The tag from Gourmont turns up in the eleventh poem of the 1919 sequence:

> "Conservatrix of Milésien"
> Habits of mind and feeling,
> Possibly. But in Ealing
> With the most bank-clerkly of Englishmen?
>
> No, "Milesian" is an exaggeration.
> No instinct has survived in her
> Older than those her grandmother
> Told her would fit her station.

And this closes the circuit back into the *Imaginary Letters*, for with the fourth of these we seem to be launched on an epistolary novel: Mrs. Bland Burn has left her husband, and Villerant rebukes her for it on the grounds that her new mate will take her into an unsavory milieu, which he calls "suburbia." Temporarily he recalls Henry James (or perhaps George Moore) when he justifies this snobbery. The suburb that Lydia has gone to (by way of "Bohemia," we understand) is Pinner; in the poem it is Ealing. The whole of this imaginary letter, dealing with woman's unsatisfactory function in society, seems a necessary gloss on the eight lines of the poem.

Meanwhile it has been established beyond much doubt that Villerant is American. In the third letter he has confessed to "anglophilia" and says, in words that recall one of Pound's letters to W.C. Williams about America, that he "was born in a more nervous and arid climate." Much of this letter is impatient about how pietism and mysticism seem to have supplanted in France, now that Gourmont is dead, the better intellectual tradition Gourmont had represented. Pound's dislike of neo-Catholicism in France appears in his correspondence but not in *Hugh Selwyn Mauberley*, unless it has to do with the anti-Christian sentiments of the third poem in the sequence.

The *Imaginary Letters* tail off disappointingly in a section called "Mr. Villerant's Morning Outburst," four letters addressed to three other ladies than Lydia. The first of these is about the unsatisfactoriness of having recourse to prostitutes. (We may remember from *Hugh Selwyn Mauberley* that "Dowson found harlots cheaper than hotels.") The second letter is of little interest; the third, however, not only rejects Christianity, but rejects it in favor of Confucianism, and Villerant even gives his version of one of the Analects—a version in startling contrast to what Pound was to make of it thirty years later, in contrast also to what he had made of it by 1924, when it was incorporated very beautifully in Canto 13.

It may not be clear why the *Imaginary Letters* are worth bothering about in relation to *Hugh Selwyn Mauberley*. But that poem has been the subject of much debate, and the disputes about it can all be reduced to the question how far at this time Pound was capable of creating and sustaining a persona, a fictitious mask to speak through. We have already found reasons for thinking that Pound's remarks about "personae" and "masks" are so many red herrings since his talent was not histrionic, like Yeats's, but rather took him toward speaking confessionally *in propria persona*. So long as Pound's criticism was unsophisticated, in *The Spirit of Romance* for instance, he responded most eagerly to precisely what a theory of the "persona" tends to exclude—that is to say, robust self-exposure on the part of the poet speaking. The *Imaginary Letters* support this view of Pound, for it is impossible to read them without at first suspecting, and later feeling sure, that Pound disliked Villerant much less than we are likely to; that Pound mistook his undergraduate superciliousness for a rather grand aristocratic disdain. Though Pound wrote in the summer of 1917 to Wyndham Lewis about Villerant's "effete and over civilised organism," [14] so much of what Villerant says is what Pound had said or was to say elsewhere, and so much more of what he says recalls men whom Pound admired, that the distance between Villerant and his creator narrows, until in the end they are identical. The identification is complete when we find Villerant in his last letter exalting Gautier above Baudelaire and discussing how hard it is to translate Gautier into English—this at the very time when the author of *Hugh Selwyn Mauberley* was throughout that poem translating Gautier, as J.J. Espey has shown.[15]

If the mask of Walter Villerant slipped so betrayingly from Pound's face, can we believe that at the same time he was capable of wearing another mask, that of H.S. Mauberley, without once betraying himself, but on the contrary keeping a constant distance between that surrogate person's character and his

[14] Donald Gallup, *A Bibliography of Ezra Pound* (London, 1963; New York, 1964), p. 73.
[15] J.J. Espey, *Ezra Pound's* Mauberley.

own? This is what many admiring commentators on *Hugh Selwyn Mauberley* ask us to believe. And they have some reason on their side. In the first place we have seen already from examples how much more sure of himself Pound was in verse than in prose, how the tight though unmetrical quatrains made sharp and distinguished in the poem what from the pen of Walter Villerant had been preenings and inanities. In the second place (a closely related point), though Pound had perhaps little talent for histrionics, he had abundant talent, as all translators have, for mimicry, for pastiche. Like the born translator he was, Pound can add cubits to his stature as soon as he begins to match himself with the master he is trying to emulate. It was a recognition of this in himself that made him stress so often the usefulness of technical apprenticeships. Pound was generous to others and serious about his vocation, as Walter Villerant could not have been; but there is evidence that otherwise, in conversation and in society, Pound in 1918 created just such an impression as Villerant creates, no more likeable, no less mannered and self-regarding. It was emulating Gautier that purified and raised to a new power attitudes that in life were callow and unresolved; for, in learning the measure of Gautier's cadence and the dynamic shape of Gautier's stanzas, Pound by that very token became, for as long as he was writing the poem, as intelligent as Gautier and as civilized.[16] This at any rate is what a comparison with the *Imaginary Letters* suggests. And, therefore, it suggests further that the appearance

[16] See Pound in "Harold Munro," *The Criterion*, XI (October 1931–July 1932), p. 590: "at a particular time in a particular room, two authors, neither engaged in picking the other's pocket, decided that the dilutation of *vers libre* ... had gone too far and that some countercurrent must be set going. Parallel situation years ago in China. Remedy prescribed '*Emaux et Camées*' (or the Bay State Hymn Book). Rhyme and regular strophes.

"Results: Poems in Mr. Eliot's second volume, not contained in his first ..., also H.S. Mauberley." (We may doubt if, despite Pound's suggestion, the Bay State Hymn Book would have served him as well as Gautier's *Emaux et Camées*.)

of intricate planning behind the interlinked sequences of *Hugh Selwyn Mauberley* is an illusion, an *ex post facto* rationalization; that the work was in fact written "by ear," by improvising and feeling forward from one poem to the next, not according to any pre-ordained scheme.

If so, it follows that most of the disputes about *Hugh Selwyn Mauberley* have been misconceived, for they have turned on the question of what Pound intended; and on this showing all that Pound intended was to do in English what Gautier had done in French.[17] On the one hand are those who find that H.S. Mauberley is a transparent fiction, who identify the poet at all points with his persona, and so read the two sequences as a clear-sighted and painfully honest judgment by Pound on the limitations of his own talent, and so on the reasons why he could never surpass the limited, though fine, achievement of this very poem. It is hard to square this reading with the fact that the author of *Hugh Selwyn Mauberley* had long before embarked on the *Cantos*, and was still working on them; and accordingly other readers have maintained that the persona, Mauberley, is at nearly all points distinct from the poet who created him—as distinct (so some have dared to suggest) as Lambert Strether was from Henry James. Pound has not unnaturally given his approval to this second reading,[18] but this may be only another rationalization after the fact.

The point at issue comes out most clearly in relation to the poem that closes the second sequence, and so closes the whole

[17] Gautier is the over-riding influence; there are others, e.g. Bion in the fourth poem of the sequence. And for the piece which is in most respects the high point of the whole work, the Envoi to the 1919 sequence, the model was Edmund Waller. Despite George Dekker's objections (*Sailing After Knowledge*, London, 1963, p. 157), I still believe with T.E. Connolly (*Accent*, Winter, 1956) that the "her" of this Envoi is England. (Canto 80 for me supports this reading of the second stanza.)
[18] See Pound, as quoted by Thomas E. Connolly in *Accent* (Winter, 1956), speaking of commentators on *Hugh Selwyn Mauberley*: "The worst muddle they make is in failing to see that Mauberley buries E.P. in the first poem; gets rid of all his troublesome energies."

work. It is called "Medallion." In order to sustain the case that Mauberley and Pound are distinct (in other words, that H.S. Mauberley is truly a created fiction), one has to believe that this poem is offered as Mauberley's work, not Pound's; that the exactness this poem achieves is in Pound's opinion bought at too great a cost, in view of the metallic inertness with which the imagery endows the subject. Yet at the end of the *Imaginary Letters*, Walter Villerant briefly discusses Joyce:

> The metal finish alarms people. They will no more endure Joyce's hardness than they will Pound's sterilized surgery. The decayed-lily verbiage which the Wilde school scattered over the decadence is much more to the popular taste.

Are we to believe that Villerant admires Joyce for the wrong reasons, or perhaps for the right reasons but without the necessary qualifications? We must believe this if we are to take "Medallion," with its conspicuously "metal finish," as Mauberley's poem rather than Pound's. In any case it looks more than ever as if Walter Villerant and Hugh Selwyn Mauberley are the same person. If so, then Pound's relation to the one fiction, Villerant, illuminates his relation to the other, Mauberley. Those who argue that Pound never loses control of the persona, Mauberley, require us to see the latter as an inadequate person whose inadequacies Pound is indicating. But as we have seen, Villerant, so largely assembled of components from men whom Pound admired (James, Ford, Gourmont), appears to differ from Pound not as a limited person whom Pound will surpass but, much of the time, as an ideally civilized person whom Pound aspires to emulate. Pound surpasses Villerant in only one particular, in the barbaric virtue of energy. And this seems true of Pound's relation to Mauberley also.

In other words, just as we are cheated of our expectations when the *Imaginary Letters* seem to be leading into an epistolary novel, so in *Hugh Selwyn Mauberley* we look in vain for the developing "plot" that commentators of all persuasions (including the present writer) have thought they found.[19] Such "plots" can indeed be found—all too many of them. The trouble is that any one of them requires that we give Pound the benefit of every doubt, on the score of elusive shifts of tone, a raised eyebrow here, a half-smile somewhere else, a momentary puckering of the brow. "Tone" will not do so much, so certainly, as the most admiring commentators ask us to believe. Therefore, the two sequences are much more loosely jointed than they seem to be. Hardly anything is lost, and much is gained, if the poems are read one at a time, as so many poems by Pound, and if the Mauberley persona is dismissed as a distracting nuisance. *Hugh Selwyn Mauberley* thus falls to pieces, though the pieces are brilliant, intelligent always, and sometimes moving (for Gautier repeatedly enabled Pound to surpass himself). As for the theory of the persona, which served Yeats so well, it seems only to have confused Pound and led him to confuse his readers.

[19] For a more generous as well as more detailed examination of *Hugh Selwyn Mauberley*, see Donald Davie, "Ezra Pound's Hugh Selwyn Mauberley,' " in *The Modern Age* (*Pelican Guide to English Literature*, London, 1961), pp. 315-29.

VI

Cavalcanti

It was in relation to Ernest Fenollosa that Pound wrote of "the romance of modern scholarship." But what he meant by that, and how vividly he responded to it, appear most plainly in a footnote to his volume of essays *Make It New*,[1] at a point where he is discussing the attribution to Guido Cavalcanti of certain disputed poems and fragments. The essay, "Cavalcanti," is dated "1910/1931," and the footnote reads:

> 1934. Whole question of authenticity of the other canzoni thrown wide open again by examination of manuscript I.ix.18 in Comunale di Siena. For further details, see my *Guido Cavalcanti: Rime*, Genova, anno x.

[1] *Make It New* (London, 1934; New Haven, 1935). Most of the essay on Cavalcanti from this volume had appeared in various issues of *The Dial* through 1928 and 1929.

The Cavalcanti: Rime to which Pound refers [2] represents his most determined bid for academic respect. The bid appears to have failed with the Romance philologists. But Pound's dealings with Cavalcanti manifest at least the scholarly virtue of pertinacity and another, rarer one, the ability to change an opinion and confess as much. From the first translation of 1912 [3] through to his edition of *Tre Canzoni* in 1949,[4] Pound has worried away at the poems of Cavalcanti more doggedly than at any other body of literature, even the Confucian scriptures. And to review Pound's dealings with this author, in chronological sequence over the years, is to follow with exceptional intimacy the poet's gradually growing awareness of what verse translation entails, or what it may entail in the case of an author so recondite as Cavalcanti. Unfortunately, the bibliography is so far from clear that it is impossible to date exactly all of the versions from Cavalcanti that Pound has made. The *Translations of Ezra Pound* (London, 1953), a book not at all so inclusive as its title suggests, gives no indication of when any given translation was made, nor of where a later version has been substituted for an earlier one. And Anne Paolucci,[5] though she usefully shows how even in 1912, despite Pound's declaration of indebtedness at that time to D.G. Rossetti's versions, his intentions were very different from Rossetti's, on the other hand weakens her case by resting it on such poems as Sonnets VII and XVI, to which Pound returned after 1912, discarding the earlier translations which she asks us to admire.

Of the thirty-five sonnets by Cavalcanti, Sonnets VII, XIII, XIV, XVI, and XVII are given in *The Translations of Ezra Pound* in versions different from those that appear in the *Son-*

[2] *Guido Cavalcanti: Rime*, texts, with notes, (Genoa, 1931).

[3] *The Sonnets and Ballate of Guido Cavalcanti*, with translation and introduction (London and Boston, 1912).

[4] *Tre Canzoni di Guido Cavalcanti*, con i fac-simili dei manoscritti senesi e la vita del poeta di Celso Cittadini (Siena, 1949).

[5] A. Paolucci, "Ezra Pound and D.G. Rossetti as Translators of Guido Cavalcanti," in *Romanic Review*, LI (1960), 256-67.

nets and Ballate of 1912. The changes were not always for the better; and Miss Paolucci's case for the first version of XVI, for instance, reflects adversely on the later version. But Sonnet VII is one case where the issue is hardly in doubt. In 1912 (and again in *Umbra*, 1920, where several of the versions were reprinted), this ran:

> Who is she coming, drawing all men's gaze,
> Who makes the air one trembling clarity
> Till none can speak but each sighs piteously
> Where she leads Love adown her trodden ways?
>
> Ah God! The thing she's like when her glance strays,
> Let Amor tell. 'Tis no fit speech for me.
> Mistress she seems of such great modesty
> That every other woman were called "Wrath."
>
> No one could ever tell the charm she hath
> For all the noble powers bend toward her
> She being beauty's godhead manifest.
>
> Our daring ne'er before held such high quest;
> But ye! There is not in you so much grace
> That we can understand her rightfully.

Miss Paolucci cites the fifth line in particular as an example of how much more closely Pound translates than Rossetti, and Pound, as will be seen, takes exception to other lines as rendered by Rossetti. Yet it is hard to have any patience with such slack poeticisms as "adown," eking out metrical regularity with a redundant prefix, or, to light upon something more important, the commercialized vulgarity of "charm" ("the charm she hath") for "la sua piacenza."

In *Make It New* Pound supplies a later translation which has rightly supplanted the earlier one:

> Who is she that comes, makyng turn every man's eye
> And makyng the air to tremble with a bright clearenesse
> That leadeth with her Love, in such nearness
> No man may proffer of speech more than a sigh?

Ah God, what she is like when her owne eye turneth, is
Fit for Amor to speak, for I cannot at all;
Such is her modesty, I would call
Every woman else but an useless uneasiness.

No one could ever tell all of her pleasauntness
In that every high noble vertu leaneth to herward,
So Beauty sheweth her forth as her Godhede;

Never before so high was our mind led,
Nor have we so much of heal as will afford
That our mind may take her immediate in its embrace.

I shall take it for granted that this version is more to modern
taste. And yet it is not easy, if the two versions are compared,
to explain what makes the later version the better one.

In the first place, if one proceeds like Miss Paolucci to look
above all for closeness, line by line and phrase by phrase, the
early version comes out better. For this is the Italian poem:

Chi è questa che vien, ch'ogni uom la mira,
Che fa dí clarità l'aer tremare,
E mena seco Amor, sí che parlare
Null' uom ne puote, ma ciascun sospira?

Ahi, Dio, che sembra quando gli occhi gira?
Dicalo Amor, ch'io nol saprei contare:
Cotanto d'umiltà donna mi pare,
Che ciascun' altra in vêr di lei chiam' ira.

Non si potria contar la sua piacenza,
Ch' a lei s'inchina ogni gentil virtute,
E la beltate per sua Dea la mostra.

Non fu sì alta già la mente nostra,
E non si è posta in noi tanta salute,
Che propriamente n'abbiam conoscenza.

Here much has been gained by reading in the penultimate line
"in noi" instead of, as in 1912, "in voi"; this gets rid of the

awkward but in 1912 inescapable switch from "ye" and "you" to "we" in the last line. There remains, however, "ira" at the end of the eighth line, which plainly underwrites the "Wrath" of the first version whereas it affords remarkably little grounds for the delightful "useless uneasiness" of the revision.

We might go further and point out that there is no justification in the original for the strenuous enjambement of the later version, "is/Fit for Amor to speake." But this would be captious. For this is not felt as an enjambement; on the contrary the syllable of "is" is felt to be necessary to the rhythmical completeness of the line it occurs in. And this surely brings out what is the really potent difference between the first version and the second: it is the difference of rhythm. In his essay in *Make It New* Pound remarks, "Another prevalent error is that of dealing with Italian hendecasyllables as if they were English 'iambic pentameter.'" It was an error into which he had fallen himself in his versions of 1912; and, although in his Introduction to those versions he had declared, gallantly and vulnerably, "I believe in an ultimate and absolute rhythm as I believe in an absolute symbol or metaphor," his use in his translations of an iambic pentameter line quite nullifies this assertion and makes nonsense of his further claim that "the rhythm set in a line of poetry connotes its symphony, which, had we a little more skill, we could score for orchestra." The tunes played in the translations of 1912 prompt no reader into dreaming up novel "symphonies," since Shakespearean and Miltonic and other symphonies come to his mind as soon as the traditional measure is sounded. In *Make It New* Pound further observes, following an unnamed authority, "that Dante's hendecasyllables were composed of combinations of rhythm units of various shapes and sizes and that these pieces were put together in lines so as to make, roughly, eleven syllables in all. I say 'roughly' because of the liberties allowed in elision." Although Pound goes on to claim that he had discovered this for himself "in Indiana," his versions of 1912 do not suggest as much. It is only in the later versions that one gets the effect of "rhythm units of various shapes and sizes." In the very first line, for instance, of "Chi è questa che vien," there is a much sharper break apart on "she that comes, makyng" in the second version, than on "she coming, drawing" in the first; and, because in the second version the iambic beat has been so much disconcerted, the ear demands another break between "turn" and "every man's eye." Where in the early version the pentameter line breaks, if at all, only weakly on the caesura, in the later version it divides itself markedly into three distinct units of rhythm. In fact, this is that dismemberment of the line from within that was noted as the distinctive rhythmical pleasure of poems in *Cathay*. Even in the Fenollosa notes on the Noh, Pound had encountered a similar notion of the poetic line as constituted, not out of so many equal feet, but out of two unequal rhythmical units in the proportions 7 to 5 or 5 to 7; and Pound had drawn attention to this in an intrigued but baffled footnote about Arnaut Daniel. Out of his own practice in *Cathay* and "The Seafarer," out of the meters of the Noh, and now out of the hendecasyllables of Dante and Cavalcanti, the same recognition was pressed upon him: there were rhythms to be found by reconstituting the line, rather than stanza or paragraph, as the poetic unit, and then by dismembering the line into musical units larger than the metrical feet of traditional prosody. "To break the pentameter, that was the first heave." Because for purposes of polemic Pound chose at times to play the iconoclast, it is easy to see his abandonment of the traditional pentameter as something deliberate and programmatic; his translations of Cavalcanti from 1912 onwards suggest on the contrary that he broke with the pentameter reluctantly, grudgingly, and, as it were, of necessity. By the time of the essay in *Make It New* he had discovered belatedly some seventeenth-century English precedents for this manner of proceeding, and he acknowledges them in his dedication to the centerpiece of the Cavalcanti essay, a translation of the canzone "Donna mi prega": "To Thomas Campion his ghost, and to the ghost of Henry Lawes, as prayer for the revival of music."

Another way in which the later version of this sonnet differs notably from the first version is in its use of archaic diction. To the translations of 1912 Pound prefixed two lines of verse:

> I have owned service to the deathless dead.
> Grudge not the gold I bear in livery.

And part of what this means is, I think, a plea by the translator to be allowed to use a lofty and ornate language—that surely is part of "the gold" which he bears "in livery." Insofar as the loftiness and ornateness is achieved by use of archaisms like "adown," most readers, rightly or wrongly, will refuse to accept Pound's plea, will not feel that the grounds on which he enters this plea are sufficient. (And one may wonder, incidentally, whether the plea was accepted by those to whom the volume was dedicated, "my friends, Violet and Ford Maddox (sic) Hueffer," for, according to Pound's later testimony, Hueffer's advice to him in these years was always that he should compete with the novelists by making his language as prosaic and hard as, for instance, Stendhal's.) Apart from this, Pound's remarks on diction in the Introduction of 1912 are limited to specific crucial words in the Italian—*gentile, mente, spiriti, valore, virtute*—and to the English words by which Pound has rendered these. But larger issues, of diction only in the first place, are opened up when Pound objects to Rossetti's version of one of the lines from Sonnet VII:

> Ch'a lei s'inchina ogni gentil virtute.

Rossetti's version—"To whom are subject all things virtuous"—will not do because, says Pound, "the *inchina* implies not the homage of an object but the direction of a force"; in other words, the "she" of the poem "acts as a magnet for every 'gentil virtute,' that is, the noble spiritual powers, the invigorating forces of life and beauty bend towards her. . . ." In both of Pound's versions this meaning of *s'inchina* is duly reproduced: in 1912, "all the noble powers bend toward her"; twenty-five years later, "every high noble vertu leaneth to herward." But it is in the later version that the point is rammed home, that the difference between Rossetti's version and Pound's is made irreconcilable. This is a function of the much denser and more conspicuous archaism of the revised version; in other words, the much heavier archaism of the second version is not for the sake of loftiness and ornateness but, on the contrary, it serves to cleave more closely to the sense as Pound perceives it. In the final version the archaism of the language is not, after all, at odds with the prosaism Hueffer had recommended; it is the archaism "to herward" that permits a precision, a hard definiteness of meaning.

A great deal is involved here, and in 1912 Pound saw much of what was involved, though he had not yet found a verse style to deal with it in his translations. For instance, if the lady in Sonnet VII acts as a magnet, this is not peculiar to her, for elsewhere in the Introduction of 1912 Pound says of Cavalcanti's world:

> Virtù is the potency, the efficient property of a substance or person. Thus modern science shows us radium with a noble virtue of energy. Each thing or person was held to send forth magnetisms of certain effect; ..."

It thus appears that, behind the problem of how to English one line by Cavalcanti, there lie considerations involving the physics and the metaphysics of the thirteenth century and of the twentieth. As he continued to work on Cavalcanti, Pound came to think that the greatness of Cavalcanti lay in the way the Italian poet could imply, by his vocabulary in a love poem, abstruse and indeed highly technical problems of speculation. And these scattered observations of 1912 about magnetism and potency and energy are elaborated and systematized in the pages of Make It New so as to produce some of Pound's most important formulations—important not only as they bear on Cavalcanti and the ultimately insoluble problem of how to translate him, but also because Pound seems to have composed his own metaphysics chiefly out of these mediaeval documents.

In the first section of the *Make It New* essay on Cavalcanti—a section which is an essay in itself, entitled "Mediaevalism"—Pound explains what he finds uniquely valuable in Cavalcanti by defining what is lost to Italian poetry as it moves from Cavalcanti to Petrarch, or as it moves (so an old-fashioned scholar might say) from the Middle Ages into the Renaissance. Between Cavalcanti and Petrarch, Pound says,

> We appear to have lost the radiant world where one thought cuts through another with clean edge, a world of moving energies *'mezzo oscuro rade,' 'risplende in se perpetuale effecto,'* magnetisms that take form, that are seen, or that border the visible, the matter of Dante's paradiso, the glass under water, the form that seems a form seen in a mirror, these realities perceptible to the sense, interacting, *'a lui si tiri.'* ...

Pound contrasts this way of thinking and feeling, which a few pages later he will attempt to illustrate from a treatise on light by a mediaeval Bishop of Lincoln,[6] to what he sees as the modern scientist's image of the same world:

> For the modern scientist energy has no borders, it is a shapeless 'mass' of force; even his capacity to differentiate it to a degree never dreamed by the ancients has not led him to think of its shape or even its loci. The rose that his magnet makes in the iron filings, does not lead him to think of the force in botanic terms, or wish to visualize that force as floral and extant (*ex stare*).
> A mediaeval "natural philosopher" would find this modern world full of enchantments, not only the light in the electric bulb, but the thought of the current hidden in air and in wire would give him a mind full of forms, "Fuor di color" or having their hyper-colours. The mediaeval philosopher would probably have been unable to think the electric world, and *not* think of it as a world of forms. ...

[6] Robert Grosseteste, *De Luce et de Incohatione Formarum*, in Etienne Gilson, *Philosophie du Moyen Age* (Paris, 1925), and *Make It New*, pp. 356-62.

This may seem a long way from the matter of archaism in poetic diction. But this is not so. Not just the diction of Pound's revised translations, but their rhythms also, hinge upon this notion that "something was lost" between Cavalcanti and Petrarch. The loss was not only in Italian poetry but also, we must say, to the mind of Western Europe, for it is a commonplace of literary history that Petrarch exerted much influence on English poetry over a period that can be defined quite exactly. (That this influence came from only a few aspects of Petrarch, not from the whole of him, is for present purposes irrelevant.) The literary histories name, as the originators of this Petrarchan vogue in England, two poets of the court of Henry VIII, Sir Thomas Wyatt and Henry Howard, Earl of Surrey; and Surrey (Wyatt admittedly is a more complicated and interesting case) also figures in the histories as the poet who established the iambic pentameter as the norm of English versification. Thus, to translate Cavalcanti into iambic pentameters, as Pound did for the most part in 1912, is to translate him into a meter devised for precisely the poet, Petrarch, from whom Pound is anxious to distinguish him. Moreover, it is again a commonplace of literary history that between Chaucer and Surrey English poets were using, though often with little success, a poetic line that rhythmically rocks apart in the middle as in the alliterative verse of Middle English. Accordingly, not just diction but rhythm also becomes archaic, simply through the endeavor after strict accuracy, as soon as Pound tries to "reach back to pre-Elizabethan English." Those are his own words for what he had in mind when he decided to try again at "Chi è questa che vien." As with some of the Odes from the *Classic Anthology*, so with Pound's Cavalcanti versions, it is not enough to observe that the diction is archaic; one is meant to ask also, "How archaic? Archaic of what period? What English precedents or analogues is this archaism meant to bring to mind?" In the present case, it might be said that the 1912 version of "Chi è questa che vien" prompts us to find the English precedent or analogue in the Earl of Surrey;

whereas the later version makes us envisage rather some non-existent, perhaps anonymous, English lyrist of a hundred years earlier than that.

When Pound, in *Make It New*, publishes the Italian text of Cavalcanti's masterpiece, the canzone "Donna mi prega," he presents to the reader's eye that rhythmical dismemberment of Cavalcanti's line that he hopes will in any case sound in the reader's ear. He does this by spacing out the line in print, making it float or step across, as well as down, the printed page:

> Donna mi priegha
>   perch'i volglio dire
> D'un accidente
>   che sovente
>   é fero

And he claims, "The melodic structure is properly indicated—and for the first time—by my disposition of the Italian text. . . ." This is an elaboration of the expedient that was announced as soon as the phrase "the swift-moving" was printed so as to hang ambiguously between the last two lines of "South Folk in Cold Country" from *Cathay*. Pound in the *Cantos* had already begun to explore more audaciously the resources modern typography provides for thus controlling very imperiously the tempo, the stops and starts, that the reader is to observe in his reading. Other poets, notably Pound's life-long associate William Carlos Williams, were to seize upon this range of expedients; and whole poems by Williams and others are stepped across the page in tripartite arrangements such as Pound's typographer gives to Cavalcanti's second line. Already, when Pound was working at Cavalcanti in the 'twenties, E.E. Cummings was making play with other devices not just of typesetting machines but of the typewriter also—devices such as upper-case and lower-case, single and double quotation marks, and punctuation stops. These devices, especially in the case of Cummings, have been crassly misunderstood by many critics and reviewers, who have frequently condemned them as "merely typographical." But why "merely"? Of course it is true that the ear will allow itself to be persuaded by the eye only up to a point; and when a poet tries by typography to persuade the ear of a rhythm that to the ear is nonexistent, then it must be allowed that his arrangement is "merely typographical," and for this he may be blamed. But not only may the reader's ear be assisted, simply by the look of verse on the printed page, to hear a rhythm it might otherwise have missed; but at times the look on the page may actually *create* a rhythm that could not be conveyed to the reader's ear by any other means. As Charles Olson remarks:

> It is the advantage of the typewriter that, due to its rigidity and its space precisions, it can, for a poet, indicate exactly the breath, the pauses, the suspensions even of syllables, the juxtapositions even of parts of phrases, which he intends. For the first time the poet has the stave and bar a musician has had. For the first time he can, without the convention of rime and meter, record the listening he has done to his own speech and by that one act indicate how he would want any reader, silently or otherwise, to voice his work.
>
> It is time we picked the fruits of the experiments of Cummings, Pound, Williams, each of whom has, after his way, already used the machine as a scoring to his composing, as a script to its vocalization.[7]

And Mr. Olson is usefully specific:

> If a contemporary poet leaves a space as long as the phrase before it, he means that space to be held, by the breath, an equal length of time. If he suspends a word or syllable at the end of a line ... he means that time to pass that it takes

[7] Charles Olson, "Projective Verse," *Poetry New York*, 3 (1950); republished as a pamphlet (New York, 1959) and as a "Statement on Poetics" in D.M. Allen, ed., *The New American Poetry: 1945-1960* (New York, 1960).

the eye—that hair of time suspended—to pick up the next line. If he wishes a pause so light it hardly separates the words, yet does not want a comma—which is an interruption of the meaning rather than the sounding of the line—follow him when he uses a symbol the typewriter has ready to hand:

What does not change/is the will to change.

Observe him, when he takes advantage of the machine's multiple margins, to juxtapose:

Sd he:

to dream takes no effort
　　to think is easy
　　　　to act is more difficult...

The examples, from Charles Olson's own poems, illustrate Pound's use, in his later work, of the conventions of the typewriter. Such devices are mannerisms or "gimmicks" only when we cannot see, in the poet's use of them, "the listening he has done to his own speech." In Pound's case he was led to them, not just by the availability of a typewriting machine, but by seeking to translate a poet of mediaeval Italy so scrupulously as to bring over even what that poet's speech sounded like in that poet's ear.

Thus the breaking down of Cavalcanti's line into its constitutive members is indicated by Pound in the typographical arrangement he gives to it. But one notices that Cavalcanti himself had taken steps to this end by rhyming:

D'un accidente
　　　che sovente...

And it is obvious that this is another way to "break the pentameter": the poet makes the rhyme-word within the line mark off one rhythmical member from another. This seems to be what Pound means when he speaks, with annoying slanginess, of how Cavalcanti uses internal rhyme to "stop the line from going heavy." Pound was thus to use typography and

rhyme together to translate the lyric choruses of Sophocles'
Trachiniae, and it is characteristic of many of his versions in
the other late translation, the Classic Odes, that he makes terminal rhyme sparse only so as to enrich internal rhyme. According to William McNaughton, there is precedent for this in
the original Chinese poems "many of which are in lines of
four syllables, rhymed on the third or penultimate syllable." [8]

The work on "Donna mi prega," however, shows Pound at-
tempting to reconstitute a longer poetic unit than the line
while still holding on to the rhythmical dismemberment of the
line from within. He speaks not of members within the line but
of "lobes" within the strophe.

> Each strophe is articulated by 14 terminal and 12 inner
> rhyme sounds, which means that 52 out of every 154 syl-
> lables are bound into the pattern. The strophe reverses the
> proportions of the sonnet, as the short lobes precede the
> longer.

It is worth dwelling on this curious word "lobe," so unexpected in this sort of context. What one is likely to feel first
is that a lobe *hangs*, like the lobe of an ear; as the Shorter Oxford English Dictionary defines it, "the lower soft pendulous
part of the external ear." And this seems a curiously inert, in-
active way to describe how one part of a poem may depend
upon, or depend from, a preceding part. And when we look
elsewhere in the dictionary definition ("A roundish projecting
part, usually one of two or more separated by a fissure. . . .
A rounded projection or part of a leaf or other organ"), it
will appear that Pound's use of the term has everything to do,
and quite exactly, with what the poem looks like on the page;
but nothing at all to do with what it sounds like, actually or
in imagination, in the reader's ear. Yet, in fact, Pound is at this
point very concerned indeed with what the poem sounds like,

[8] W. McNaughton, "Ezra Pound's Meters and Rhythms," *PMLA*,
LXXVIII (March 1963), 136-46.

since he is talking of how it was written for musical setting and how the exigencies of music determine its form:

> The strophes of canzoni are perforce symmetrical as the musical composition is only one-fifth or one-sixth the length of the verbal composition and has to be repeated.

Thus, unless we are to believe that Pound is at this point unbelievably confused between the senses of sight and of sound, we are forced to find some meaning in terms of sound for an expression like "hanging suspended." And we can do this: we can speak meaningfully of how a sound "hung in the air." In fact, when we spoke of how "the swift-moving" hangs between the last two lines of a poem from *Cathay*, we meant that the sound it makes hangs between the sounds that they make. And thus what we have to conceive of, as the effect of Cavalcanti's canzone, is an effect by which, just as units of a few syllables float free of the line of verse and the sound of them hangs in the air, so units of three or four lines of verse at a time float free or hang free of the strophe which, taken together, they constitute.

It cannot be said that the translation Pound offers in *Make It New* does in the event create this effect. When he says in his commentary that "The melodic structure is properly indicated ... by my disposition of the Italian text," he seems to mean that his own translation, on the other hand, is devoted to bringing out other features of the poem than this. For he warns us:

> I have not given an English "equivalent" for the *Donna mi Prega;* at the utmost I have provided the reader, unfamiliar with old Italian, an instrument that may assist him in gauging *some* of the qualities of the original.

The italics are Pound's.

The most cursory look at the translation reveals one quality of the original that is being emphasized: it is a feature of Cavalcanti's vocabulary to which Pound gives much space in his commentary. There he argues that the Italian poet was using with philosophical strictness terms from the physics and meta-physics of his time. And it is this emphasis that produces in Pound's English the string of words "affect," "*virtu*," "force," "essence," "mode," "placation," "locus," "sensate," "modus," "quality," "postulate," "intention," "property," "emanation." When Pound speaks of "the atrocities of my translation," we may take him to mean, among other things, these rebarbative locutions, especially at points where they are crammed one upon another. He will hammer this point home even if it means emphasizing this feature of the diction out of all proportion with other features of the poem. This is why he can confess to "atrocities," and yet go on to declare them "intentional."

One of these words deserves to detain us if only because it rouses an echo—the word "locus":

> In memory's locus taketh he his state
> Formed there in manner as a mist of light
> Upon a dusk that is come from Mars and stays

The word is used again, though not at quite the same point, in another translation Pound made of this poem, which stands as the first part of Canto 36. But we have encountered it already in Pound's introduction to the *Make It New* translation:

> For the modern scientist energy has no borders, it is a shapeless "mass" of force; even his capacity to differentiate it to a degree never dreamed by the ancients has not led him to think of its shape or even its loci. The rose that his magnet makes in the iron filings, does not lead him to think of the force in botanic terms, or wish to visualize that force as floral and extant.

Among the energies that animate the created world is that one which Cavalcanti calls Amor or Love, which he can talk of therefore in the technical vocabulary usual in his day for defining other sorts of energy, physical or metaphysical. Such at least is Pound's contention. Another such animating energy (if indeed all of them are not different modes of one) is the psychic energy that creates poems, of which accordingly Pound may talk as something "floral," borrowing the botanical term "lobe."

This explains why this poem which is so concerned with energy is so unenergetic. For this is surely the case. In either of Pound's versions the last thing we would ascribe to Cavalcanti's poem is impetus, momentum. The same thing is true of his "Who is she that comes, makyng turn every man's eye," just as it is true also of *Cathay*. And, indeed, how could it be otherwise? The metrical sign of kinetic energy, of impetus, is inevitably the enjambement, which swings or whirls the reader on a torrent of feeling out of one line and into the next. Yet Pound the translator, as we have seen, had to eschew enjambement, for in no other way could that breaking of the pentameter which his originals forced upon him, the rhythmical dismemberment of the verse-line from within, be brought about. For the members of the line to achieve some rhythmical independence of the line, it was essential that the rhythmical impetus through the line as a whole be slackened; for the "lobes" to achieve status independent of the strophe, it was essential that the momentum through the strophe be slackened. And so the poetry of *Cathay* and of the later Cavalcanti versions is a static poetry; its constituent parts seem to be almost as much components of an arrangement in space, as phases of a process through time. In *Cathay*, for instance, one might have expected that the reinstatement of the sentence as a poetic unit would have brought with it the impetus of active transitive verbs—indeed, Fenollosa, in his essay on the Chinese written character, assumed that this would be the case. But in the event, precisely because a line ends when a sentence ends, in "South-Folk in Cold Country" the active verbs have none of the activating force they would have had if the sentence had been strung across the line by enjambement. Accordingly, of the lines in this poem it seems more accurate to say that they are placed one beneath another, than to say that one comes after another.

Several commentators have been struck by the paradox that a dynamic character such as Pound should have produced such undynamic poetry as in these translations. And it has been taken to show that the goal of his poetic endeavors was no different from that of the so-called Aesthetic Movement of the previous generation: the deliberate prolongation of what Walter Pater calls the "intervals of time" in which aesthetic perception occurs, the isolation of these not for analysis of them (as by Mallarmé sometimes), but simply for their artificial prolongation in a tranced stillness. Pound would claim, it seems, that the stillness is achieved for the purposes of analysis —analysis, that is, of the sort that poetry practises, notably by rhythm—but that the analysis was conducted, in the Italian poems as in the Chinese poems, from a standpoint and according to categories which to the modern reader are strange, though he is impoverished for lack of them.

However this may be, it is true that poetry of this kind, whether practised by Pound himself or by others such as William Carlos Williams and Charles Olson and Robert Creeley, is a poetry that characteristically moves forward only hesitantly, gropingly, and slowly; which often seems to float across the page as much as it moves down it; in which, if the perceptions are cast in the form of sentences, the sentence is bracketed off and, as it were, folded in on itself so as to seem equal with a disjointed phrase; a poetry (we might almost say) of the noun rather than the verb.

VII

A *Draft of XXX Cantos*
The Malatesta Cantos · Canto 17 · Canto 20

Pound left London and England at the end of 1920, when he was thirty-four; from 1921 to 1924 he was domiciled in Paris, though traveling frequently, especially in Italy; and in 1925 he set up house in what was to be the most permanent of his homes, Rapallo, on the Ligurian coast.

He was still in London when in 1920 he got a rude shock from the oldest of his friends, William Carlos Williams. In this year the radical disagreements between them, which can be heard muttering and grumbling on several pages of the *Letters* from 1908 onwards, came to a head when Williams published a piece he had composed in 1918, the Prologue to his *Kora in Hell: Improvisations*. Here Williams defends some stay-at-home American poets, such as himself, against the successful expatriates Eliot and Pound. He scores some entertaining hits:

I do not overlook De Gourmont's plea for a meeting of the nations, but I do believe that when they meet Paris will be more than slightly abashed to find parodies of the middle ages, Dante and Langue d'Oc foisted upon it as the best in United States poetry.[1]

As a debating point this is unanswerable, and when Pound tried to answer it in a letter he came off very lamely. But of course a debating point is all it is. More interesting are some of the positive points that Williams makes about his own ideas of what poetry should be:

> The true value is that peculiarity which gives an object a character by itself. The associational or sentimental value is the false. Its imposition is due to lack of imagination, to an easy lateral sliding....
>
> ... The imagination goes from one thing to another. Given many things of nearly totally divergent natures but possessing one-thousandth part of a quality in common, provided that be new, distinguished, these things belong to an imaginative category and not in a gross natural array. To me this is the gist of the whole matter....
>
> ... the thing that stands eternally in the way of really good writing is always one: the virtual impossibility of lifting to the imagination those things which lie under the direct scrutiny of the senses, close to the nose. It is this difficulty that sets a value upon all works of art and makes them a necessity.[2]

To all of this, with its emphasis on "the direct scrutiny of the senses," Pound would give a hearty assent, schooled as he had been (by Fenollosa and Gourmont alike) into admiring the controlled observations of empirical science as akin to poetic apprehensions. The heroism of the scientist was to be celebrated in a naïvely generous way in the figure of Pierre Curie, in Cantos 23 and 27, which Pound was shortly to write. Wil-

[1] Quoted in *Letters*, footnote to p. 225.
[2] "Prologue to 'Kora in Hell,'" in *Selected Essays of William Carlos Williams* (New York, 1954), p. 11.

liams was a practising physician and to that extent a scientist himself; and he can see, as the men of letters Pound and Gourmont do not, how natural science can lend its prestige to an itemizing, inert apprehension of particulars that is thoroughly anti-poetic:

> The senses witnessing what is immediately before them in detail see a finality which they cling to in despair, not knowing which way to turn. Thus the so-called natural or scientific array becomes fixed, the walking devil of modern life. (Williams, pp. 11-12.)

What Williams rightly insists on is an imaginative "category" of inter-related items, not an inert "array" of items as items; it is a distinction that Pound, at least in theory, overlooked. But for Williams too the items that offer themselves for apprehension by the poet as "images" are the same as those the scientist isolates for observation. Although the items are thereafter inter-related by the poet's imagination, they retain first and last their character as items, sharply distinct. Williams, like Pound and indeed T.E. Hulme, sets great store by this distinctness; it is a part of the hard-edgedness which imagism demanded of poetic images.

When Williams more than a dozen years later jotted down his impressions of the first thirty of Pound's *Cantos*, it was this quality that he singled out for praise:

> It stands out from almost all other verse by a faceted quality that is not muzzy, painty, wet. It is a dry, clean use of words.[3]

One of Pound's words for this was "cut." It is the word he uses for a quality of perception to be found in Cavalcanti's world and since lost, but he uses it in other contexts also, and it can be related to a context that Pound overlooks—to the

[3] "Excerpts from a Critical Sketch. A Draft of XXX Cantos by Ezra Pound" (*The Symposium*, 1931), in *Selected Essays of William Carlos Williams*, p. 111.

world of the cinema where an Eisenstein "cuts" from one shot to the next. It was the principle of "cut" that necessitated a fresh start after the three cantos, later abandoned, which appeared in *Quia Pauper Amavi;* there were to be no more transitions from image to image by "an easy lateral sliding," but gaps were to be left between images as the poet, like a film director, cut from one to the next. In Canto 4, for instance, Pound cuts rapidly from mediaeval Provence to mythopoeic Greece and back again, as he shuttles the reader from the troubadour biographies of Guillem de Cabestanh and Piere Vidal to the myths of Procne and of Actaeon respectively. More than one commentary is available,[4] and several commentators have followed Hugh Kenner in seeing here what is to be a common procedure in many of the cantos, a procedure that they call "cultural overlayering." (For instance, in the next two or three cantos mediaeval Provence seems frequently to correspond to Homeric Greece, Renaissance Italy to late Greece and republican Rome, contemporary Europe to Rome's decline). But the important point was made by Williams:

> Only superficially do the Cantos fuse the various temporal phases of the material Pound has chosen, into a synthesis. (p. 110.)

One culture may "overlayer" another; but the layers remain, and are meant to remain, distinct. What is intended is a sort of lamination, by no means a compounding or fusing of distinct historical phases into an undifferentiated amalgam. This is what Pater had asked for, confusedly, as early as 1868 in his essay "Aesthetic Poetry." And it is what Williams means by insisting that Pound's object is analysis, not synthesis.

This has to be true because, as Williams rightly insists, it goes down into the structure of the verse-line. The breaking of the pentameter made possible, indeed it enforced, the breaking down of experience into related but distinct items. On the

4 See, for instance, Warren Ramsey, "Pound, Laforgue, and Dramatic Structure," in *Comparative Literature*, III (Winter 1951) 47-56.

123

other hand, any submergence of the line by enjambement into larger units inevitably produced that blurring of edges that Pound and all the imagists, no less than Williams, would castigate as "muzzy"; this is why these poets had to denigrate Milton, the master of the blank-verse paragraph. After the fresh start on the *Cantos*, the verse-line there often dismembers itself into two members or sometimes three or four, cranking apart as the Anglo-Saxon line did, or the line of mediaeval English alliterative verse, or the hendecasyllables of Cavalcanti, or the Japanese verse-line of the Noh plays. Sometimes typography makes this clear, as in Canto 2, a story sumptuously retold from the *Metamorphoses* of Ovid:

> Olive grey in the near,
>   far, smoke grey of the rock-slide,
> Salmon-pink wings of the fish-hawk
>   cast grey shadows in water,
> The tower like a one-eyed great goose
>   cranes up out of the olive-grove.

More often the dismemberment of the line (its integrity despite dismemberment is often, as here, a matter of grammar) is too complex to be indicated by typography, resourceful as Pound is in juggling with variations of type. But the principle is always the same: this is verse in which enjambement is impossible; what has been reinstated as the poetic unit is the verse-line—continually dismembered, but never disintegrated.

How close Williams and Pound were in their purposes, despite their much publicized disagreements, appears if Williams's prose masterpiece of 1925, *In The American Grain*, is compared with Cantos 8 to 11, published in *The Criterion* in 1923 under the title *Malatesta Cantos*. On these cantos too the spade work of exegesis has been carried out very thoroughly.[5] They present, by way of much reproduction of original documents,

[5] See John Drummond, "The Italian Background to the Cantos," in *Ezra Pound: A Collection of Essays for Ezra Pound on His Sixty-fifth Birthday*, ed. Peter Russell (London, 1950).

a telescoped and jumbled account of the *condottiere*, Sigismundo Malatesta, Lord of Rimini; and Pound's method is precisely that of Williams when in his book the latter deals with Cotton Mather or Franklin or John Paul Jones. "Where possible," Williams writes,[6] "I copied and used the original writings. . . . I did this with malice aforethought to prove the truth of my book, since the originals fitted into it without effort on my part, perfectly, leaving not a seam." And thus Williams can add exultantly, of his chapter given to John Paul Jones, "no word is my own," meaning that the whole section is a scissors-and-paste fabrication out of Jones's own dispatches. "Leaving not a seam" is no part of Pound's intention; on the contrary, he leaves the original documents to stand out as foreign bodies embedded in his poem. But his motive, surely, is that of Williams: "to prove the truth of my book." Pound's inclusion of such foreign bodies, his refusal to mask his quotations by translating them out of their original language—these features of the *Cantos* are sometimes taken as proof of incurable dilettantism in the author; but they may just as well prove the direct opposite: his determination to hew to the contours of his subject, to "prove the truth" of his book. Pound in the *Cantos* and Williams in *In the American Grain* are writing as historians. But in history too (so they would maintain) many of the rules of scientific method apply; in particular, the specimens to be examined must not be tampered with before being offered for inspection. And in this way Williams, critical as he is on other counts, can blithely accept what sticks in the gullets of so many, the undeniable fact that Pound's poem, in these cantos and in many others, includes much that must be called prose.

We are no wiser when we have read the Malatesta cantos about what was involved for Malatesta at any point in his in-

[6] *Selected Letters of William Carlos Williams*, ed., J.C. Thirlwall (New York, 1957) p. 187.

cessant campaigning. Indeed, "reading" is an unsatisfactory word for what the eye does as it resentfully labors over and among these blocks of dusty historical debris. We get lost in ever murkier chaos, an ever more tangled web of alliances, counteralliances, betrayals, changing of sides, sieges and the raising of sieges, marches and countermarches; it is impossible to remember whose side Malatesta is on at any time or why. But this is precisely what we were promised by the lines that introduce the sequence:

> These fragments you have shelved (shored).
> 'Slut!' 'Bitch!' Truth and Calliope
> Slanging each other sous les lauriers:

The fragments that Pound has shored against his ruins [7] turn out to be snarled imprecations, a hubbub of charge and counter-charge, the truth inextricably tangled, all wasteful, all remote. All Malatesta's military exploits were wasted, pointless, a hand-to-mouth snatching at eleventh-hour expedients. Yet out of this ignoble maneuvering we hear Malatesta writing to Florence for a painter, meeting the philosopher Gemistus Pletho, getting stone from Verona for the building he projected in Rimini, receiving illiterate letters from his builder about the plans of his architect, Alberti. The only thing that justifies Malatesta's warfare and his shabby diplomacy is the work of art that was coming out of it, the Tempio.

For it is important to remember another of the meanings Pound, especially in his *Gaudier-Brzeska* and *Hugh Selwyn Mauberley*, had given to "cut." "Cut" for him involves an admiration for cut stone, and for related arts like intaglio and

[7] Cf. T.S. Eliot, *The Waste Land* (London, 1922). George Dekker, in *Sailing After Knowledge* (London, 1963) perceives a pun in Pound's "shelved," which makes this allusion to *The Waste Land* a hostile one: "Eliot's poetic method in *The Waste Land*, far from making the useful part of the past more available, rather 'shelves' it again. Pound, on the other hand, will 'unshelve' the useful part of the past, as he does in the Malatesta Cantos." Dekker's case rests on his brilliant reading of the preceding Canto 7 (op. cit., pp. 14-28).

the making of medals, as the image of a moral and cultural positive. In particular, he has been very interested in bas-relief; no more than Adrian Stokes could Pound agree with writers on aesthetics who see carving in low relief as a bastard form between sculpture and painting.

Adrian Stokes, who met Pound many times in 1927, 1928, and 1929, both in Rapallo and in Venice, has written several books that make an illuminating, perhaps indispensable commentary on the *Cantos*. The most important of these is *The Stones of Rimini* (1934). Here Stokes makes a great deal of the derivation of marble from limestone, which is of all stones the one that has most affinity with the element of water. He maintains that great carvers of marble, such as Agostino di Duccio, the sculptor of Sigismundo's Tempio,[8] express their material through the medium of figures they carve from it; and that in doing so they try (unconsciously) to do justice to the stone's watery origin. This fantasy, he argues, would be particularly common and potent in Venice, built upon water, its power and prosperity based on naval supremacy and sea-going trade. Hence, he is particularly interested in the Istrian marble used by the Venetian builders and carvers:

> Istrian marble blackens in the shade, is snow or salt-white where exposed to the sun. . . .
> . . . For this Istrian stone seems compact of salt's bright yet shaggy crystals. Air eats into it, the brightness remains. Amid the sea Venice is built from the essence of the sea. . . .
> Again, if in fantasy the stones of Venice appear as the wave's petrifaction, then Venetian glass, compost of Venetian sand and water, expresses the taut curvature of the cold undersea, the slow, oppressed yet brittle curves of dimly translucent water.
> If we would understand a visual art, we ourselves must cherish some fantasy of the material that stimulated the

[8] According to John Pope-Hennessy, *Italian Renaissance Sculpture* (London, 1958), p. 328, much of this carving is now attributed to Matteo de Pasti.

artist, and ourselves feel some emotional reason why his imagination chose...to employ one material rather than another. Poets alone are trustworthy interpreters. They alone possess the insight with which to re-create subjectively the unconscious fantasies that are general.[9]

Those last sentences seem to be Stokes's oblique acknowledgment that he draws authority here from the early cantos, which, as we know, he had read with excitement some seven years before, and from one of these in particular, Canto 17, which Yeats was later to choose for inclusion in his *Oxford Book of Modern Verse*.

In Canto 17 there appears, to begin with, the very epithet for stone which Stokes was to use, "salt-white." Elsewhere in the Canto Pound compresses into a single perception the whole process of the composition of marble from the incrustation of sunken timber by algae, through shell-encrusted cliff and cave, to the hewn stone of the palazzo with its feet in water. Thus "Marble trunks out of stillness" are balks of timber encrusted by limestone deposits, but they are no less ("On past the palazzi") the hewn columns of some Venetian portico, which is "the rock sea-worn" as well as the wood stone-encrusted. The light is said to be "not of the sun," and this for all sorts of reasons: because it is light as reflected off water in the open air or inside a cave or inside a Venetian portico, because it is light refracted through water when we imagine ourselves submerged along with the just-forming limestone.

When, a few lines later, a man comes by boat talking of "stone trees" and "the forest of marble," he may be taken as one who brings to a Venice not yet revetted in stone the news of marble to be quarried, together with his excited sense of an affinity between city and quarry, a fittingness about bringing the stone of the one to dress the other; or he may be conceived as one who returns to another part of Italy with excited news of the city of stone on water that the Venetians are making.

[9] Adrian Stokes, *The Stones of Rimini* (London, 1934), pp. 19-20.

He speaks of the beaks of gondolas rising and falling, and of the glass-blowers from Murano in terms that look forward to Stokes's argument about the marine fantasies inspiring them. The transition from this, in two lines of verse, to "Dye-pots in the torch-light," may be glossed from another book by Adrian Stokes:

> There is no doubt that the Venetian painters were directly inspired in their use of oil paint by the achievements of the glass makers at Murano.[10]

This stone Venice is seen in the poem as a product of Mediterranean sensibility (related, for instance, to the Greek culture, similarly maritime, similarly marble-loving) and not, as Ruskin thought, related northward to Gothic. The place spoken of is identified as Venice only at the end of the Canto, and then only obliquely (by way of two names, Borso and Carmagnola). And this is right, for the pleached arbor of stone, besides being Venice and besides being the quarries from which Venice was built, is the good place, a sort of heaven of cut and squared masonry, which the broken but indomitable hero earns by his resolution and courage.

The *Cantos* force us to dismiss from our minds most of the familiar connotations of "marmoreal" or "stony." Where "marble" appears, or "stone," it is a sign of resurgence and renewed hope. The most striking example is in Canto 16, where the first glimmer of convalescence after the passage through infernal regions, which occupied Cantos 14 and 15 also, is a hand clutching marble. After the marble comes the new inflow, the embryonic, the new potential; and twelve lines later in Canto 16 a new amplitude and tranquillity: "The grey stone posts,/and the stair of gray stone...."

It is this casing in hewn and chiselled stone that, in the *Cantos*, justifies Sigismundo Malatesta. It may seem that all is to be forgiven Sigismundo—and there is much to forgive—just because he was good to artists, because he chose them well

10 Adrian Stokes, *Colour and Form* (London, 1937), p. 111.

and set them to work on a worthwhile project. And it is true, as Williams noticed, that at times in these early cantos there is a disconcertingly great weight attached to enlightened patronage of the arts in a quite general sense, such as Pound had argued for in his *Patria Mia*.[11] But Malatesta is established as a type of individual for whom the modern sense of "patron" is inadequate, just as it is inadequate for the "onlie begetter" celebrated in Shakespeare's sonnets. Adrian Stokes exclaims, of the Tempio, "It is a tight fit, this holding of one man's emblem"; and he elaborates on this:

> Sigismundo's Tempio expresses Sigismundo. There he is, projected directly into stone, not as a succession or a story, but as something immediate. It is an effect impossible to other generations. All the fifteenth century genius for emblem, for outwardness, centred in Sigismundo.... Each characteristic passed easily into a form of art, non-musical, tense.[12]

Clearly, if this is a sort of patronage quite different from what may be found and hoped for in the twentieth century, it is different also from, for instance, the mediaeval patronage of Abbot Suger of St. Denis, "onlie begetter" of French Gothic:

> The great man of the Renaissance asserted his personality centripetally, so to speak: he swallowed up the world that surrounded him until his whole environment had been absorbed by his own self. Suger asserted his personality centrifugally: he projected his ego into the world that surrounded him until his whole self had been absorbed by his environment.[13]

Malatesta was the sort of patron who "swallowed up the world that surrounded him until his whole environment had been

[11] (Chicago, 1950), but written 40 years earlier.
[12] Adrian Stokes, *The Quattro Cento* (London, 1932), p. 188.
[13] Erwin Panofsky, *Meaning in the Visual Arts* (Garden City, N.Y., 1955), p. 137.

absorbed by his own self." That is the achievement which Pound celebrates. And, if we understand why, we go near to the nerve of all the early cantos, for of all spiritual manifestations, the one that Pound at this stage showed himself surest about, and most excited by, was that which in the Renaissance went by the name of *virtù*:

> That hath the light of the doer, as it were
> a form cleaving to it.

The virtù which is the light of a personality cleaving to act or artifact, molding and forming it, is all the more impressively *there*, all the more certainly a proof that the spiritual resources of the person can modify and indelibly mark the physical, when we perceive it as in the Rimini Tempio transmitted through intermediaries as well as through a medium—the *virtù* not of doer or artificer, but of the patron who caused things to be done, caused artifacts to be made. For the Tempio, according to Adrian Stokes, expresses not Alberti's personality nor Agostino di Duccio's, but Sigismundo's. This was the emphasis Pound was to give to Sigismundo in *Guide to Kulchur*: "There is no other single man's effort equally registered."

The man of Pound's own time who might come nearest to registering his effort with equal authority, Pound would come to think, was Mussolini. Thus this powerful strain of feeling in the poet had its sinister side, as Williams perceived:

> It is still a Lenin, striking through the mass, whipping it about, that engages his attention. That is the force Pound believes in. (op. cit., p. 111.)

When Pound opens Canto 30 with the haunting mediaeval pastiche of his "complaint of Artemis," reversing Chaucer's "Complaint unto Pity" into an argument for a proper ruthlessness (because "Pity spareth so many an evil thing"), although we may realize that the point is well taken, we have to feel with the benefit of hindsight that this was a woefully inappropriate time for taking it. It was characteristic of the whole of Pound's generation to sway toward totalitarian politics in the late 'twenties and early 'thirties: Eliot in "Coriolan," D.H. Lawrence in his letters, Wyndham Lewis in *The Art of Being Ruled*, Yeats in his marching songs for O'Duffy's blueshirts—all similarly failed to read the signs of the times. Pound was the only one of them to persist in his misreading and to be brought to book for it.

When Adrian Stokes wrote of the Tempio as Sigismundo's emblem, he was making another distinction besides that between the Renaissance patron and other kinds of patron. He insists that Sigismundo is "projected directly into stone, not as a succession or a story," and that "each characteristic passed easily into a form of art, non-musical, tense." When he writes "not as a succession . . . non-musical," he is deploring the confusion of non-successive arts like sculpture and architecture with the "successive" art of music, a confusion that he lays at the door of Brunelleschi. Pound had made the same protest, but from the side of, and on behalf of, music:

> The early students of harmony were so accustomed to think of music as something with a strong lateral or horizontal motion that they never imagined any one, ANY ONE could be stupid enough to think of it as static; it never entered their heads that people would make music like steam ascending from a morass.[14]

But what of literature, of poetry? Is not poetry necessarily a "successive" art like music, carving its structures out of lapsing time? Certainly the symbolists thought so, with their "De la musique avant toute chose." But Pound as early as *Gaudier-Brzeska* was opposed to symbolism on these grounds as on others, and was speculating about poetry by analogy with the spatial art of sculpture rather than the temporal art of music. Moreover, in his typographical laying out of "Donna

[14] Pound, *Patria Mia and The Treatise on Harmony* (London, 1962), p. 80.

mi prega," a layout which seems to have been the model for many pages of the *Cantos*, Pound had contrived at least the illusion of a poetry that is ranged across as well as down in the space of the printed page.

In 1927 he was still imagining his poetry in these sculptural and spatial terms. This appears from a letter written in that year to his father, a document which is invaluable in any case as it is the nearest we come to an exegesis by the poet of one of his own cantos, specifically, of Canto 20.

This canto opens with interlarded scraps of verse from the Provençal of Bernart de Ventadour and the Latin of Catullus and Propertius. It moves into a pleasantly relaxed and affectionate reminiscence of Pound's visit, on the advice of his teacher Hugo Rennert, to the scholar of Provençal, Emile Lévy, with a problem of vocabulary from Arnaut Daniel. There ensues a passage of natural description, whether of Provence or of Lévy's Freiburg is not clear. Pound's exegesis for his father begins with the first line of a fourth section, "He was playing there at the palla." Pound writes that this section represents "Nicolo d'Este in sort of delirium after execution of Parisina and Ugo" (that is, of Nicolo's wife and his own natural son, who had been her lover). And Pound's note goes on:

> The whole reminiscence jumbled or 'candied' in Nicolo's delirium. Take that as a sort of bounding surface from which one gives the main subject of the Canto, the loto-phagoi: lotus eaters, or respectable dope smokers; and general paradiso. You have had a hell in Canti XIV, XV; purgatorio in XVI etc. (*Letters*, p. 285.)

Nicolo's delirium plays with or plays over a great deal more than this. It includes, as Pound notes, memories of a passage of the *Iliad* when the old men of Troy talk of returning Helen to the Greeks and so ending the war; and this is confounded with another beautiful woman on another wall—Elvira, in Lope's play *Las Almenas de Toro*, which is described

133

in *The Spirit of Romance*. Another episode that weaves in and out of Nicolo d'Este's disordered mind is the death of Roland; and it is in *The Spirit of Romance* that Pound objects to the treatment of this in *The Song of Roland* as stiff and frigid. Pound's extremely shrill and wooden retelling of it is open to Williams's objection:

> His words affect modernity with too much violence (at times)—a straining after slang effects, engendered by their effort to escape from that which is their instinctive quality —a taking character from classic similes and modes. (op. cit., p. 107.)

And this makes something unintentionally warped and coarsely textured out of the "bounding surface" that the delirium was meant to provide. However, if Pound had spoken of this as "a background," there would have been no difficulty in approving at least the intention: against the tumultuous violence of love and war in Nicolo's delirium the serenity of what follows was to stand out seductively. By speaking instead of "a bounding surface" (one imagines something like a rough-hewn concave shell, half-enclosing sculpted masses in its shadow), Pound shows that he is conceiving of his poetic space in three dimensions, in sculptural terms rather than painterly.

As for the subsequent treatment of the lotus-eaters, this has been much admired, for instance by Hugh Kenner. Yet one can only be astonished at the impression the passage gives, which Pound's letter to his father confirms, that the lotus-eaters are offered naïvely to be admired by the reader as having attained one stage toward an all-important illumination. In cantos written twenty-five years after this, Pound was to insist that "Le Paradis n'est pas artificiel"; but at this stage the Paradiso certainly is very close to the "paradis artificiel" of the drug-takers. A paradiso thus infected with nineteenth-century diabolism and self-admiring "decadence" is surely damned by the Dantesque parallel which Pound too presumptuously invites.

VIII

C antos 30-36 · Guide to Kulchur

Cantos 31 to 34, first published in magazines in the years 1931-33, are the first installment of what have come to be called the American History cantos. Cantos 31 and 32 and the first half of 33 have been put together out of snippets from letters exchanged between John Adams and Thomas Jefferson. According to William Vasse, these pages are devoted to "outlining some of the main points of the early American economic, political, legal and ideological struggles." [1] But the only struggle we find documented in the verse (and even this we find with difficulty) is the ideological difference between Jefferson's respect for doctrinaire theorists like Tom Paine and

[1] W. Vasse, "American History and the Cantos," *The Pound Newsletter*, 5 (Jan. 1955).

Condorcet and even Franklin, and Adams's distrust of them. Thus ten lines of Canto 31 are made up from a very respectful letter from Jefferson to Paine, whom Adams on the contrary (though this is not in the canto) described as "a disastrous meteor." [2] Elsewhere in the canto Adams is quoted describing Condorcet, Franklin, and others as grossly ignorant; and in still other lines Adams mocks Franklin for his notions of "the exalted dignity of human nature." Yet in Canto 33, when Adams renews his attacks on what he calls "ideology" (borrowing the word from Napoleon), the point is blurred because Pound omits from the beginning of his quotation the words "establishing a free republican government." It is kindest, therefore, to suppose that Pound intended by these cantos to do no more than tease the reader into looking up his sources.

This is not true, however, of Canto 34, which is similarly a catena of quotations from a selected edition of the diaries of John Quincy Adams, son of John Adams.[3] Though in this canto too there are teasingly cryptic references, and though I think Vasse takes the will for the deed in finding that some citations from John Quincy Adams's term as president contrast him with his father as more the observer and less the actor, yet the canto by itself, without recourse to the *Diary* it is hewn from, establishes John Quincy Adams as a rounded and sympathetic character. This is effected by strictly poetic means; the rhythms, while necessarily still prosaic, are repeatedly tauter than in the preceding cantos. Moreover, the alleged decline in standards of taste and enlightenment from the heyday of John Adams to that of his son is wittily and convincingly depicted. And there are lines at the end of the canto which can sustain comparison with Eliot's "Coriolan," to which indeed they appear to be related:

[2] *The Works of John Adams,* ed. Charles Francis Adams, 10 vols. (Boston, 1850-57), II, 507.
[3] *The Diary of John Quincy Adams, 1794-1845,* ed. Allan Nevins (New York, 1928).

The firemen's torchlight procession,
Firemen's torchlight procession,
Science as a principle of political action

Firemen's torchlight procession!

The exclamation mark does an amusing amount of work. The *Diary* records that Adams was accorded this peculiar honor three times running—in Buffalo, in Rochester, in Utica. "Science as a principle of political action" refers, however, to a visit to Cincinnati that succeeded the visit to these towns of New York State. Thus the *Diary* confirms what the lineation of the verse suggests: the second repetition of "Firemen's torchlight procession" represents a delayed reaction to the absurdity of a piece of *ad hoc* ceremonial which at first was accepted bemusedly. And it stands, with its exclamation mark, as a self-sufficient comment upon a society where the ceremonies are pompous and on a gross scale, yet uninformed by precedent or by any symbolic aptness of invention; the Diary confirms that the public life of America in 1843, as Adams saw it, was indeed the tasteless and raucous America that Dickens was to hold up to exasperated mockery in *American Notes* and *Martin Chuzzlewit*.

This is the America also of Canto 37, which is quarried from the autobiography of yet another President of the United States, Martin Van Buren. Unfortunately, the vulgarity of Van Buren, the extent to which he was himself a product of tasteless demagoguery, is concealed in Pound's canto and is revealed only when we inspect in the autobiography the language of Van Buren himself which, with its fulsome capital letters on "the People" and "the Party," is an eloquent witness to that tyranny of the majority that John Adams had foreseen ("a country where popularity had more omnipotence than the British parliament assumed"[4]), that Fenimore Cooper fought against and suffered by throughout his life, that Dickens rightly

[4] Adams, *Works*, X, 53.

mocked and castigated. Pound declared, in *The A.B.C. of Reading*, "A people that grows accustomed to sloppy writing is a people in process of losing grip on its empire and on itself." [5] And yet he finds a hero of sorts in a man whose own language is sloppy and blowsy in the extreme. It is here one has the right to say that Pound's new-found "conspiracy" theory of fiscal history was distorting and over-riding his own earlier insights. For Van Buren earns his place in the *Cantos* and is accorded the title of "fisci liberator" because he was the champion of Jacksonian democracy in its war with the Banks. It is true that in Canto 34 John Quincy Adams was allowed to record "L'ami de tout le monde, Martin Van Buren." But it is worth returning this judgment to its context:

> Finished reading Holland's Life of Martin Van Buren, a partisan electioneering work, written with much of that fraudulent democracy by the profession of which Thomas Jefferson rose to power in this country, and of which he set the first successful example. Van Buren's personal character bears, however, a stronger resemblance to that of Mr. Madison than to Jefferson's. These are both remarkable for their extreme caution in avoiding and averting personal collisions. Van Buren, like the Sosie of Molière's *Amphitryon*, is "l'ami de tout le monde." This is perhaps the great secret of his success in public life....[6]

This reveals, if it reveals nothing else, the animosity of the Adamses to many of their famous contemporaries, something that Pound's treatment of American history conceals. Of course the principle may be wrong; perhaps we should judge Martin Van Buren as much by his recorded actions as by his utterances. But Pound had seemed to maintain that integrity in action and integrity in language necessarily go together. And a reading in Van Buren's autobiography confirms, by the language Van Buren employs, John Quincy Adams's estimate of him as a crafty, fulsome, and slippery demagogue.

[5] (London and New Haven, 1934), p. 86.
[6] *The Diary of John Quincy Adams*, p. 465 (Apr. 13, 1836).

Between the John Quincy Adams canto and the Van Buren canto stand Cantos 35 and 36. Canto 35 contains the first display of Pound's anti-Semitism. There is no point in denying that this is what it is. And yet we must observe that, without the appalling hindsight we have from subsequent history and subsequent cantos, Canto 35, though it would in any case give offence to many Jews, is seen to make an arguable and interesting point about Jewish social life:

> this is Mitteleuropa
>   and Tsievitz
> has explained to me the warmth of affections,
> the intramural, the almost intravaginal warmth of
> hebrew affections, in the family, and nearly everything else....
> pointing out that Mr. Lewinesholme has suffered by deprivation
> of same and exposure to American snobbery ... 'I am a product,'
> said the young lady, 'of Mitteleuropa,'
> but she seemed to have been able to mobilize
> and the fine thing was that the family did not
> wire about papa's death for fear of disturbing the concert
> which might seem to contradict the general indefinite wobble.
> It must be rather like some internal organ,
> some communal life of the pancreas ... sensitivity
> without direction ... this is ...

If Pound had never gone further than this into anti-Semitism, one could argue that this has as much to do with his ideas about music as expressed in *Antheil and The Treatise on Harmony*, and that, most of the executants being Jewish, there is a witty and legitimate connection between their music and the rest of their emotional life. What is in any case equally disturbing in this canto is the increased abstractness of Pound's thought: this permits him, as elsewhere to write off with a confident generalization whole tracts of recorded history, so here to dispose with absurd jauntiness of a large tract of the earth's surface—"So this is (may we take it) Mitteleuropa."

Canto 35 ends with an extended reference to Mantua, and this is carried on in the next canto in a reference to the Mantuan Sordello, who survives into the *Cantos* out of the Browningesque first draft of the first three, where he had played the lead. But most of Canto 36 is taken up, surprisingly enough, with a new translation of "Donna mi prega," a translation even more opaque than the already all but impenetrable version given in *Make It New*. The best explanation of this is George Dekker's,[7] who argues that the point is precisely the opacity. In literature and history, as in the sciences, there are phenomena surviving that for certain reasons (in this case, the erosion through time of the intellectual context of Cavalcanti's poem) are simply and blankly unaccountable, inscrutable. In such cases the most faithful translation is the one making least sense, and this corresponds to what Pound has always required of historians—that they leave blanks in their writings for "what they don't know."[8] Thus Cavalcanti's poem is lodged in the center of the Cantos, a hard nugget of foreign matter, to enforce humility.

Pound's *Guide to Kulchur*[9] is an incomparable book—not incomparably good, just incomparable. In what other work could one find the author conceding after thirty pages: "I cd. by opening volumes I haven't seen for 25 or more years find data that run counter to what I am saying or what I shall say in the next ten pages"? No doubt many authors have admitted this to themselves on their thirtieth page, and yet gone on to write three hundred and forty pages more. But who has done this who has made the admission not to himself but his readers? None, surely, whose purpose is, as Pound's is, peda-

[7] *Sailing After Knowledge* (London, 1963), pp. 126-8.
[8] Canto 13: And Kung said "Wang ruled with moderation,
    "In his day the State was well kept,
    "And even I can remember
    "A day when the historians left blanks in their writings,
    "I mean for things they didn't know, ..."
[9] (London, 1938); *Culture* is the title of the American printing in the same year.

gogical; for no pedagogue can afford such an admission. Pound can afford it, and that is his unique qualification, as he realizes:

> It is my intention in this booklet to COMMIT myself on as many points as possible, that means that I shall make a number of statements which very few men can AFFORD to make, for the simple reason that such taking sides might jeopard their incomes (directly) or their prestige or "position" in one or other of the professional "worlds." Given my freedom, I may be a fool to use it, but I wd. be a cad not to.

Some may think that Pound, having used the poet's freedom to the pedagogue's ends, has misled as many readers as, for instance, Robert Graves, who in some of his prose has made the same use of his poet's freedom; but Pound saw that the freedom involved responsibility. This appears from the passage just quoted from the Preface, but the best evidence is the damaging admission we started with, to which there is no parallel in Graves. And halfway through the book, at the start of Section VIII, Pound reminds himself again of what he is doing, and how risky it is:

> Ridiculous title, stunt piece. Challenge? Guide,
> ought to mean help other fellow to get there.

What is involved is a genuine educational experiment. The experiment may fail, but it was undertaken in all seriousness, not irresponsibly. And the same is true of the earlier pilot experiments, *How To Read* and *The A.B.C. of Reading*. After all, Pound commenced life as a pedagogue, and in 1938 he was still the man who had written *The Spirit of Romance*.

The method he experiments with is determined by certain self-imposed ordinances. Not all of these are clear at first, but one of them is:

> In the main, I am to write this new Vade Mecum without opening other volumes, I am to put down so far as possible only what has resisted the erosion of time, and forgetfulness.

"In the main" is a saving clause. And with that qualification the rule might seem to have been followed as much in the *Cantos* as in the pedagogical treatise. In the poem, however, there is far more "opening other volumes"—more's the pity, perhaps, for it means that in the poem, when we come on inaccuracies (as we do, repeatedly), they are far more damaging than they are in *Guide to Kulchur*, where we have been forewarned of them. At any rate, the reason for relying on memory is the same in the prose as in the poetry; the knowledge that has "resisted the erosion of time, and forgetfulness" is a different sort of knowledge from the sort that has to be refreshed, the knowledge of "where to look it up." And there are plausible reasons for thinking that knowledge of the first sort is superior to the second sort, so superior that perhaps the second is not properly to be called knowledge at all. We have not read many pages of *Guide to Kulchur* before we find that the distinction between the two kinds of knowledge not only determines Pound's way of writing, it is also, quite centrally, what he is talking about.

The knowledge we have of the Ionian philosophers is necessarily, he suggests, knowledge of the second sort; if we want to recall what Heraclitus said besides "everything flows," or what he meant by that gnomic, because too inclusive, proposition, we always have to "look it up." This knowledge we have of Heraclitus is obviously different from knowledge we have which, once acquired, is a permanent possession. Pound's example of the second sort of knowledge is connoisseurship, in painting and in literature; the sort of "feel," or rule of thumb, derived from experience, by which in the first place the connoisseur makes his attributions. Pound identifies this sort of knowledge as that which the Confucian tradition deals with and deals in, whereas the Greek tradition (even in Plato, even in Aristotle) deals always in knowledge of the other, academic sort. Pound's attempt to demonstrate this by excerpts from the Analects is unconvincing. Yet the failure of this example does not invalidate the distinction as such between the two kinds of knowledge; in fact, the distinction is endorsed always by common sense, and, as Pound realizes, it has been made many times before. Keats was making it when he distinguished between knowledge that is "felt on the pulses" and other kinds of knowledge. And Pound is surely in a very strong position when he implies that the distinction, since it exists, ought to be the first distinction made in pedagogical theory and that all pedagogical practice should be conducted in the light of it.

In fact, even as Pound wrote *Guide to Kulchur*, an attempt was being made to apply just these insights to the teaching of literature—an attempt sustained mostly in the University of Cambridge and associated with the name of F.R. Leavis and the magazine that he founded, *Scrutiny*. This Cambridge experiment is not irrelevant to a discussion of Pound, since Leavis, in his *How To Teach Reading, A Primer for Ezra Pound*, was the only academic figure to take anything by Pound (in this case, *How To Read*) seriously enough to retort to it; and in his *New Bearings in English Poetry* Leavis at a later date drew admiring attention to *Hugh Selwyn Mauberley* at the same time as he condemned the *Cantos* and nearly everything else by Pound except *Homage to Sextus Propertius*. In fact, Leavis condemns *How To Read* and the *Cantos* by Poundian principles, since he seems to believe in the last resort that there can be no knowledge of literature "on the pulses" except of literature in one's native language. It is reasonable for any self-respecting pedagogue to decide that the only knowledge that is worth imparting is knowledge that shall be a permanent acquisition, not mere book-learning; and yet inevitably, with Pound as more conspicuously with Leavis, this position produces a canon of approved authors and an index of proscribed books. Among their opponents, a slack irresponsibility, taste at the whim of fashion and idiosyncrasy, masquerades as open-mindedness. Yet open-mindedness *is* the cornerstone of the edifice of learning; and Pound's anathemas, like Leavis's, close the minds of their disciples. The dispute is a bitter one, and interminable, because both parties are in the right. Every man's mind is closed eventually, when time and energy run out on him before he has acquainted himself with more than a tiny fraction of what is worth knowing; and it is Pound's sense of the sands running out for his pupils, and of the unmanageable copiousness of what may be known, that justifies Pound, like Leavis, in trying to close the student's mind to what seems sterile or inessential. Moreover, in Pound this concern takes the very practical form of demanding better co-ordination internationally inside the world of learning.

Pound does not in any case proscribe whole bodies of knowledge. On the contrary, unlike Leavis but like many pedagogues of the 'thirties, Pound urges the student of literature and philosophy into, for instance, economic theory and economic history. He differs from the majority, who made this recommendation under Marxist auspices, by considering particularly important the history of fiscal policy. It soon appears that his lukewarmness about Plato and Aristotle (he stops far short of proscription of these authors) has to do with their being Athenians, citizens of a state where fiscal and economic practice was determined by the needs of maritime commerce. Like Pater in *Plato and Platonism*, Pound's sympathies are instead with Sparta, a totalitarian state with a less mercantile economy, and with Rome. And as Pound boldly associates the figure of 30 per cent interest with Athens, and of 6 per cent with Rome, as he credits St. Ambrose with transmitting the best of imperial Rome into the mediaeval Church, as he reprints Gaudier's "Vortex" as a "history of sculpture," we perceive that Pound is not the sort of educator who proscribes whole subjects as useless; he is, on the contrary, the more buoyant but perhaps more dangerous kind who will save the time that he and his students so desperately need, by using mnemonics, on the understanding that in most subjects of discourse the essential truths can be stated on the back of a postcard or at most on a few sheets of notepaper. His "gists and piths," as he calls them, are the mnemonics, the essential truths. The mnemonic for St. Ambrose, for instance, from this time forward in

Pound's writing, is "captans annonam" or "hoggers of harvest"; there is no intimation that we need to know more of St. Ambrose than this single phrase in order to esteem him as highly as Pound does. Quite consistently, when he rightly comes to consider how a culture can be maintained by social custom and habit for some time after creative minds have ceased to fructify it, he gives as proof and example an observation and an anecdote from the conversation of an acquaintance, Urquell, a Russian White Guard émigré. It is easy to laugh this out of court, indignantly; but it must be agreed that if the only "real" knowledge is that which stays in the memory permanently, then perhaps a mnemonic is all that stands between St. Ambrose and oblivion, and all that he deserves in the unmanageable plenitude of so much else that is worth knowing.

In Part II of *Guide to Kulchur* (five chapters), the disorder is not just apparent but real. Yet the observant reader will perceive that Pound is here making a new estimate of his own career to date. Already on an earlier page he had written (Chapter 4):

> My generation found criticism of the arts cluttered with work of men who persistently defined the works of one art in terms of another.
> For a decade or so we tried to get the arts sorted out.

And to any reader who remembers the memoir of Gaudier, and Pound's definition of his own poetry as "painting or sculpture just coming over into speech," this will seem disingenuous to say the least. For Pound himself had been one of those men who, in the climate of opinion inaugurated by Pater, "persistently defined the works of one art in terms of another." The Pound of 1938 is disowning the Pound of 1916, and to set the record straight he needs to make this explicit. He does so when in Part II he relates his own activities between 1916 and 1921 to contemporaneous French movements connected with the names of Picabia, Marcel Duchamp, and Erik Satie; that is to say, his and Wyndham Lewis's work for *Blast* (no less, in a rather special way, Joyce's in *Ulysses*) are now considered as wholly, though necessarily, destructive or at least disruptive— the vorticist movement corresponds to Dadaism across the Channel in being deliberately anarchical, a summing up or clinical clearing out and breaking down of categories and conventions inherited from the nineteenth century. It can be justified only retrospectively when it produced by reaction Cocteau's *Rappel à l'ordre*. Cocteau is declared to be a poet of genius, the presiding genius of the 'twenties, and yet his work too is only preparatory. It prepares for "the new synthesis, the totalitarian." "Totalitarian" as used by Pound refers to more than politics, but it is a term of politics in the first place, and *Guide to Kulchur* is an overtly Fascist book.[10] Pound even compliments Wyndham Lewis on having discovered Hitler before he, Pound, discovered Mussolini. Though one dislikes admitting it, nothing has happened since to invalidate this logical and chronological connection between modernism in the arts and Fascism in politics; Thomas Mann discerned it also. There is further corroboration in Chapter 20, where the Vou club in totalitarian Japan, with which Pound corresponds through Katue Kitasono, is said to have been founded by ad- mirers of Satie.

In some places Pound's Fascism is just a straightforward en- thusiasm for all things Italian, no more sophisticated (despite his years of residence in Rapallo) than the enthusiasm of any British or American middle-aged couple after a holiday in Sestri Levante. In Chapter 16 he is unashamedly the tourist, telling his readers to take walking tours in France but in Italy to take the bus, and (pretentiously knowledgeable) declaring gravely that "Le Voyage Gastronomique is a French pai- deuma." On the other hand, Chapter 21, on the excellence of the textbooks in Italian schools, gives food for thought. And elsewhere the totalitarianism is much more serious. For in-

[10] As had been, for instance, Pound's *Jefferson And/Or Mussolini* (Lon- don, 1935).

stance, what Pound envisages as totalitarianism in art ("the new synthesis") becomes clearer with an interesting passage in Chapter 19, where he speaks of Bartók's Fifth Quartet, as played at Rapallo in 1937 by the New Hungarian Four, as "the record of a personal struggle," as "too interesting," as having "the defects inherent in a record of struggle," which are "the defects or disadvantages of my Cantos." Set against the Bartók is a work by Boccherini, played on the same occasion by the same musicians, in which "no trace of effort remained," any more than it remains in the disconcerting limpidity of the Analects or in the simplicity of "the jokes in Boccaccio." Totalitarian art will be simple and transparent; the obscurity and oddity of modernist art like the *Cantos* will nowhere be treated with such contumely as in the totalitarian states—and Pound almost brings himself to admit this. However, such totalitarian art is not just round the corner; for the necessary preparatory labor of clarification, co-ordination, and research is all to be done—as Pound vividly illustrates in respect to the very composers he is talking about, Boccherini and Vivaldi.[11] The difference between Boccherini and Bartók is not, in any ordinary sense of "totalitarian," the difference between totalitarian and non-totalitarian art. As Pound acutely and instructively says, it is the difference between an art that has a culture behind it and an art (Bartók's, Pound's, perhaps even Beethoven's) that is produced out of a solitary artist's struggle *against* the cultural conditions he is born to. The two kinds of art correspond to the two kinds of knowledge. As Pound says:

> Knowledge is NOT culture. The domain of culture begins when one HAS 'forgotten-what-book'.

[11] Pound, himself the composer of an opera, *The Testament of François Villon*, was not only a pioneer in the appreciation of Vivaldi, but gave to the locating of Vivaldi's manuscripts (and their interpretation) the benefit of his experience years before in locating manuscripts of troubadour songs for the edition he did with Walter Morse Rummel. (See *Hesternae Rosae* by Walter Morse Rummel, London, 1911.) Pound the musician and musicologist deserves a book to himself.

The knowledge that one possesses securely is not safeguarded consciously, nor even is it so acquired; it is like a trained reflex, not maintained nor extended by any act of will. Commonsense knows that this is so, but it is difficult and perilous for educators to acknowledge it.

Pound is repeatedly aware of the perils to education, and to scholarship. Academic freedom, like the freedom of the press, is worthless unless freedom brings responsibility. Even open-mindedness is worthless except in the service of curiosity. Pound knows that he himself is a man with bees in his bonnet. In Chapter 28 he calls himself "a credit-crank." And in Chapter 31 he says, "I am not satisfied with my own journalism. I suspect it of being coloured by my convictions." Yet, he says, "even this mania, this one-trackness occasionally ploughs up more truth than mere lack of direction," because "some kind of line to hang one's facts on is better than no line at all." Thus:

> The indifferent or "cold" historian may leave a more accurate account of what happens, but he will never understand WHY it happens.
>
> I have seen the nitchevo journalists missing the mainspring, almost always missing the mainsprings.
>
> A complete laissez-faire, a conviction of universal vanity, a disgust with the metier itself, a belief in their own impotence, an attribution of similar lack of motivation, of constructivity, of volition to all other men, leaves them on the outside.

The dilemma is familiar to every literary scholar, and there are none who are not, wittingly or unwittingly, caught upon the horns of it, as Pound is. Unless an investigation is made with an open mind it cannot be scholarly, but will ignore whatever does not fall in with the investigator's preconceptions. And yet there is open-mindedness that is indistinguishable from indifference; and indifference, under the specious masks of impartiality and detachment, may be scholarly indeed, but it is also sterile and sterilizing. Even curiosity is worth very little if it is omnivorous, if it makes every item of information equal to every other. Nevertheless, Pound is superior to, for instance, F.R. Leavis, who at this period was making similar points with similar courage, because Pound holds on to curiosity as the irreplaceable saving grace. Scholarship is damned, and its pretensions to open-mindedness are seen to be hollow, if it can be shown to be incurious. And Pound, who has pointed out how incurious the musicologists are (for instance, about Vivaldi), can easily make the same charge stick upon the scholars of literature. "Philology," in the inclusive German sense which was taken over from the Germans in Europe generally and in the United States, was the discipline of literary scholarship into which Pound was initiated at the University of Pennsylvania in 1907, just as the young graduate is initiated into it today in Pennsylvania or in Cambridge, England. Pound blames it, as others have done, for fostering and depending upon an impartiality which is really indifference, which recognizes no hierarchy of significance by which some items of information are more important than others. The peculiar strength of Pound's case is that he also shows how incurious it is. The Germans who initiated this scholarly method are the least to be blamed for it; and Anglo-American sneers at "Teutonic scholarship" are particularly out of place since, as Pound shows, not only is German scholarship better co-ordinated than any other (for instance in the Institute that Frobenius founded at Frankfurt), but also, in each field Pound turns to for examples of how incurious the literary scholars are, such solitary pioneers as can be found turn out to be Germans, like Klabund in the field of ancient Chinese poetry. When Pound compares Klabund's versions with the eighteenth-century Latin versions of Lacharme (a Frenchman, but reprinted in the present century by Germans), he is inspired by the Latin to a rough English version which is the first intimation of his translation of the *Classic Anthology* twenty years later. And this, like the admirable versions of African folk-poems in the preceding two chapters of *Guide to Kulchur*, is not only an example of the effortless limpidity to be expected of totalitarian art; it stands also as evidence of how incurious literary scholarship is, which will allow such poems to lie hidden in unknown languages or in the archives of anthropologists.

Nobody can suppose that *Guide to Kulchur* was written according to a plan worked out beforehand. Chapter by chapter, even paragraph by paragraph, Pound is improvising, and no one can be deceived for more than a moment by Pound's pretense that the abruptness of his transitions is really a matter of pregnant juxtapositions, contrived according to the so-called "ideogrammic method" as recommended by Fenollosa. On the contrary, the appeal of *Guide to Kulchur*, and its uniqueness, are in its being so desperate and so harried, and in Pound's vulnerability which, in consequence, he exposes consciously as well as unconsciously. For Pound surprises himself as well as surprising his readers. Ever more discouraged as the book drags toward its close, Pound is compelled for a second time to review his own half-century of effort, and to see his achievement as partial, limited, in part misdirected, and at best eccentric. Most unexpectedly (since the most strident of Pound's diatribes have throughout been reserved for England), it is a British writer, Hardy, who provokes Pound to this second and more painful self-assessment. In a letter of 1937 he had written of Hardy's *Collected Poems*, "Now *there is* the harvest of having written 20 novels first" (*Letters*, p. 386). And this is the note struck in *Guide to Kulchur* also (Chapter 52):

> 20 novels form as good a gradus ad Parnassum as does metrical exercise, I dare say they form a better if the gods have granted light by that route. Hardy is Gautier's successor as Swinburne could not be.

In consequence,

> a craft that occupies itself solely with imitating Gerard Hopkins or in any other metrical experiment is a craft misdirected. We engage in technical exercise faute de mieux, a necessary defensive activity.

Here Pound is not quite unsaying what he had said many times in earlier years, for he saves himself (with a spurt of renewed pugnacity) by observing, "Out of these sentences you may omit neither the 'solely' nor the 'necessary' without destroying their meaning." But the emphasis of the earlier Pound had been so consistently the other way, in favor of "technique," and of "technique" that could be learned, that even so close an associate as Wyndham Lewis had, in *Men Without Art*, taken this to be Pound's central and distinguishing characteristic. And so, in these pages on Hardy, we see more clearly than before what a *volte-face* was involved when Pound disavowed modernist intricacy and technical sophistication in favor of a limpidity he considered "totalitarian." Of Hardy's generation, the last generation of British Victorian artists, Pound now says, "they bred a generation of experimenters, my generation, which was unable to work out a code for action." Hardy, with his insularity and his clumsiness (sometimes calculated, often not) is so much the last poet one would have expected Pound to admire, that this tribute to him gives us a new respect for Pound's generosity and open-mindedness, the genuine catholicity of his taste. Yet there is no blinking the fact that it makes nonsense of many of Pound's other professions, at this date as well as earlier. And, indeed, Pound is so discouraged by this time that he can no longer find enthusiasm for a totalitarian New Dawn. We hear again about the "new synthesis," but Pound's heart is not in it. Instead, after acknowledging and dismissing "the rocks anyone can throw at Hardy for romance and sentiment," Pound observes:

> Whether in a communist age we can, or will in our time be able to, concede such emphasis to the individual elegy and the personal sadness, I doubt. And if not? the transition may have been from literary to rhetorical.

"Communist" in that passage seems to refer to much more than the Soviet Union. And if so, this is a betraying admission. Pound, for all his epic pretensions, is ready to think that in his lifetime the only true poetry will be elegiac, all else rhetoric. And indeed, the poetry that remained for him to write, like most of the poems he had written already, was to be poetry of "the individual elegy and the personal sadness." At least it is permissible to think so. And one does not thereby dismiss that poetry as of little worth, for the uncomfortable challenge of Hardy forces Pound in the end, after an exceptionally abject apology for obscurity, into formulating what would be the great and peculiar virtue of the Pisan and Rock-Drill cantos, as it had been of earlier work:

> I mean or imply that certain truth exists. Certain colours exist in nature though great painters have striven vainly, and though the colour film is not yet perfected. Truth is not untrue'd by reason of our failing to fix it on paper.

From "A Song of the Degrees" in *Lustra* ("certain colours exist in nature") through to "Le Paradis n'est pas artificiel" in the latest cantos, this is the burden of Pound's poetry at its most bracing and beautiful:

> Pull down thy vanity, it is not man
> Made courage, or made order, or made grace,
> Pull down thy vanity, I say pull down.
> (Canto 82)

"Le Paradis n'est pas artificiel," it is not man who made it.

"Paradise" is not altogether metaphorical, for *Guide to Kulchur* reveals, to many of Pound's readers if not for the first time to Pound himself, that he is a religious poet. On religion as on other matters Pound's observations veer disconcertingly between the superficial and the penetrating. On the one hand he spends many pages vindicating the Roman Catholic Church at its best against Protestantism, which latter, according to Pound, is a fundamentally usurious institution. These pages are most interesting when Pound argues, as in the Usura canto (45), that Protestant toleration of or complicity with usury infects not only its art but also its ethics and norms of conduct in the apparently unrelated field of sexual relations. But the discussion of religion becomes something better than sectarian in Chapter 17, where Pound deals (sympathetically on the whole) with Stoicism, in Chapter 39 under the head of "Neo-Platonicks Etc.," and in Chapter 53, where Pound contends that "our time has overshadowed the mysteries by an overemphasis on the individual" whereas "Eleusis did not distort truth by exaggerating the individual," that "only in the high air and the great clarity can there be a just estimation of values," that "the Gods exist," and that "a great treasure of verity exists for mankind in Ovid and in the subject matter of Ovid's long poem, and that only in this form could it be registered." States of mystical exaltation "exist in nature" (in human nature), as do, so Pound will believe, the metaphysical realities that are revealed to such states. It is notoriously difficult to embody these states and these realities in art, but this is no proof that they do not exist, for here too "truth is not untrue'd by reason of our failing to fix it on paper." And, in the event, Pound will rise time and again to the challenge of expressing these traditionally inexpressible experiences.

IX

The Fifth Decad of Cantos ·
The Chinese History Cantos · The Adams Cantos

It is not often observed that the art of sculpture, as tradition-ally conceived, comprises two very different kinds of activity. Yeats applauds Robert Gregory

> As he that practised or that understood
> All work in metal or in wood,
> In moulded plaster or in carven stone...

But the carving of stone and the molding of plaster (or of clay, so as later to make a bronze casting) are very different opera-tions, and profoundly different because the artist's way with his material represents in miniature his way of dealing with the whole material world.

Some have thought that molding and carving are not just

different but antithetical. Adrian Stokes observed, in *The Stones of Rimini:*

> Today, and not before, do we commence to emerge from the Stone Age: that is to say, for the first time on so vast a scale throughout Europe does hewn stone give way to plastic materials. An attitude to material, an attitude conceived . . . as being far more than the visual-aesthetic basis of Western civilization, can hardly survive long. The use in building of quarried stone must . . . increasingly diminish, and with it one nucleus of those dominant fantasies which have coloured the European perception of the visual world. In the work of men, manufacture, the process of fashioning or moulding, supersedes, wherever it is possible, the process of enhancing or carving material, the process that imitates those gradual natural forces that vivify or destroy nature before our eyes (p. 24).

And elsewhere Stokes elaborates:

> In the two activities there lies a vast difference that symbolizes not only the main aspects of labour, but even the respective roles of male and female (p. 110).

This last erotic analogy is several times pursued by Pound, nowhere more clearly and powerfully than in Canto 47:

> And the small stars now fall from the olive branch,
> Forked shadow falls dark on the terrace
> More black than the floating martin
>   that has no care for your presence,
> His wing-print is black on the roof tiles
> And the print is gone with his cry.
> So light is thy weight on Tellus
> Thy notch no deeper indented
> Thy weight less than the shadow
> Yet hast thou gnawed through the mountain,
>   Scilla's white teeth less sharp.
> Hast thou found a nest softer than cunnus
> Or hast thou found better rest

> Hast 'ou a deeper planting, doth thy death year
> Bring swifter shoot?
> Hast thou entered more deeply the mountain?

But, if the mountain is the female body ("By prong have I entered these hills"), it is also literally the mountain from which the sculptor quarries his marble block ("Yet hast thou gnawed through the mountain"), the quarrying being itself a sort of sculpture, a first stage in the carving. It is also ("Begin thy plowing... Think thus of thy plowing"—out of Hesiod in this same canto) the mountain that the farmer scores with his plough. And in *The Stones of Rimini* Adrian Stokes makes this analogy too: carving is not only like a man's way with a woman, it is also like a ploughman's way with the land. And let it not be thought that for Pound, any more than for Stokes, these analogies are fanciful; when Stokes speaks of "fantasy" he means something as far as possible from free association— he means that in man's profoundest awareness of what he is doing, these actions are not just alike but identical. It seems clear that we should range with them that way of dealing with words which regards them, as Pound says, as "consequences of things"; and with the other, the female role, the way of the modeler, that symbolist way with words which regards things, in the last analysis, as the consequences of the words that name them.

In Stokes's book on the Venetian use of color, the analogous distinction in painting is between hue and tone; hue is the "intrinsic" color, tone that color which is imparted to objects by the light as it strikes them this way or that, with this or that degree of intensity: and the distinctive achievement of Venetian painters, we are asked to think, lies in their attachment to hue as against tone. In Canto 52, an extremely beautiful redaction of the *Li Ki* or Chinese Book of Rites, Pound evokes in terms of ancient China a way of life that becomes ritual in its observance of the seasonable; and we learn, concerning one month in the year:

> The lake warden to gather rushes
> > to take grain for the *manes*
> to take grain for the beasts you will sacrifice
> to the Lords of the Mountains
> > To the Lords of great rivers
> Inspector of dye-works, inspector of colour and broideries
> see that the white, black, green be in order
> let no false colour exist here
> black, yellow, green be of quality

There is nothing arbitrary about introducing the inspector of dye-works. In an ideally good society his office, the keeping of colors true, is a crucial one. In the canto preceding this we have read:

> Usury rusts the man and his chisel
> It destroys the craftsman; destroying craft
> Azure is caught with cancer. Emerald comes to no Memling
> Usury kills the child in the womb
> And breaks short the young man's courting.

And this in turn has repeated Canto 45:

> Azure has a canker by usura; cramoisi is unbroidered
> Emerald findeth no Memling....

For that matter Pound years before, in "A Song of the Degrees" from *Lustra,* had already ranged himself with hue against tone:

I

> Rest me with Chinese colours,
> For I think the glass is evil.

II

> The wind moves above the wheat—
> With a silver crashing,
> A thin war of metal.
>
> I have known the golden disc,
> I have seen it melting above me.

I have known the stone-bright place,
     The hall of clear colours.

III

O glass subtly evil, O confusion of colours!
O light bound and bent in, O soul of the captive,
Why am I warned? Why am I sent away?
Why is your glitter full of curious mistrust?
O glass subtle and cunning, O powdery gold!
O filaments of amber, two-faced iridescence!

For Pound, color inheres in the colored object, it is of its
nature; just as the carved or hewn shape inheres in the stone
block before it has been touched; just as words inhere in the
natures they name, not in the minds that do the naming. Not
in painting any more than in poetry will Pound agree that
"it all depends how you look at it." Nature exists as other,
bodied against us, with real attributes and her own laws which
it is our duty to observe.

In Canto 46, "The bank makes it *ex nihil*," associated with the
name of William Paterson, chief founder of the Bank of England, reveals an imagination still in command of its material and
giving to the distinction between carving and molding, between stone and brick, a new slant that is totally unexpected
and yet persuasive. For, as the carver strikes the block with his
chisel, so the ploughman grooves the earth—in each case to
draw out of nature the wealth that lies concealed in it. On the
other hand, to mold a ball of clay in the hands is to draw no
wealth out of that material, but to impose the wealth of significance upon it by an act of will; and this is like giving to
paper money a value that is not inherent in the paper as paper.
If the only reliable symbol of true wealth is the grain which
the earth may be made to yield, a national currency can be a
true register of wealth only when the amount of money in
circulation corresponds to the wealth of the natural resources

known to exist in that nation's lands and in the known aptitudes of its citizens. To create money out of nothing, in excess of natural wealth, to buy and sell money, to set money chasing after money—this is the way of the molder and the brickmaker, not the way of stonemason and ploughman. And this is what Pound means by "usura."

The analogy holds, logically. Whether it can be seen at work chronologically—usurious practices in any economy reflected at once in decadence of artistic styles—this, which Pound seems to believe, is open to doubt. But at least it is not true, as is often believed, that Pound's conversion to the economics of Major C.H. Douglas and of Silvio Gesell represented a wholly new departure in his thought, which was accommodated in the *Cantos* only by distorting the emphases initially emergent and apparent; the economic doctrines arise, though unexpectedly all the more impressively, out of cardinal distinctions already made. And in Cantos 42 to 51 inclusive, which Pound called *The Fifth Decad of Cantos* (1937), the shaping hand is more than usually apparent. The measured and ominous condemnation of usury in Canto 45 has been much anthologized and much admired; but the case there stated has been argued through the three preceding cantos, which forbiddingly accumulate the necessary documentation. Our admiration and sympathy for Canto 45 is worthless because it is unscientific unless we see how the conclusions to be drawn arise unavoidably from the case in point there documented from Tuscan history—the case of the reforms instituted by Leopold, Grand Duke of Tuscany from 1765 to 1790. Righteous indignation is worse than worthless, it is a vicious self-indulgence, unless it is indeed "righteous," unless we have earned the right to it. And so after Canto 45 the reader is forced back into the circles of Pound's hell, the snapping and snarling contradictory voices of recorded history, before in Canto 51 he has once again earned the right to join in with measured condemnation. The second immersion, as it happens, is less painful than the first, for the accidental reason that on

159

the second time round the evidence is accumulated also from virtually unrecorded history, from the prehistory of the Mediterranean basin (Canto 47) and of ancient China (Canto 49). The evidence that reaches us, accordingly, is in the singing voice of the poet rather than the dry or snappish voice of the chronicler and diplomat.

Cantos 53 to 61 inclusive, which Pound was working at in the late 1930's, comprise the so-called Chinese History cantos, in which the most fervent of Pound's apologists have found little good. Pound's principal source for these cantos is the *Histoire générale de la Chine, ou Annales de cet empire*, traduites... par ... Père Joseph-Anne-Marie de Moyriac de Mailla,[1] though Canto 56 draws also on two poems by Li Po, and elsewhere, for instance in Canto 59, there are quotations from the Latin of another Jesuit sinologist of the French Enlightenment, Père Lacharme.[2] In the seven lines quoted from Lacharme in Canto 59 (they contain a phrase, *libidinis expers*, to be quoted often in subsequent cantos), there are no less than three errors of transcription.[3] And this is not the only evidence of extraordinary heedlessness in these pages. To work through some of them with Mailla's *Histoire générale* at hand is to realize how thoroughly dependent Pound is on this source; but the poet's decisions about what to take from Mailla, and what to leave behind, seem wholly arbitrary. In Canto 53, for instance, out of the many details that Mailla gives about the prehistoric ruler Hoang Ti, Pound chooses to emphasize that Hoang Ti learned and taught brick-making—and we prick up our ears. For, in line with Adrian Stokes's distinction, whereas building with stone is a case of "carving," building with brick is a case of

[1] In 12 volumes (Paris, 1777-83).
[2] *Confucii Chi-King sive Liber Carminum*, ex latine P. Lacharme interpretationis edidit Julius Mohl, Stuttgartiae & Tubingae Sumptibus J.C. Cottae, 1930.
[3] See Achilles Fang, in *Harvard Journal of Asiatic Studies*, 20 (1957), 213-38.

the other, plastic principle, molding or modeling; and so, in Pound's scheme of things as it has developed to this point, the invention of brick should appear an acquisition of dubious value. Sure enough, in a later canto, Canto 76, when Pound writes of "bricks thought into being ex nihil," the reference is disapproving. There appears to be no disapproval of Hoang Ti, however. This might not matter if the Chinese History cantos were offered as simple narrative chronicle, in which no judgments are passed. But in fact the non-Confucian (Buddhist and Taoist) influences on Chinese history are consistently condemned in strident language ("taozers," "shave-heads") that recalls fisticuffs in the schoolyard and brutal and contemptible rabble-rousing. There is no alternative to writing off this whole section of Pound's poem as pathological and sterile.

The John Adams cantos, Cantos 62 to 71, are composed in the same way as the Chinese History cantos that precede them. In favor of the later sequence it can be said that there is more point, for most readers, in being made to read the works of John Adams, second President of the United States,[4] than in consulting the *Histoire générale de la Chine*. And, indeed, Pound's pedagogical purpose is constant: undoubtedly part of his intention in writing these cantos was to find readers for an author who, on literary no less than historical grounds, deserves to be read closely and often—and not just by Americans. But even if such a pedagogical intention is legitimate in poetry (as no doubt it is), it can hardly be by itself a *sufficient* reason for poetry, least of all for ten whole cantos, even in a poem on such a massive scale as this one.

Does Pound, then, do nothing by way of modifying or re-creating the material that he borrows? Very occasionally he does something. For instance, in Canto 64:

[4] *The Works of John Adams*, ed. Charles Francis Adams, 10 vols. (Boston, 1850-57).

Cumis ego occulis meis
sleeping under a window: pray for me,
withered to skin and nerves *tu theleis* respondebat illa
apothanein; pray for me gentlemen
my prayers used to be answered, She prayed for deliverance
110 years of age, and some say she is over that

The tags of Greek and Latin which here juxtapose the Cumaean sybil with an old woman in New England certainly modify an anecdote from Adams's diary. But it would be wrong to say that Pound universalizes the anecdote, for the universality is in the humanity that Pound's mythopoeic treatment tends to diminish. John Adams's unaffected prose is more aghast and more compassionate, and this makes it more universal:

> Stopped at James Sullivan's, at Biddeford, and drank punch; dined at Allen's, a tavern at the bridge. After dinner, Farnham, Winthrop, Sewall, Sullivan, and I, walked a quarter of a mile down the river to see one Poke, a woman at least one hundred and ten years of age, some say one hundred and fifteen. When we came to the house, nobody was at home but the old woman, and she lay in bed asleep under the window, We looked in at the window and saw an object of horror;—strong muscles withered and wrinkled to a degree that I never saw before. After some time her daughter came from a neighbor's house, and we went in. The old woman roused herself, and looked round very composedly upon us, without saying a word. The daughter told her, "here is a number of gentlemen come to see you." "Gentlemen," says the old antediluvian, "I am glad to see them; I want them to pray for me; my prayers, I fear, are not answered; I used to think my prayers were answered, but of late I think they are not; I have been praying so long for deliverance;—Oh, living God, come in mercy! Lord Jesus, come in mercy! Sweet Christ, come in mercy! I used to have comfort in God, and set a good example; but I fear, etc."
> Her mouth was full of large, ragged teeth, and her daugh-

ter says, since she was one hundred years old, she had two new double teeth come out. Her hair is white as snow, but there is a large quantity of it on her head; her arms are nothing but bones covered over with a withered, wrinkled skin and nerves; in short, any person will be convinced, from the sight of her, that she is as old as they say, at least. She told us she was born in Ireland, within a mile of Derry; came here in the reign of King William. She remembers the reign of King Charles II, James II, William and Mary; she remembers King James's wars, etc. but has got quite lost about her age. Her daughter asked her how old she was? She said, "upwards of threescore, but she could not tell." (*Works,* II, 244-5.)

The most one can say for Pound's redaction is that it is, in its different way, equal to the original; and perhaps one cannot say even so much. Certainly for the most part one cannot; Pound's cuts and compressions and juxtapositions make a non-sensical hurly-burly of Adams's life, a life that was harried indeed but admirably purposeful. Adams's politicking was not senseless and desperate, like Sigismundo Malatesta's. And indeed Pound knows this. Yet his method, ruinously wasteful and repeatedly arbitrary, blurs all distinctions. An example is some lines from Canto 71 (they begin, "I am a church-going animal"), which juxtapose snippets from an admirable letter written by Adams at the end of his life to Benjamin Rush (*Works,* IX, 635-40); the lines are pointless unless one realizes that Adams, refusing to comply with Rush's suggestion that he compose a posthumous testament to the nation, is giving examples of how malice would misconstrue any recommendations he might make. Thus Pound's redaction fails even in its intention of sending the reader to Adams's works; for Adams is far more lively, interesting, and consistent than the Adams cantos suggest. Above all Adams is more humane. Irascible and impulsive as he was, his judgments on his opponents, such as Hutchinson or Dickinson (Pound misspells the name), show up Pound's shrill interjections ("Hutchinson undoubtedly scrofulous"—Canto 64) for the infinitely dangerous simplifications of a political naïf, to whom politics appears in the black and white of abstractions. The poetic method presses to its limit the notion that all truth is in particulars; the mind behind the method is thinking in the abstract.

Cantos 52 to 71 were published early in 1940, and William Vasse, who has usefully tabulated all their numerous misspellings and apparent errors of transcription, says indulgently, "Many are of the kind to suggest a typographical error, not caught in the proofreading, perhaps because of the rush and uncertainty of things at that time." [5] An essay that Pound published in 1937 [6] is far more illuminating than his poetry is, about how his enthusiasm for Adams and Jefferson fits in with his other enthusiasms. It does not fit very well. In the essay an extraordinary muddle supervenes as soon as Pound, having "placed" Adams and Jefferson as heirs of the Encyclopedists, finds that in his scheme of European or world culture the Encyclopedists do not rank high; certainly not so high as he wants to rank Jefferson and Adams:

> Can we not say that the mental integrity of the Encyclopedists dwindled into bare intellect by dropping that *ethical* simplicity which makes the canonists, *any* canonist, so much more 'modern', so much more scientific than any eighteenth century 'intellectual'?

"The Encyclopedists" is one thing; "any eighteenth century intellectual" is another. Is there no ethical simplicity in Doctor Johnson, for instance? The question is to the point, for, although John Adams could not be expected to sympathize with Johnson, the author of "Taxation No Tyranny," yet in

[5] "American History and the Cantos," *The Pound Newsletter*, 5 (Jan. 1955). Mr. Vasse is far more generous to the Adams cantos than I can be.
[6] "The Jefferson-Adams Correspondence," *North American Review*, 244 (Dec. 1937), 314-24.

general Adams appeals to British precedents and British authorities and to the model of the British Constitution; and his distrust of French authorities, like the Encyclopedists, was what distinguished him most sharply from Jefferson.[7] Yet Pound says, of Jefferson and Adams alike, "Their sanity and civilization, their varied culture and omnivorous curiosity stem from the encyclopedists. . . ." So far as Adams is concerned, this seems to be just not true.

For Pound the eighteenth century had always been a French century, almost exclusively. This appears to have come about through the influence of Gourmont, yet there was a deeper reason for it. For only in French was the century seen as the *siècle des lumiéres*, in terms of that metaphor from light that Pound had found likewise at the center of Confucian thought, and of the thought of Dante and Cavalcanti, Richard of Saint Victor and Scotus Erigena. This is why he compares the Encyclopedists with "the canonists" and decides that in the Encyclopedists the metaphor from light, though it persisted, was no longer taken in all seriousness:

> They are brilliant. Bayle is robust with the heritage of Rabelais and Brantome, Voltaire a bit finer, down almost to silver point. But the idea and/or habit of gradations of value, and the infinitely more vital custom of digging down into principles gradually fade out of the picture. The degrees of light and motion, the whole metaphoric richness begin to perish. From a musical concept of man they dwindle downward to a mathematical concept. . . .[8]

But if the Encyclopedists can thus be found wanting, what of Jefferson and Adams whom Pound has agreed to regard as the Encyclopedists' transplanted heirs? In 1937 he extricates himself by asserting boldly that these American Founding Fathers had all the Encyclopedists' virtues but not their vices, having

[7] See Z. Haraszti, *John Adams and the Prophets of Progress* (Cambridge, Mass., 1952).
[8] "The Jefferson-Adams Correspondence," *North American Review*, 244 (Dec. 1937), pp. 314-24.

on the contrary a substantiality in their thought that goes back (he dares to think) to Aquinas:

> Their sanity and civilization, their varied culture and omnivorous curiosity stem from the encyclopedists, but they are not accompanied by the thinning, the impoverishment of mental life, which lack of structural order was to produce in a few decades.

But in a curiously modified version of this essay, which was published in 1960,[9] the emphasis is subtly different:

> The sanity and civilization of Adams-Jefferson stems from the Encyclopedists. You find in their letters a varied culture, and an omnivorous (or apparently so) curiosity. And yet the thinning, the impoverishment of mental life shows in the decades after their death, and not, I think, without cause.

Wise after the event—after, that is, the Second World War, in which Pound rested on Adams and Jefferson his conviction that he acted as an American patriot in broadcasting from Rome—Pound is prepared to think that, from the Encyclopedists or elsewhere, the canker was already in the rose, even in 1776. "Omnivorous (or apparently so) ...," "and not, I think, without cause"—these are the saving clauses that make the point.

In any case there was from the first a contradiction in Pound's thought, that made his eighteenth-century enthusiasms, however true to his natural temperament, anomalous in his conscious thought. It was a contradiction inherited from Gourmont. For in Gourmont and Pound alike the eighteenth-century enthusiasms cannot be squared with their enthusiasm for Flaubert and behind him for Stendhal, for "realism" as understood by the nineteenth-century novelists, with its faith in the particular. Eighteenth-century theory (the theory much more

[9] *Impact: Essays on Ignorance and the Decline of American Civilization,* edited by Noel Stock (Chicago, 1960).

166

than the practice) was, on the contrary, whether in France or in Britain, contemptuous of particulars unless they could be marshalled and abstracted into generalized maxims. And when Pound considers an English poem of the eighteenth century, Johnson's "Vanity of Human Wishes," in some engaging and sensible pages of his *Guide to Kulchur*,[10] it is consistently enough Stendhal's strictures on eighteenth-century poetry that prevent Pound from accepting Eliot's claims for Johnson's poem. But in the essay on Adams and Jefferson, though there is a worried acknowledgment of nineteenth-century realism ("The whole gist of Flaubert was a fight against maxims, against abstractions..."), Pound cannot bring himself to press home the damaging implications of this for the case he is arguing. Indeed, how could he? For Confucius too delivers himself of maxims, though in his translations, particularly of the Analects, Pound was to go to all lengths to obscure the fact.

[10] Pp. 179-81, 183-4, 193.

X

The Pisan Cantos

In an interesting passage from *Modern Painters* (vol. IV, ch. xx) Ruskin speaks of "the kind of admiration with which a southern artist regarded the *stone* he worked in; and the pride which populace or priest took in the possession of precious mountain substance, worked into the pavements of their cathedrals, and the shafts of their tombs." Thus to regard the worked stone as "mountain substance," and to assert that the Italians thus regarded it, is to move at once into the area of interest of Adrian Stokes and of Canto 17. And it is significant that to illustrate his point Ruskin quotes aptly from "The Bishop Orders His Tomb in St. Praxed's Church" by the poet, Browning, whom Pound has never ceased to honor as one of his first masters—"pourquoi nier son père?" Taking into account some of Pound's even less fashionable allegiances, for example, to Ford Madox Ford and to Whistler, it would not be hard to trace for him a direct line of descent from Ruskin.

But this is hardly worth doing where the affinities are in any case so many and so clear. G.S. Fraser, for instance, considering Pound's position as a thinker about society, very justly sees it as Ruskinian:

> "By their fruits ye shall know them." There must be something right about the society that produces Chartres and something wrong that produces, say London south of the river. Men like Adams and Jefferson respect the arts, but they are not in Mauberley's sense "aesthetes," and indeed throughout *The Cantos* Pound seems to be moving away from Mauberley's still faintly ninetyish attitude towards one more like Ruskin's in *Unto this Last;* it must be good men, in a good society, who build a good cathedral.[1]

Rather plainly Fraser feels that the relationship between healthy art and healthy society is somehow more complicated than this. And one may agree with him, while still applauding both Pound and Ruskin for asserting that *some* connection there must be, and a close one, too. This is the less satisfactory side of Ruskin, just as, in the long run, it is the frightening and repellent side of Pound. Both men, who are very wise about trees and swans, mountains and skies and clouds, wasps and ants ("And now the ants seem to stagger/as the dawn sun has trapped their shadows"—Canto 83), and about buildings and paintings and bas-reliefs, become rather dangerously unwise—in particular, unwisely too sure of themselves—when they move, as they are right to do, to regarding the conduct of men in societies. This tragic discontinuity runs, perhaps, through the whole Ruskinian tradition; Gerard Manley Hopkins, for instance, who belongs in this tradition, is much less wise about bugler-boys than he is about highland burns and windhovers.

But in the much more persuasive matter of how they regard the world of natural beings and the world of human artifacts,

[1] G.S. Fraser, *Vision and Rhetoric* (London, 1959), pp. 90-91.

Ruskin and Pound represent, each in his own period, a traditional wisdom much older than nineteenth-century romanticism. Mr. Fraser goes on:

> The odd thing is that in religion Pound is a kind of eighteenth-century deist (one of his literary heroes, and an oddly assorted set they are, is Voltaire), and there must be a sense in which the cathedral, and the whole outer fabric of mediaeval life that he loves so passionately, is nothing for him but an adorable mockery or a beautiful empty shell. Critics have noted, and very rightly, the new and very moving note of religious humility in the "Pull down thy vanity" passage in the *Pisan Cantos;* but none of them have noted that the divinity not exactly invoked but hinted at there—the deity that sheathes a blade of grass more elegantly than a Parisian dressmaker sheathes a beautiful woman—is just the divinity of the Deists: Nature, or Nature's God, it hardly matters which one calls it, for it is just enough of a God to keep Nature running smoothly....
> (*Vision and Rhetoric*, p. 91)

It was Yeats who in the 1920's struck off, in a brilliant phrase already quoted, this sympathy for the eighteenth century which is constant with Pound:

> Ezra Pound arrived the other day,... and being warned by his wife tried to be very peaceable but couldn't help being very litigious about Confucius who I consider should have worn an Eighteenth Century wig and preached in St. Paul's, and he thinks the perfect man.[2]

Chinese thought, pre-eminently Confucian thought, was introduced to the West by representatives of the European Enlightenment, and Pound is devoted to it as were those earliest translators; partly what Pound does with it is to read back into ancient Chinese an Enlightenment scheme of things. Similarly Jefferson, together with the whole American culture that

[2] *The Letters of W.B. Yeats*, ed. Allan Wade (New York, 1955), p. 774.

he and other Founding Fathers stand for in the *Cantos*, is for Pound an Enlightenment product; Jefferson's personality and way of life exemplify the ideals of a Goldsmith or a Montesquieu. What is more, Pound's whole philosophy of history is in the strictest sense "Augustan"; that is to say, like Pope and Swift (but not Addison) he sees the course of human history in terms of prolonged "dark ages" interrupted by tragically brief luminous islands of achieved civilization, for which the Rome of Augustus stands as the type. (Pound's very marked preference for the Roman as against the Greek culture is another aspect of his Augustanism). Like Pope at the end of the *Dunciad*, Pound has written and acted as if the precarious islands of achieved civility were maintained only by unremitting vigilance on the part of a tiny minority, typically a group of friends, who must continually (and in the end, always vainly) stop up the holes in the dikes against which the sea of human stupidity, anarchy, and barbarism washes incessantly. In fact, if Pound's loyalty to the Enlightenment is taken seriously, most (though not all) of his other interests and commitments fall into a rationally coherent, massive, and impressive pattern; and his "literary heroes" will appear to be much less of "an oddly assorted set."

His mediaevalism, and also that element in him that may be called "Ruskinian," look rather different if related to a prime controlling sympathy with the Enlightenment. Fraser, for instance, is very just and perceptive about the passage he refers to from Canto 81:

> The ant's a centaur in his dragon world.
> Pull down thy vanity, it is not man
> Made courage, or made order, or made grace,
>   Pull down thy vanity, I say pull down.
> Learn of the green world what can be thy place
> In scaled invention or true artistry,
> Pull down thy vanity,
>   Paquin pull down!
> The green casque has outdone your elegance.

The feeling and import of this is indeed, as Fraser suggests, very close to Pope's:

> Far as Creation's ample range extends,
> The scale of sensual, mental pow'rs ascends:
> Mark how it mounts, to Man's imperial race,
> From the green myriads in the peopled grass:
> What modes of sight betwixt each wide extreme,
> The mole's dim curtain, and the lynx's beam:
> Of smell, the headlong lioness between,
> And hound sagacious on the tainted green:
> Of hearing, from the life that fills the flood,
> To that which warbles thro' the vernal wood:
> The spider's touch, how exquisitely fine!
> Feels at each thread, and lives along the line: ...

"The ant's a centaur in his dragon world" is as near as Pound chooses to come to what interests Pope centrally, the idea of a ladder and of the Great Chain of Being with never a link missing. Faithful to his manifesto in *Gaudier-Brzeska*, and along with Hopkins and Ruskin, Pound's attention has shifted somewhat from this grand design to the tight "designs" achieved on a smaller scale, which the natural world throws up momentarily and incessantly. All the same, Nature is still seen primarily as a designer, and for just this reason is wittily described as a "couturier" in Canto 80:

> as the young lizard extends his leopard spots
>   along the grass-blade seeking the green midge half an ant-size
>
> and the Serpentine will look just the same
> and the gulls be as neat on the pond
> and the sunken garden unchanged
> and God knows what else is left of our London
>   my London, your London
> and if her green elegance
>   remains on this side of my rain ditch
>   puss lizard will lunch on some other T-bone
>
> sunset grand couturier.

It is easy in fact to be so aware of the difference between Pope on the one hand, Ruskin and Hopkins on the other, as to miss the essential identity of their concerns. This is true at least of the Pope of the *Essay on Man*. It was the *Essay on Man* that prompted Ruskin to write of "the serene and just benevolence which placed Pope, in his theology, two centuries in advance of his time."[3] And it was Ruskin who memorably clinched and explained the difference between his interest in nature, and Pope's: "exactly in proportion as the idea of definite spiritual presence in material nature was lost, the mysterious sense of unaccountable life in the things themselves would be increased."[4] As the conviction of an abiding Presence is lost, so the observer expects all the more urgently "presences." Pound manifests this loss of faith, as do Hopkins and Ruskin and, for that matter, Wordsworth. Nevertheless, the essential similarity with Pope remains, between "the green midge half an ant-size" and "the green myriads in the peopled grass." These perceptions are possible only in an attitude of humility about the place of the human in relation to the non-human creation. And it was the shock of Pound's appalling predicament in the American prison-camp in 1945, awaiting trial for treason, that restored to him this humility, after the steady crescendo of raucous arrogance through the Chinese History and American History cantos of the years before.

It may be said that W.B. Yeats shares with the symbolist poets, and with a poet squarely in their tradition, such as T.S. Eliot, an imperious, appropriating attitude toward the perceived world. When swans get into Yeats's verse, the swan loses all its swanliness except what it needs to symbolize something in the person who observes it: "Another emblem there!"

[3] John Ruskin, *Lectures on Art* (Oxford, 1870), para. 70.
[4] Quoted by Maynard Mack, Introduction to *An Essay on Man* (Twickenham Edition of the Poems of Pope, Vol. III-i), p. lxxv—where the context is immediately apposite and illuminating.

And the poet at the end of "Coole Park and Ballylee" says explicitly that this is also what has happened to Lady Gregory. Similarly, Frank Kermode has demonstrated how far "In Memory of Major Robert Gregory" is concerned with Major Gregory, much less for what he is or was in himself than for what the poet chooses to make him stand for in his (the poet's) private pantheon. It is for this reason, to give an example, that Gregory's activities as a landscape painter are made so salient—so that Yeats may applaud this imperious attitude to the natural world at just the point where it would seem least likely, in landscape painting:

> We dreamed that a great painter had been born
> To cold Clare rock and Galway rock and thorn,
> To that stern colour and that delicate line
> That are our secret discipline
> Wherein the gazing heart doubles her might.

We attend to natural landscape, not for the sake of delighting in it, nor for what it may tell us of supernatural purpose or design, but so that the imperious personality, seeing itself there reflected, may become the more conscious of its own power—"the gazing heart doubles her might." As Marion Witt was first to show, Yeats intends here to relate Gregory's practice as a landscape painter with that of Samuel Palmer and Edward Calvert, the nineteenth-century artists who, true to the Blakean tradition, which was Yeats's tradition also, reject the discipline that is the scientist's as much as the artist's, exact and intent observation, setting up instead the discipline of the visionary, who sees through the perceivable to what lies beyond.

This is a matter not of mutually exclusive categories but only of where the emphasis characteristically falls. For examples of vivid and exact observation can, of course, be found in Yeats the visionary; and conversely Ezra Pound, who characteristically sees scientific observation as not at all at odds with the poet's kind of attention, also shows himself sympathetic to the Platonist John Heydon ("Secretary of Nature, J. Heydon," in

Canto 91) who attends to natural appearances only so as to read them as "signatures" of the realm of essence. The point is best made, therefore, by quotation from Canto 83:

> and Brother Wasp is building a very neat house
> of four rooms, one shaped like a squat indian bottle
> La vespa, *la* vespa, mud, swallow system
> So that dreaming of Bracelonde and of Perugia
> and the great fountain in the Piazza
> or of old Bulagaio's cat that with a well timed leap
> could turn the lever-shaped door handle
> It comes over me that Mr. Walls must be a ten-strike
> with the signorinas
> and in the warmth after chill sunrise
> an infant, green as new grass,
> has stuck its head or tip
> out of Madame La Vespa's bottle
>
> mint springs up again
> in spite of Jones' rodents
> as had the clover by the gorilla cage
> with a four-leaf
>
> When the mind swings by a grass-blade
> an ant's forefoot shall save you
> the clover leaf smells and tastes as its flower
>
> The infant has descended
> from mud on the tent roof to Tellus,
> like to like colour he goes amid grass-blades
> greeting them that dwell under XTHONOS $X\Theta ONO\Sigma$
> OI $X\Theta ONIOI$;   to carry our news
> $\varepsilon i\varsigma\ \chi\theta o\nu\iota o\nu\varsigma$ to them that dwell under the earth,
> begotten of air, that shall sing in the bower
> of Kore, $\Pi\varepsilon\varrho\sigma\varepsilon\varphi\delta\nu\varepsilon\iota\alpha$
> and have speech with Tiresias, Thebae

If we say that neither Yeats nor Eliot could have written this passage, we should have in mind, not in the first place any question of poetic method or strategy, but the quality of the sensibility, the sort of attitude and attention to the natural world, that is here displayed. It is not helpful to recall Words-worth and "a heart/That watches and receives," for this sort of contemplation is as much an active participation of the mind as are the more imperious operations of a Yeats.[5] One is re-minded rather of passages in Coleridge's and Ruskin's note-books, in some of the letters of Keats, in the essays and poems of D.H. Lawrence, above all in the writings of Hopkins. In fact, what lies behind a passage such as this (and they occur throughout the *Cantos*, though seldom at such length) is an attitude of mind that is incompatible with the symbolist poet's liberation of himself from the laws of time and space as those operate in the observable world. In order to achieve that liber-ation the poet had to forego any hope or conviction that the world outside himself was meaningful precisely insofar as it existed in its own right, something other than himself and bodied against him. There is all the difference in the world between identifying a swan with one's self, and identifying one's self with a swan. It may be the difference between Shelley's "Ode to a Skylark" (where the lark is important be-cause it is identified with Shelley) and a famous letter by Keats in which he identifies himself with a sparrow (where the sparrow is important because Keats can identify himself with it, and so explore an order of being other than his own.) Pound identifies himself with the baby wasp as Keats with the sparrow. The wasp burrows into the earth to greet the chthonic powers of under-earth, just as Odysseus, in the *Odys-sey* and time and again in the *Cantos*, must descend to the un-derworld to consult the Theban sage Tiresias. But at no point in the passage—not even if we remember how important for Pound, as for Lawrence, is such encountering of the chthonic powers of the loins and the libido—at no point does the wasp become a symbol for something in Pound's predicament, or

[5] Such reliance on the special Wordsworthian case tends to blunt the point of an otherwise admirably penetrating essay by Peter Ure, "Yeats's 'Demon and Beast,'" in *Irish Writing* (Dublin, 1955), which makes very much the point about Yeats that I have sought to make.

for his ethical or other programs, or for his personality. The wasp retains its otherness as an independent form of life; it is only by doing so that it can be a source of comfort to the human observer:

> When the mind swings by a grass-blade
> an ant's forefoot shall save you

For, only if the ant is outside the human mind, can it, as we say, "take us out of ourselves" when we observe it and try to enter into its life. This quality of tenderness, and this capacity for sympathetic identification with inhuman forms of life, make up an attitude of reverent vigilance before the natural world, an attitude which, if it is no longer the attitude of the physicist, is still surely the habit of the biologist, in the field and the laboratory alike.

These are not the terms in which Pound is usually considered, partly because these are not the terms in which he talks of himself; nor is this lineage—Coleridge, Keats, Ruskin, Hopkins—the sort of family tree that Pound draws up for himself. Moreover, it is taken for granted that, if Pound has any claim on our attention at all, it is for what he has in common with Yeats and Eliot, not for that in him which distinguishes him from his old allies, whose names are so much more respectable. Yet it should be clear that if this sort of attention is not to be found in Yeats, it is unthinkable in Eliot, as in any man whose main interest in the external world is as a repertoire of objective correlatives for his own states of mind. "Old Possum's Book of Favourite Cats," for instance, is Eliot's one venture into light verse; and the assumption behind it, that cats cannot be taken seriously in poetry, seems arbitrary when set beside the seriousness on just this subject of Christopher Smart, for instance, or Baudelaire. Pound's cat, "Old Bulagaio's cat that with a well-timed leap/could turn the lever-shaped door handle" ("lever-shaped"—the exact observation anticipating the natural question, "how?") is more alive, more of a cat, than any of Eliot's.

Almost from the first, sure enough, Pound has defined his poetry as radically opposed to symbolist poetry. He confesses to having learned from Laforgue and from Corbière, still more from Rimbaud; but these poets he obviously does not regard as "symbolist." He claims to have learned much more from the non-symbolist Théophile Gautier than even from Rimbaud —a claim that J.J. Espey, in his book on *Hugh Selwyn Mauberley*, shows to be well founded. Pound puts it on record "que les poètes *essentiels* [as texts for English poets to study] se réduisent à Gautier, Corbière, Laforgue, Rimbaud. Que depuis Rimbaud, aucun poète en France n'a inventé rien de fondamental." [6] In 1918 he writes that "Mallarmé, perhaps unread, is apt to be sightly overestimated . . ." [7] and that "Imagisme is not symbolism. The symbolists dealt in 'association,' that is, in a sort of allusion, almost of allegory. They degraded the symbol to the status of a word. . . ." "Moreover," he says, writing in the period of the First World War, "one does not want to be called a symbolist, because symbolism has usually been associated with mushy technique." (*Gaudier-Brzeska*, p. 97.)

Yeats and Pound were close and constant friends, and some of Pound's remarks on symbolism are beside the point because, like many people since, he takes Yeats as a typical symbolist; and this is far from the truth. In the Pisan Canto 83 there are two passages on Yeats. One of them, which follows almost immediately the page of sympathetic identification with the baby wasp, is Pound's hilarious account of the life at Stone Cottage, Coleman's Hatch, Sussex, where Yeats and Pound lived together at several periods between 1913 and 1916:

> There is fatigue deep as the grave.
> The Kakemono grows in flat land out of mist
>   sun rises lop-sided over the mountain
>   so that I recalled the noise in the chimney
>   as it were the wind in the chimney

[6] *Letters*, p. 293 (letter to René Taupin, 1928).
[7] "French Poets," *The Little Review* (Feb. 1918); reprinted in *Make It New* (1934), p. 161.

                    but was in reality Uncle William
downstairs composing
that had made a great Peeeeacock
        in the proide ov his oiye
            had made a great peeeeeeecock in the . . .
made a great peacock
                in the proide of his oyyee

proide ov his oy-ee
as indeed he had, and perdurable

a great peacock aere perennius
        or as in the advice to the young man to
breed and get married (or not)
            as you choose to regard it

at Stone Cottage in Sussex by the waste moor
(or whatever) and the holly bush
        who would not eat ham for dinner
because peasants eat ham for dinner
        despite the excellent quality
and the pleasure of having it hot

well those days are gone forever
        and the travelling rug with the coon-skin tabs
and his hearing nearly all Wordsworth
        for the sake of his conscience but
preferring Ennemosor on Witches

did we ever get to the end of Doughty:
        The Dawn in Britain?
                                perhaps not
    (Summons withdrawn, sir.)
    (bein' aliens in prohibited area)
    clouds lift their small mountains
        before the elder hills

The fineness of this is identical with the fineness of the passage
on the wasp. The whole man, Yeats, is carried before us; we
delight, as the poet has delighted, in his alien mode of being.
His foibles, recorded with affectionate and amused indulgence
—his way of *keening* rather than reading poetry, his "Gothick"

interests ("preferring Ennemosor on Witches"), his preposterous snobbery ("because peasants eat ham for dinner")—do not in the least detract from, they only substantiate, the perception of his greatness. Out of this personality, with all its quirky eccentricities, comes something in the splendid Horatian phrase "aere perennius," more lasting than bronze, equal in its achieved conclusiveness to the metal singing-bird of Yeats's own "Byzantium" and to those sonnets by Shakespeare ("the advice to the young man to/breed and get married"), where Shakespeare himself makes the proud Horatian claim,

> Not marble, nor the gilded monuments
> Of princes, shall outlive this powerful rhyme;

It should be plain that this is very far indeed, in human terms, from Yeats's treatment of the Gregories, the Pollexfens, John O'Leary, Lionel Johnson, John Synge. It manifests a respect for the uniqueness and otherness of the other person, a flexibility of feeling incompatible with the Yeatsian private pantheon and his deliberately noble style, even in such a splendid poem as "The Municipal Gallery Revisited."

The other passage on Yeats in Canto 83 is shorter, but more immediately apposite, for it considers Yeats specifically as a symbolist, and at this point not unfairly:

> Le Paradis n'est pas artificiel
> and Uncle William dawdling around Notre Dame
> in search of whatever
>   paused to admire the symbol
> with Notre Dame standing inside it
> Whereas in St Etienne
>   or why not Dei Miracoli:
> mermaids, that carving,
>
>   in the drenched tent there is quiet
>   sered eyes are at rest

"Le Paradis Artificiel" is the title of a book by Baudelaire about drugs and the beatific hallucinations they induce. Pound's rejection of the assumption behind it sounds as one of the strongest of many refrains that knit the later cantos together; it reappears, for instance, in an especially moving way in the Rock-Drill Canto 92. Pound's repeated assertion that the paradisal is *real*, out there in the real world, is a conscious challenge to the whole symbolist aesthetic. Hugh Kenner's gloss on this passage makes the essential point: "Yeats' incorrigibly symbologizing mind infected much of his verse with significance imposed on materials by an effort of will ('artificiel')...." [8] Yeats can see Notre Dame as an artifact, a presence created in masonry and sculpture, only inside the symbol, only for the sake of what it answers to in him, not for what it is in itself. He must always arrange the perspective, and project upon the object the significance he can then read out of it. For Pound, to whom, ever since his friendship with Gaudier-Brzeska, cut and worked stone has been an especially fruitful source of presences and inscapes, this attitude is intolerable. Only when he sees stone in and for itself, the artist's working of it only a drawing out of what was latent in the stone to begin with— only then, as in the sculptures of S. Maria dei Miracoli in Venice, can it save him as the ant's forefoot could save him. Only by contemplating it thus can the "sered eyes" (both "seared" and "fallen into the sere, the yellow leaf") come to be "at rest."

[8] Hugh Kenner, *The Poetry of Ezra Pound* (London, 1951), p. 210.

XI

Confucius

Among the papers of Fenollosa that his widow gave to Pound in 1913 was the text of a Confucian classic variously entitled, by English and French translators, "The Doctrine of the Mean," "Juste Milieu," "L'Invariable Milieu," "The Golden Medium."[1] By 1937, Pound was calling it "Standing Fast in the Middle." [2] But the title he found for it when he translated it, nearly forty years after it came into his hands, was "The Unwobbling Pivot." [3] This work is grouped by the Chinese along

[1] See, on how the text came to Pound from Fenollosa, Pound's Dedication to Amiya Chakravarty, in *Confucius: The Unwobbling Pivot & The Great Digest Translated by Ezra Pound* (Calcutta, 1949).
[2] *The Letters of Ezra Pound, 1907-1941*, ed. D.D. Paige (London, 1951), p. 384.
[3] *Confucius: The Unwobbling Pivot & the Great Digest* (Norfolk, Conn., 1947). A translation into Italian had appeared in Venice in 1945.

with the Analects, with the work known simply as "Mencius," and with another called *Ta Hio*, "The Great Learning": these are "The Four Books," which constitute an introductory course in Confucianism preparing the student for the more exacting study of other ancient scriptures called "The Five Classics." Pound has made formal translations of the Analects and of "The Great Learning" (which he calls "The Great Digest"), as well as "The Unwobbling Pivot." And his cantos contain extended translations, by Pound or adapted by him from others, out of Mencius and also out of the Five Classics.

Only one of these works at most, "The Great Learning," can be regarded as the literary composition of Confucius himself, and that one only partially. His part in the Five Classics seems to have been that of a compiler or editor for the most part. As for the Four Books, the Analects were compiled by Confucius's disciples, or by the disciples of those disciples, out of anecdotes by and about the Master and sayings handed down as having come from him; the "Mencius" records the sayings and doings of the most illustrious of Confucius's disciples, born in 372 B.C., more than a century after Confucius died; "The Great Learning" credits Confucius with only the seven paragraphs of the first chapter, the nine further chapters being commentary by a disciple; while "The Unwobbling Pivot" is presented as a treatise by Confucius's grandson.

The Analects is the only one of these works known even by name to the common reader in the West. But very often the Confucius of the Analects is the one of "Confucius him say," the enunciator of stupefying platitudes. And Pound's version, though he jazzed it up with slang and affected terseness, is not much more readable than any other.[4] *The Unwobbling Pivot* is a very different matter, as will be seen.

The first fruit of Pound's work on the Fenollosa manuscripts was *Cathay;* the second was his book of Noh plays; the third

[4] Pound's translation of the Analects appeared in *The Hudson Review*, III (1950). It was reprinted as *Confucian Analects* in New York in 1951, and in London in 1956.

his edition of Fenollosa's essay "On the Chinese Written Character as a Medium for Poetry." It seems to have been this last that brought Chinese literature, and Confucius, into the center of Pound's life. It was his urgency about getting this essay into print that led him to declare to John Quinn, at the beginning of 1917:

> China is fundamental, Japan is not. Japan is a special interest, like Provence, or 12th-13th Century Italy (apart from Dante). I don't mean to say there aren't interesting things in Fenollosa's Japanese stuff (or fine things, like the end of Kagekiyo, which is, I think, "Homeric"). But China is solid. One can't go back of the "Exile's Letter," or the "Song of the Bowmen," or the "North Gate." (*Letters*, p. 155.)

And within the month Pound is offering to write an essay on Confucius for Margaret Anderson's *Little Review* (Letters, p. 161).

Of course Pound thought better of what he had written to John Quinn. His readiness to dismiss his mediaeval interests goes along with fears he had expressed in 1916 that these interests had betrayed him into Browningesque styles and into excessive archaisms of language (*Letters*, pp. 138, 141). The work he was yet to do on Cavalcanti, with his essay on "Mediaevalism," shows that thirteenth-century Italy, even apart from Dante, was in no sense for him "a special interest." And yet the volume in which that work appeared professed by its very title, *Make It New*, his Confucian allegiance:
"In letters of gold on T'ang's bath-tub:

AS THE SUN MAKES IT NEW
DAY BY DAY MAKE IT NEW
YET AGAIN MAKE IT NEW" [5]

---

[5] Surprisingly, there is no evidence that Pound knew of an earlier occasion when this Confucian motto had got into American literature, in Thoreau's *Walden*.

The mediaevalist or Romance philologist had not changed into an Orientalist, a sinologue. And yet the two lines of interest were not just concurrent; they had come together, and pointed in one direction.

This does not appear, however, from the first of the sustained Confucian translations. It was from Rapallo in 1927 that he dispatched to a small press in America the manuscript of *Ta Hio. The Great Learning. Newly rendered into the American Language.*[6] There is nothing very "American" about this language:

> The ancient princes who wished to develop and make apparent, in their states, the luminous principle of reason which we receive from the sky, set themselves first to govern well their kingdoms; those who wished to govern their kingdoms well, began by keeping their own families in order; those who wished good order in their families, began by correcting themselves; those who wished to correct themselves tried first to attain rectitude of spirit; those who desired this rectitude of spirit, tried first to make their intentions pure and sincere; those who desired to render their intentions pure and sincere, attempted first to perfect their moral intelligence; the making as perfect as possible, that is the giving fullest scope to the moral intelligence (or the acquaintance with morals), consists in penetrating and getting to the bottom of the principles (motivations) of actions.

So far from being American, this language is quite precisely, in its structure and vocabulary, French. For it is a transliteration from the French of the nineteenth-century translator, Guillaume Pauthier.[7] And, though Pauthier doubtless is, as Pound declared, "a magnificent scholar" (*Letters*, p. 384) and capable

[6] Seattle, 1928; also London, 1936, and Norfolk, Conn., 1939.
[7] Cf. M.G. Pauthier, *Confucius et Mencius: Les Quatre Livres* (Paris, 1868), p. 42.

moreover of elegance in his French, he is being used to poor purpose when his "rendre leurs intentions pures et sincères" produces in Pound's English "render their intentions pure and sincere."

"American" figures in Pound's title for reasons that have little or nothing to do with his language. They are connected rather with what he wrote to a French correspondent in 1928:

> je viens de donner une nouvelle version du *Ta Hio* de Confucius, parce que j'y trouve des formulations d'idées qui me paraissent utiles pour civiliser l'Amérique.... Je révère plutôt le bon sens que l'originalité.... (*Letters*, p. 293.)

And it appears that Pound only at a late stage decided not to introduce his translation with an "acrid and querulous preface" attacking the American State Department and the administrations of President Wilson and President Harding (*Letters*, pp. 289-90). In fact, what we encounter here for the first time is the strain of thought and feeling that ultimately brought the poet to face a charge of treason, and then into a mental home. This is the sinister side of Pound's interest in Confucius, and it is worth seeing what there is in the Confucian texts that can lend itself to such perilous applications as Pound was to make. Another earlier translator whom Pound has consulted and honored (*Letters*, pp. 390-91), James Legge, remarked of the *Ta Hio*:

> the execution is not equal to the design; and, moreover, underneath all the reasoning...there lies the assumption that example is all but omnipotent. We find this principle pervading all the Confucian philosophy. And doubtless it is a truth, most important in education and government, that the influence of example is very great.... It will be well if the study of the Chinese Classics should call attention to it. Yet in them the subject is pushed to an extreme, and represented in an extravagant manner. Proceeding

from the view of human nature that it is entirely good, and led astray only by influences from without, the sage of China and his followers attribute to personal example and to instruction a power which we do not find that they actually possess.[8]

It would be laughable to find a necessary connection between Confucianism and Fascism. On the other hand, the point is not merely that the politics the Confucians envisage is necessarily authoritarian. As Legge implies, the characteristic emphasis on the exemplary function of the ruler obviously leads itself to the aggrandizing of "the leader." And indeed, as Legge says elsewhere, the conduct recommended in the treatise seems available, if not to no one but the Emperor himself, at least to the leader rather than to the common individual. For this reason, though for others also, one sympathizes with those Chinese who expressed to Legge "the difficulty they felt in making the book a practical directory for their conduct"; especially with one of them who complained, "It is so vague and vast" (Legge, p. 29).

Legge raises other objections that are not so obviously just and yet are not easy to deal with. Of the paragraph that has been quoted, for instance, he remarks:

> ... we feel that this explanation cannot be correct, or that, if it be correct, the teaching of the Chinese sage is far beyond and above the condition and capacity of men. How can we suppose that, in order to secure sincerity of thought and our self-cultivation, there is necessarily [sic] the study of all the phenomena of physics and metaphysics, and of the events of history? (Legge, p. 267.)

To see the point of this objection we need to re-read the paragraph, not in the muffled and flaccid language of Pound's first version, but from *Ta Hio. The Great Digest*, his second

[8] James Legge, *The Chinese Classics: Translated into English, with Preliminary Essays and Explanatory Notes*, Vol. I: *The Life and Teachings of Confucius* (London, 1867), p. 31.

translation which he published along with *The Unwobbling Pivot* in 1947:

> The men of old wanting to clarify and diffuse throughout the empire that light which comes from looking straight into the heart and then acting, first set up good government in their own states; wanting good government in their states, they first disciplined themselves; desiring self-discipline, they rectified their own hearts; and wanting to rectify their hearts, they sought precise verbal definitions of their inarticulate thoughts (the tones given off by the heart); wishing to attain precise verbal definitions, they set to extend their knowledge to the utmost. This completion of knowledge is rooted in sorting things into organic categories.

"Sorting things into organic categories" (like Legge's balder version, "the investigation of things") is very different from Pauthier's "getting to the bottom of the principles of actions"; and it asserts, just as Legge says it does, that an inescapable preliminary to any scheme of moral self-improvement is "the study of all the phenomena of physics and metaphysics, and of the events of history." But in Cavalcanti too, as Pound presents him to us, if the study of physics and metaphysics is not a *preliminary* to the moral improvement involved in loving truly, such study seems to be at any rate a necessary *implication* of so doing. The refusal to specialize, or to regard existing categories and fields of study as more than a working arrangement—this is not only what Pound asks us to admire in Cavalcanti, it has to be noted also as a constant and determining feature of Pound himself, as a man and as a writer. Legge's common-sensical objection to this, like the common-sensical objections to Pound's work in general and to the encyclopaedic cantos in particular, is irrefutable: the body of available knowledge has expanded so vastly since Confucius's day, or even since Cavalcanti's, that if a man wants exact and trustworthy knowledge in any field he must restrict himself to that field. However, no man does this: it is a professional rule, not a human possibility. Since the poet is not a professional among professionals, but a man who aspires to be more completely human than other men, it is he, the poet, who has a duty to break down or overleap boundaries. When Pope in *The Dunciad* mocks the natural historian of his day, such as the conchologist, common sense declares him wrong, since the event has shown that the pedestrian omnivorousness of the eighteenth-century virtuoso was necessary at that stage if scientific knowledge was to advance; but another faculty than common sense declares Pope right, since the conchologist whom he pictured had come by his specialized expertise only at excessive cost to his own humanity, by an inexcusably narrow sense of the scope of human possibilities:

> The most recluse, discreetly open'd, find
> Congenial matter in the cockle-kind.

The conchologist, as it happens, would not have been Pound's example of the narrow specialist, for he took over from Fenollosa an admiration for the scientific method as exemplified by the great naturalists such as Louis Agassiz.[9] But the same reasons that vindicate Pope against the objections of common sense, vindicate Pound also. And rather plainly the man who had consulted Grosseteste in order to understand a canzone of Cavalcanti would find attractive in Confucian thought precisely that overleaping of boundaries, that determination to regard human experience as all one, which Legge objects to as impractical. The issue is even clearer with *The Unwobbling Pivot*.

[9] See Norman Holmes Pearson, in *Shenandoah*, VII, 1 (Autumn 1955), 81-2: "Louis Agassiz becomes a landmark. It was he in his laboratory at Harvard who trained Edward S. Morse, the Salem natural scientist who taught at the Imperial University of Tokyo and became the influential collector and curator of Oriental art..., not forgetting to carry over the lessons of Agassiz into the new field. And it was Morse who in turn persuaded Ernest Fenollosa, also from Salem and fresh from Harvard, to go out as instructor in rhetoric to the Imperial University, where Fenollosa's interest like that of Morse expanded to include the stimulation of Oriental culture."

There is another observation by Legge which is more far-reaching still. This arises from the next paragraph (the fifth) of Chapter I of the *Ta Hio*. Legge's version of this runs as follows:

> Things being investigated, knowledge became complete. Their knowledge being complete, their thoughts were sincere. Their thoughts being sincere, their hearts were then rectified. Their hearts being rectified, their persons were cultivated. Their persons being cultivated, their families were regulated. Their families being regulated, their States were rightly governed. Their States being rightly governed, the whole empire was made tranquil and happy.

Legge observes that what Confucius offers here are the seven steps of a climax, "the end of which is the empire tranquillized." He goes on: "Pauthier calls the paragraphs where they occur instances of the sorites, or abridged syllogism. But they belong to *rhetoric*, and not to *logic* (pp. 29-30)." Fenollosa might have had this comment specifically in mind when he wrote indignantly, after analyzing the nature of the Chinese written character:

> In diction and in grammatical form science is utterly opposed to logic. Primitive men who created language agreed with science and not with logic. Logic has abused the language which they left to her mercy.
> Poetry agrees with science and not with logic.[10]

But it is better to be more temperate. What Fenollosa means, as his context makes clear, is that there have been, historically, more kinds of logic than one; and that, in consequence, logic and rhetoric have not always been so flatly opposed one to the other, nor so easy to distinguish one from the other, as Legge supposes. As Fenollosa implies, and elsewhere asserts,

[10] Fenollosa, *The Chinese Written Character as a Medium for Poetry* (*Square Dollar Series*, Washington, D.C., 1951). See the discussion in the present author's *Articulate Energy: An Enquiry into the Syntax of English Verse* (London, 1955), pp. 33-42 and Appendix.

the pioneers of the experimental method in the sciences found themselves committed to a struggle among the variously competing logics of Bacon, of Descartes, and of mediaeval Scholasticism, for instance. It may be held that the subjects of the *Ta Hio*, ethics and politics, can be reliably studied only empirically, through the accumulation of specific instances closely observed and scrupulously recorded, as Pope's conchologist observed and recorded shells; and in such a case the method would properly be described as neither "logical" nor "rhetorical," but "scientific." In fact, the Confucian writings, with their constant use of the illustrative anecdote and their reliance on accumulated instances from recorded history, do seem to use such a method. (Thus, whereas Pound's first translation of this fifth paragraph had agreed with Pauthier's in being cast in the present tense, his second agrees with Legge's in using the past; and this swings it into line with the Confucian reliance on recorded instances, and generalizations from these.)

What Fenollosa maintained was that not just Confucius, but all Chinese thinkers were necessarily committed to this method, since their written language compelled it. The Chinese written character, so he maintained, had escaped or resisted the antiscientific attentions of the logicians who had perverted the structures of Western languages. In consequence, not only was Chinese a highly, indeed essentially, metaphorical language (as English is also), but also it was a language (such as English is not) in which it was impossible for "live" metaphors to go "dead," a language which it was impossible to read or to write without being aware that metaphors were what you were using, what you were *thinking with*. Perhaps most readers still will think, with Legge, that a highly metaphorical discourse is likely to be rhetorical; Fenollosa argues on the contrary that its being highly metaphorical is what makes it scientific. His position, however unlikely it may seem, is a strong one; though this is not the place to examine it.[11]

[11] See the treatment in my *Articulate Energy*, loc. cit.

As for his contention that no Chinese can read Chinese characters without being aware of how they are built up out of pictorial metaphors, most authorities now appear to disagree with him. It is in any case something that can be neither proven nor disproven. Just as most speakers of English use the word "discourse" without being aware of the metaphor of running about concealed in its etymology, so one concedes that a slow-witted Chinese, or a sharp-witted Chinese in a state of fatigue, would not register the pictorial metaphors in the Chinese he was reading. The argument can then be pushed further only by unprofitably speculating on what is the statistically normal degree of slow-wittedness or exhaustion among Chinese.

Pound at any rate was convinced by Fenollosa (though not to much purpose when he first translated the *Ta Hio*) that previous translators of Chinese had erred in not bringing out the highly metaphorical, and therefore highly concrete, nature of the original. The first sentence of the fourth paragraph shows the very interesting issues that are involved. In 1928 Pound, following Pauthier, gave for this:

> The ancient princes who wished to develop and make apparent, in their states, the luminous principle of reason which we receive from the sky, set themselves first to govern well their kingdoms....

Twenty years later, wanting to bring to life the dead, or at least somnolent, metaphor in "luminous," he wrote:

> The men of old wanting to clarify and diffuse throughout the empire that light...

(The metaphorical force comes from "clarify and diffuse" replacing "develop and make apparent," more than it comes from "light" replacing "luminous principle.") But in 1867 Legge had written:

> The ancients who wished to illustrate illustrious virtue throughout the empire...

And there is the light shining just as brightly as ever for any reader who knows and remembers how both "illustrious" and "illustrate" incorporate "luster," and what "luster" means! This suggests that, however it may be in Chinese, in English a metaphor that is dead for one reader will be live for another. I suspect there are readers of English for whom "clarify" does not "make clear," or not at any rate in the sense in which a day is "clear"; and to such readers the metaphor in Pound's second version may be as "dead" as in his first. On the other hand there may be those whose visual imagination is so prompt and lively that out of "make apparent" in the version of 1928 they conjure up an image of an apparition glowing in light against darkness. If the second version is an improvement on the first, it is partly because nowadays, unfortunately, there are more readers of the first sort than of the second; in Legge's time things may have been different.

It is not by accident that these metaphors from the start of the *Ta Hio*, like the metaphors in Cavalcanti's "Donna mi prega" that Pound examines in discussing that poem, are metaphors drawn from the nature, the structure, and the behavior of light. Such metaphors are central to the Confucian experience as we encounter it in Pound's translations of the *Ta Hio* and "The Unwobbling Pivot," just as they seem central to the experience of Cavalcanti and Dante. In a sumptuous edition of the two Confucian translations,[12] Pound prefaces them by a table of what he calls "Terminology," presenting some seventeen Chinese characters that he considers crucial, with an English gloss on each; the gloss to the second runs:

> The sun and moon, the total light process, the radiation, reception and reflection of light; hence, the intelligence.

12 *Confucius: The Great Digest & Unwobbling Pivot*, translated by Ezra Pound, with Chinese "stone" text from rubbings supplied by William Hawley, and a note on the stone editions by Achilles Fang (Norfolk, Conn., 1951).

193

> Bright, brightness, shining. Refer to Scotus Erigena, Grosseteste and the notes on light in my *Cavalcanti*.

There can be no doubt that long before 1947, when the Confucian translations first appeared together, it was this common ground between the two areas which convinced Pound that by these two distinct avenues he was moving toward one body of insights.

The metaphors from light are even more insistent in "The Unwobbling Pivot" than in the *Ta Hio*, as is only to be expected from a work which, as Pound says, "contains what is usually supposed not to exist, namely the Confucian metaphysics." Accordingly, to Legge, a Christian missionary, "The Unwobbling Pivot" commends itself even less than the *Ta Hio* or "Great Learning." He finds in it

> the same combination which we found in the Great Learning,—a combination of the ordinary and the extraordinary, the plain and the vague, which is very perplexing to the mind, and renders the Book unfit for the purposes of mental and moral discipline (p. 45).

The writer, he says, "belongs to the intuitional school more than to the logical" (p. 43). And as early as the fifth paragraph he finds that

> From the path of duty, where we tread on solid ground, the writer suddenly raises us aloft on wings of air, and will carry us we know not where, and to we know not what (pp. 44-5).

Legge is a sturdy thinker and a distinguished writer, as this splendidly Johnsonian cadence shows, and as Pound has insisted. When he refers to "the path of duty," he is quoting his own translation of a term in the very first paragraph, a term that Pound translates as "the process." Pound here, it may be thought, is being not more concrete but more abstract than Legge (or than Pauthier, who gives "*règle de conduite morale ou droite voie*—Pauthier offers not so much translation as interpretation or concealed commentary). But a moment's thought reveals how inadequate "abstract" and "concrete" are as words to use in such a case; for on the one hand "path of duty," though a metaphor, is a dead one, an inert commonplace of countless homilies, while on the other hand "process," considered by way of its Latin etymology, releases precisely the same metaphor, thoroughly alive. The case is reversed when in the fourth paragraph Legge gives "state of equilibrium" where Pound writes "the axis." Legge writes sourly, "It is difficult to translate the paragraph, because it is difficult to understand it" (p. 283 n.). And we see what he means when in his translation he has to mix his metaphors:

> This EQUILIBRIUM is the great root *from which grow all the human actings* in the world, and this HARMONY is the universal path which they all pursue.

But Pound at this point has to mix his metaphors no less:

> That axis in the center is the great root of the universe; that harmony is the universe's outspread process (of existence).

Where metaphors are thus mixed in from mechanics ("axis"), from botany ("root"), from music ("harmony"), and from traveling ("process" or "path"), we may well feel, with Legge, that we are in "an obscurity where we can hardly grope our way" (p. 54). But if our speculations so far have had any point at all, not just as regards the nature of the Chinese language, but as regards the nature of English also, we should have realized that metaphors *have to be* mixed, and that the prejudice against mixing them is unfounded. For, if every word of the language is metaphorical (as it is, if we learn from Fenollosa to be alert to etymology), then the metaphors released by any passage of language will hang together only in nothing less than the totality of human experience. The implications of this for poetics are revolutionary.

For the moment, however, Legge's honest confession ("It is

difficult to translate the paragraph, because it is difficult to understand it") leads to something more commonplace, but more immediately useful: to the possibility that, where Pound's translation differs most strikingly from those of his predecessors, it is very often because he is at least making some sense where they make none. A good example is at the end of the very difficult Chapter XVI, where the Chinese talks of *Kweishin;* that is, according to Legge, "ghosts and spirits, spiritual beings." Pound here breaks into verse:

> Intangible and abstruse
> the bright silk of the sunlight
> Pours down in manifest splendor,
> You can neither stroke
> the precise word with your hand
> Nor shut it down under a box-lid.

Pauthier gives:

> Ces esprits cependant, quelque subtils et imperceptibles qu'ils soient, se manifestent dans les formes corporelles des êtres; leur essence êtant une essence réelle, vraie, elle ne peut pas se manifester sous une forme quelconque.

And Legge:

> Such is the manifestness of what is minute! Such is the impossibility of repressing the outgoings of sincerity!

Where authorities like Pauthier and Legge differ so comically, the outlandishness of Pound's version turns out to be at least not gratuitous; something outlandish was called for, in order to reconcile such variants. Even so, distinctions have to be made. When Pauthier says "elle ne peut pas se manifester sous une forme quelconque" he is after his fashion saying just what Pound says, with his talk of stroking with the hand and the shutting of a box-lid; the difference comes from Pound's determination to bring over the images he sees in the components of the Chinese characters before him. Pauthier at least makes sense, and in a way the same sense as Pound. Legge on the other hand makes nonsense, because nonsense is all that he finds; as he says contemptuously, "It is difficult—not to say impossible—to conceive to one's self what is meant by such descriptions." [13] In the context of the chapter as a whole Pound makes difficult sense where Legge makes none at all. And if Pound makes more difficult sense than Pauthier, the sense that he makes is not only more vivid; it is also more interesting. For he makes of the *Kwei-shin* not "spooks" but embodied energies such as sunlight, informing the Creation; and for this he has the authority of some Chinese commentators whom Legge rejects even as he cites them—notably of one who asserts, "The *Kwei-shin* are the energetic operations of Heaven and Earth, and the traces of production and transformation."

The reader who has no Chinese can in this way read Pound, along with Pauthier and Legge, so as to assure himself that he is not at the mercy of the translator's whims. There *are* places where Pound's version seems, on this showing, willfully eccentric—for instance, a reference to a chicken-coop in Chapter VIII; a string of epithets in Chapter XII, paragraph 1; and paragraph 14 of Chapter XX, where Pound suppresses, or transforms past recognition, something that Legge and Pauthier alike take for a recommendation about propriety in dress. But most of the time one finds with surprise that, quite apart from the greater raciness and physicality of Pound's prose, his versions reconcile the sense of Legge and of Pauthier, who differ from each other as to sense more than Pound differs from either. There are good examples of this in Chapter II and Chapter IV, in Chapter X, and also in Chapter XXIII. In the last, Pound and Legge take one view of a word, which they translate as "shoots" in something the sense of Henry Vaughan's "bright shoots of everlastingness." Pauthier takes another and

13 Legge, pp. 292-3. Pound may have found "abstruse" (meaning "remote from apprehension; recondite," but also "hidden, secret") in a rendering that Legge quotes and rejects.

opposite view. Moreover, Pauthier, who is always diffuse, extends the tail of the paragraph in what looks like an inexcusable Christian-pietistic gloss, making "change" (Pound) and "transform" (Legge) into "convert." On the other hand Pauthier is more aware of metaphorical life in the original than Legge appears to be: he gives "étant manifestés, alors ils jetteront un grand éclat" for Pound's "manifest, it will start to illuminate" and Legge's "From being manifest, it becomes brilliant." As this last example shows, this is another place where the cardinal metaphor from the behavior of light is so embedded in the original that it shows up (uncontrolledly) even in Legge.

The Unwobbling Pivot is worth this sort of effort, certainly in the context of Pound's development, but on its own account also. Legge's difficulties with it derive from what hindered him with the *Ta Hio* also: his adherence to a logic that proceeds by making sharp and final distinctions, dividing and subdividing. "The Unwobbling Pivot" moves contrary to this habit of mind, seeking to inculcate instead a readiness to see one principle operating in metaphysics and in physics, in politics and in ethics, changing its mode of operation but not its essential nature. It sees "sincerity," for instance, not as a specifically human quality but as the operation in a human mode of a principle that in other modes is an energy, as of sunlight, operating in the physical world. The word Legge sometimes translates as "sincerity," he renders elsewhere as "singleness," or "singleness of soul." And Pound takes off from the idea of singleness to translate it as "the unmixed." As such it makes its most memorable and momentous appearance at the very end of Pound's version:

> This unmixed is the tensile light, the
> Immaculata. There is no end
> to its action.

With these words Pound ends Chapter XXVI, an extremely eloquent passage which Pound presents as peroration to the whole since (as he gives notice) he does not proceed to the seven chapters remaining. The writer's excited re-creation of the plenitude of Creation ("This water is but a spoonful mid many; it goes forth and in its deep eddies that you can in no wise fathom there be terrapin and great turtles....") is something that recalls the Hebrew psalmist, and its eloquence informs even the translation of Legge, whose comment is "The confusion and error in such representations are very lamentable" (p. 311).

The word "tensile" we encountered earlier, when it gave us trouble in the translations of the Classic Anthology of the Odes. And since the Classic Anthology or *Shi King* (Book of Songs) is itself one of the Confucian scriptures, one of the Five Classics, it is proper to return to it at this point. Indeed, it is impossible not to do so, since passages from the Odes are quoted repeatedly in both the *Ta Hio* and "The Unwobbling Pivot." Confucius, we are told, insisted that the Odes be studied continually; and the *Shi King* holds its place among the Five Classics because it seemed to Confucius to constitute, no less than the chronicles of ancient history, a body of recorded instances that any generalization, if it were to be useful, must draw upon and allow for.

If we start with Part III of the Anthology, as we did in our earlier consideration of the Odes, we encounter at once, in the epigraph to Poem 235 and the first couplet of that poem, verses that are otherwise translated when quoted in Chapter II of the *Ta Hio*, in juxtaposition with "Make it new" as inscribed on T'ang's bathtub. The imagery of light running through this ode, especially as carried in words like "splendid" and "candour" which lose their abstractness in this metaphorically charged context, is far more meaningful when we return to it after a reading of *The Unwobbling Pivot*. The fourth strophe ("Wen, like a field of grain beneath the sun") is quoted in Chapter III of the *Ta Hio*, where Pound translates it more diffusely than in the *Classic Anthology* but at least as memorably, though to disconcertingly different effect.

As for "tensile," this cropped up initially in poem 238:

> Thick oak, scrub oak men pile
> for fagots; order in government
> hath power, to left and right, tensile
> to zest men's interest.

And the word at least has *some* meaning after reading *The Unwobbling Pivot* where at first it had none, since even if we knew its dictionary meaning this still seemed not to fit it into this context. What we should have learned from *The Unwobbling Pivot* is that contexts are not so immutably delimited as we tend to suppose; that in a political context, as here, a word like "tensile," a word out of physics, may still be in place, may be quite crucially in place, since it enforces the perception that the worlds of physics and of politics are not distinct but interpenetrating.

If we consult the Analects also, the relationships between Confucian poetry and Confucian prose become very intricate indeed, and present problems that are not always worth the solving. In Analects I, xv, for example, Tze-king asks Confucius what value he places on a poor man without servility, or a rich man without arrogance. Confucius replies that such characters are to be esteemed, but not so highly as "a fellow who is poor and cheerful, or rich and in love with precise observance." (This is Pound's version in which he agrees with Legge and with Soothill, but not with Pauthier, who alters the force of the whole anecdote.[14]) Tze-king asks if Confucius's distinction is not that made in the Odes, quoting Poem 55 from the Classic Anthology; Confucius agrees, and applauds Tze-king for making the application. The relevant portion of Poem 55 stands as follows, in Pound's translation, the *Classic Anthology:*

> Dry in the sun by corner of K'i
> green bamboo, bole after bole:

[14] Legge, op. cit.; W.E. Soothill, *The Analects* (London, 1910), also in *World's Classics* series, ed. by Lady Hosie (London, 1937); Pauthier, *Confucius et Mencius.*

> Such subtle prince is ours
> to grind and file his powers
> as jade is ground by wheel;
> he careth his people's weal,
> stern in attent,
> steady as sun's turn bent
> on his folk's betterment
>   nor will he fail.

This is in line with Legge's note about this poem:

> ... the first of the songs of Wei, praising the prince Woo,
> who had dealt with himself as an ivory-worker who first
> cuts the bone, and then files it smooth; or a lapidary whose
> hammer and chisel are followed by all the appliances for
> smoothing and polishing (p. 20).

Having followed the trail so far, we shall feel impatiently that
Tze-king hardly deserved Confucius's emphatic approval for
quoting to the point—it required no insight to do so; we shall
feel this the more sharply if we recall that in the *Ta Hio*
(III.4) the same passage is quoted, and given explicitly just the
gloss that Tze-king is applauded for. (Pound's more diffuse
translation in *The Great Digest* brings out the admirable con-
ciseness of his *Classic Anthology* rendering). We have to go
back to Pauthier's version of the Shi-King [15] to see that in the
poem itself there is no explicit simile such as is implied by
Legge's gloss, "had dealt with himself as...." The upshot is
that the point of Analects I.xv seems to be much less the drawing of distinctions between degrees of estimable behavior,
though the distinction is firm enough between negative virtue
and positive; rather it is an illustration of "how to read a
poem." But to take this point we need to realize how far from
explicit the Odes are, how they proceed suggestively, by allusion. And this is brought home to us by neither of Pound's
versions so much as by Pauthier's.

[15] *Chi-king ou Livre des vers traduit pour la première fois en français
par G. Pauthier* (Paris, 1872), p. 280.

XII

The Rock-Drill Cantos

I have said that one may read quite a long way into the *Cantos* in the spirit of "Lordly men are to earth o'er given" ("The Seafarer") or of "We seem to have lost the radiant world" (as in the essay on Cavalcanti). This is the point indeed at which Pound is most clearly a man of his generation; T.S. Eliot's extraordinarily influential notion of "the dissociation of sensibility" is only one version of the belief in a calamitous Fall, an expulsion from some historical Eden, that seems to have been an imaginative necessity as well for Yeats and Pound, for T.E. Hulme, and for Henry Adams before any of them.[1] For Pound as a young man the Fall came between Cavalcanti and Petrarch, and he seems to have persuaded Hulme to agree with him; for Yeats it came about 1550; for Eliot, some time

[1] See Frank Kermode, *Romantic Image* (London, 1957), ch. VIII.

between 1590 and 1650. Pound's position as he later developed it, however, was closer to Yeats's than to Eliot's, for he and Yeats embraced a cyclical view of historical change that permitted them to conceive of such calamities as having happened more than once, at corresponding stages in other cultural cycles than that of recorded history in Western Europe. Whereas Yeats interested himself in the cyclical theories of Spengler, Pound from about 1925 onwards pledged himself to Spengler's master, the neglected German thinker and explorer Leo Frobenius, who is accordingly drawn upon in later cantos.[2] Pound differs from all his old associates, characteristically, by choosing for his hero not a theorist but a scientist, whose conclusions are arrived at inductively from observations "in the field"; and, in fact, since Frobenius like Louis Agassiz can be regarded as the pupil of Friedrich Heinrich Alexander, Baron von Humboldt (1769-1859), he takes his place (along with Ernest Fenollosa) in the line of succession, as Pound sees it, of the heroes of modern science. This gives to Pound's historical nostalgia an altogether sturdier and more substantial, though also a more cluttered, appearance than the nostalgias of Eliot and of Yeats.

All the same, in the case of all these men, those of their writings that rely most heavily on this pseudo-history are already tiresome. In Eliot's case little damage is done, for he mostly reserved this kind of thinking for his essays, which, having served their vast polemical purpose, are already "dated" and outdated, as the poems are not. And in Yeats's work there are only a few poems, like "The Statues," that seem irretrievably damaged. Unfortunately, whole tracts of the Cantos are laid waste in this way, because they rest, if they are to be persuasive, on an encyclopaedic knowledge of recorded history such as we know that Pound neither possesses nor could possess. The failure of the American History and Chinese History cantos can be explained in other ways; but they would have been barren in the long run, even if they had been writ-

[2] See Guy Davenport, "Pound and Frobenius," in Motive and Method in the Cantos of Ezra Pound (New York, 1954).

ten according to a less perverse poetic method, and by a man more in control of himself than Pound was in the 1930's. For, although they derive in one way from a genuinely scientific humility, and seek to inculcate such humility in the reader, the whole plan of them is absurdly, even insanely, presumptuous; there is simply too much recorded history available for any one to offer to speak of it with such confidence as Pound does.

It is the arrogance that is damaging, not the nostalgia, for time and again in the *Cantos* the nostalgia for a vanished Europe is controlled and personal enough to rise to the level of elegy, as it did in "Provincia Deserta," and as it does in a recent interview, when Pound endorses the description of himself as "the last American living the tragedy of Europe." [3] Nothing is so mean-minded nor so wide of the mark as the common British sneer at Eliot and Pound alike that, being Americans, the Europe they speak of is a never-never land. The spectator sees most of the play, and if these Americans can see European civilization as a whole in a way no European can, that is their advantage, and something their European readers can profit from. It is abundantly possible and profitable to read the *Cantos* for the sake of the recurrent passages of elegiac lament; the landscape in Canto 20, for example, can be enjoyed in the same way as "Provincia Deserta," whether the landscape is taken as that of Freiburg or Provence. This elegiac feeling pervades the Pisan cantos.

On the other hand, the Pisan sequence is so refreshing after the score or more of cantos that precede it largely because the poet is here content to let his mind play mournfully over the past without pretending to understand it or pass judgment on it. It is, therefore, all the more discouraging that the next several cantos to appear (85 to 89) thrust us back into Chinese and American history in a way that seems to be sadly familiar. However, it is not so familiar as it seems. The mere look of

[3] "The Art of Poetry, V," *The Paris Review*, 28 (Summer-Fall, 1962), 51.

Canto 85 on the page, especially in the very beautiful Italian printing of *Rock-Drill*,[4] announces it as "unreadable": bold black Chinese characters, in various sizes, are ranged up and down and across, interspersed with sparse print which includes Roman and Arabic numerals, Greek, Latin, French, and phonetic transcriptions of Chinese, as well as English. This is at least an advance on the Chinese History and American History cantos, which looked readable but were not. All the same, what are we to do with it? Most readers will understandably decide that life is too short, and will close the book—though reluctantly, because of the beauty in the look of it. For others, the way out is in a note at the end to the effect that "the numerical references are to Couvreur's Chou King." For, whereas the Chinese History cantos become no more readable if they are taken page by page along with their source in Mailla's *Histoire générale*, nor do the Adams cantos become readable along with John Adams's Diaries, Canto 85, which is unreadable in isolation, becomes, if not in the normal sense readable, at any rate fascinating and instructive when beside Couvreur. What we experience then is certainly not in any normal sense a poem in the English language. On the other hand, William Blake's marginalia to Reynolds's *Discourses* are more interesting than all but the best of Blake's poems; and they require, to be appreciated fully, that we have a volume of Reynolds open before us, beside a volume of Blake. In the same way Pound's marginalia to Couvreur are more interesting than all but the best of the other cantos. The analogy breaks down, however, in that the interest of Blake's marginalia is in Blake's ideas, whereas the ideas of the *Chou King* become interesting only by virtue of the language that first Couvreur and then Pound have discovered for them. It is this that makes Canto 85 nearer to poetry as normally conceived than Blake's marginalia are.

Couvreur offers both a French and a Latin translation of

[4] *Section: Rock-Drill, 85-95 de los cantares* (Milan, 1955).

his Chinese text, and his versions in both languages are very distinguished, as Pound acknowledges by reproducing so much of both. The marginal translations that Pound offers in English—"Our dynasty came in because of a great sensibility," "We flop if we cannot maintain the awareness," "Awareness restful and fake is fatiguing"—emerge all the more salient and memorable from this polyglot context. But the most important of them are carefully embedded in this context so that to take the force of them we have to reconstruct, with Couvreur's volume before us, the whole linguistic situation from which they derive. For instance, between the phrase, "not water, ôu iu chouèi," and the phrase, "There be thy mirrour in men," there come, in column down the middle of the page, three Chinese characters, with to the right of them phonetic transcriptions of two of them and a numerical reference. We have to follow the reference to the page of Couvreur in order to unearth the ancient adage, "Take not for glass the water's crystal, but other men"—a very important prefiguring of what will be the governing metaphor of Canto 90. Any one is at liberty to decide that he cannot afford to take this trouble. But at least Canto 85 is the logical conclusion of ways of writing that in earlier cantos were adopted sporadically and inconsistently. In particular, it represents a recognition by Pound that for him a poem could be almost as much a composition in the space of the printed page as a shape emerging out of the time it takes in the reading; and it shows him also settling with himself, as he had not settled when he wrote the Adams cantos, how far a poem made up of marginalia upon a source can stand independent of that source. Canto 85 has to be read along with its source; there is no other way to read it. Of course the ideal reader whom Pound envisages will no longer be blank in front of Chinese characters; he will have learned from *The Unwobbling Pivot* to recognize such old acquaintances as the characters for "the total light-process" and for "tensile light."

However, it is in Cantos 86 to 89 that our lack of confidence in Pound as a historian does most damage. The plan and the intention are understandable enough: Canto 85 has established, being a digest of the history classic, the *Chou King*, a standard for moral judgments of historical eras; and so in the next few cantos we plunge into the time of recorded history, just as we had to do before and after the Usura canto (45). But inevitably our hearts sink as we face yet more pages of historical anecdotes capsulated and mangled, obiter dicta of past statesmen torn from their historical context, and roll-calls of names from the past. In particular, we may be mutinous when we discover that Cantos 88 and 89 draw on yet another source-book in American history, Thomas Hart Benton's *Thirty Years' View*. There are things of value and interest in for instance Canto 87, but to most readers, even devoted ones, these appear only when they glance back over these pages from the vantage point of the later cantos in the *Rock-Drill* sequence.

We seem to move, from Canto 90 onwards, into a blessedly different world from that in which Polk and Tyler and Randolph of Roanoke play their imperfectly apprehended roles on the stage of nineteenth-century America. Clark Emery defines this world by contrast with the Pisan Cantos:

> In Canto 90 (and those following) of the Rock-Drill group, the myth becomes of extreme importance. We seem to be witnessing the gradual but inevitable victory of the paradisal—a victory taking place in the heart and mind of Pound himself. Throughout these cantos, Castalia appears to be the objective correlative of the place in which Pound, through prayer, humility, agony, comes to union with the process. The union—or the approach to the union—is imagized by the return of the altar to the grove, the "substantiation" of Tyro and Alcmene, the ascension of a procession, and the upward climb of a new mythic component, the Princess Ra-Set. Where, in Canto 82, Pound was drawn by Gea Terra, and in 83 found no basis under Taishan (a holy mountain whose summit is to be achieved, as the city of Dioce is to be built) but the

brightness of Hudor, in the *Rock-Drill* cantos he has moved into air, into light, and beyond. And where, in Canto 80, the raft broke and the waters went over the Odysseus-Pound, in 95 Leucothoe has pity and rescues him.[5]

What Emery calls "the myth" might as well be called, quite simply, "myth." With Canto 90 we ascend from the world of history to the world of myth. It was this world to which we were introduced in the first two cantos of all, and we have never been allowed to lose sight of it altogether. Canto 47, for instance, which took us, nothing loath, from history into pre-history, by that token took us into myth—from the labor of trying to understand history into the relief of transcending it. In cantos like Canto 90, which are based on myth, the ethics that the poet commends are underpinned by metaphysical or religious intuitions, rather than by historical evidence; and yet it is the basic assumption of the *Cantos* that we have no right to our religious apprehensions unless we have taken the historical evidence into consideration.

Indeed, the myths that are useful to us, the only myths we apprehend and enter into with all seriousness, are those that raise as it were to a new power, or into a new dimension, perceptions we have already arrived at by other means. Canto 90, for example, presents as myth perceptions about the use of hewn stone by sculptor and architect, perceptions with which we are already familiar from the memoir of Gaudier-Brzeska, Canto 17, and many other passages. Hugh Kenner, it is true, in what is the most valuable account yet given of the *Rock-Drill* cantos,[6] declares that in them, "the precision of natural renewal has replaced the cut stone of the early cantos." But in Canto 90 marble plays very much the same role as in Canto 17:

[5] Clark Emery, *Ideas into Action: A Study of Pound's Cantos* (Coral Gables, Fla., 1958), p. 109.
[6] "Under the Larches of Paradise," in *Gnomon* (New York, 1958).

> "From the colour the nature
>   & by the nature the sign!"
> Beatific spirits welding together
>   as in one ash-tree in Ygdrasail.
>   Baucis, Philemon.
> Castalia is the name of that fount in the hill's fold,
>   the sea below,
>   narrow beach.
> Templum aedificans, not yet marble,
>   "Amphion!"

Amphion, thus invoked, stands inevitably for music and the power of music, especially as defined in *Guide to Kulchur* (p. 283):

> The magic of music is in its effect on volition.
> A sudden clearing of the mind of rubbish and the re-establishment of a sense of proportion.

For the Canto proceeds a few lines later to precisely "sense of proportion":

> Builders had kept the proportion,
>   did Jacques de Molay
>   know these proportions?

And the masonic associations of Jacques de Molay (accompanied by a reference we have met before, to a shadowless room in Poitiers [7]) look forward to the achieved act, on the way to which music's cleansing was only a necessary first stage. For the achieved act is a stone or marble artifact:

> The architect from the painter,
>   the stone under elm
> Taking form now,
>   the rilievi,
>   the curled stone at the marge

[7] See *Guide to Kulchur*, p. 109.

From "not yet marble" to "the curled stone at the marge" graphs the movement toward perfection.

What the architect makes, however, is in the first place an altar, as Clark Emery points out. For in between "not yet marble" and "the curled stone" has come, along with material familiar from earlier cantos (for instance the Adonis ritual at the mouth of the river):

> Grove hath its altar
>> under elms, in that temple, in silence
> a lone nymph by the pool.
>> Wei and Han rushing together
> two rivers together
>> bright fish and flotsam
> torn bough in the flood
>> and the waters clear with the flowing

Thus, the act is less an artistic achievement than a religious one; or rather it is a particularly solemn and worthy act of art in that it is a religious act also. For Pound's dislike of the Judaic element in Christianity stems specifically from the prohibition of graven images, since whenever religious apprehensions are not fixed in the images that an artist makes of them they are handed over instead to those who will codify them in prohibitions, and so betray them:

> To replace the marble goddess on her pedestal at Terracina is worth more than a metaphysical argument.[8]

And it is for this reason that Pound always wishes the Hellenic element in Christianity to outweigh the Hebraic:

> Tradition inheres ... in the images of the gods and gets lost in dogmatic definitions. History is recorded in monuments, and *that* is why they get destroyed.[9]

[8] *Carta Da Visita* (Rome, 1942); translated by J. Drummond as *A Visiting Card* (London, 1952). Cf. *Guide to Kulchur*, Ch. 30.
[9] *A Visiting Card.*

It is not an uncommon attitude, but Pound's expression of it is uncommon. For instance, in an earlier passage that we encounter as we move from the music of Amphion to the architecture of the altar, the distinction between Hellenic and Hebraic is carried in two words, "Sibylla" and "Isis":

> Castalia like the moonlight
>   and the waves rise and fall,
> Evita, beer-halls, semina motuum,
>   to parched grass, now is rain
> not arrogant from habit,
>   but furious from perception,
>   Sibylla,
> from under the rubble heap
>   m'elevasti
> from the dulled edge beyond pain,
>   m'elevasti
> out of Erebus, the deep-lying
>   from the wind under the earth,
>   m'elevasti
> from the dulled air and the dust
>   m'elevasti
> by the great flight,
>   m'elevasti,
>   Isis Kuanon
>   from the cusp of the moon,
>   m'elevasti
> the viper stirs in the dust,
>   the blue serpent
> glides from the rock pool
>   And they take lights now down to the water . . .

"Sibylla" and also "Isis" seem to come in here out of Thaddeus Zielinski's *La Sibylle*, which argues that the Christianity of the Roman Church "was psychologically prepared for by the cult of Eleusis, the cult of the Great Goddesses, the cult of Apollo, and the cult of Isis" (Emery, p. 9). And it follows, as Emery says, "that when Christian theologians turned from pagan teaching to Judaic, from Ovid and Hesiod to Moses and David, they falsified the true faith."

Of course, there is much more to the passage just quoted than this cryptic allusion. And all of it—the beer-halls no less than Isis Kuanon—can be glossed without much difficulty. What needs to be noticed, however, is that, as we lend ourselves to the liturgical sway of the powerful rhythms, we do not ask for glosses because after a while we are letting the rhythm carry us over details half-understood or not understood at all. However little we like the snapped-off, jerking rhythms of the cantos that try to comprehend history, we need them to offset these rhythms of the myth that surpasses history; we need the one to validate the other, and, although Pound may have got the proportions between them wrong, some proportion there has to be.

Thus, it is not too soon to look back at one of the unattractive cantos preceding Canto 90. We may permit "semina motuum" in the passage just quoted to call up "causa motuum" from Canto 87:

> in pochi,
> > causa motuum,
> > > pine seed splitting cliff's edge.
> Only sequoias are slow enough.
> > BinBin "is beauty."
> "Slowness is beauty.":

"BinBin" conceals, maddeningly enough, the identity of Laurence Binyon, whose "Slowness is beauty" was applauded as a partial but moving truth in *Guide to Kulchur*. But more than beauty is being spoken of, for elsewhere in this canto we have heard (echoing *Guide to Kulchur* again):

> But an economic idea will not (Mencken auctor) go into them
> in less than a geological epoch.

Thus the few who are "causa motuum," by processes as gradual as those by which a pine splits the edge of a cliff or by which the sequoia grows, are men who originate ideas as well as men who create art. But immediately after this, there comes in Canto 87 precisely the same sequence of references as those we have traced, following Hugh Kenner, in Canto 90. After Binyon here, as after "Amphion!" there, come the characters for the San Ku, the Chinese council of three which in the Tcheou dynasty had the function, according to Couvreur, "à faire briller l'action du ciel et de la terre." And then, precisely as in Canto 90, we get the unshadowed room at Poitiers, Jacques de Molay and "the proportion":

> to Poictiers.
> The tower wherein, at one point, is no shadow,
> and Jacques de Molay, is where?
> and the "Section", the proportions,
> lending, perhaps, not at interest, but resisting.
> Then false fronts, barocco.
> "We have", said Mencius, "but phenomena."
> monumenta. In nature are signatures
> needing no verbal tradition,
> oak leaf never plane leaf. John Heydon.
> Σελλοί sleep there on the ground
> And old Jarge held there was a tradition,
> that was not mere epistemology.

The identical sequence of references which, in Canto 90, takes place in the personal time of an artist proceeding to his artifact or the man of affairs to significant action, in Canto 87 takes place on the time-scale of historical epochs. The right ideas about economic morality, and with them the right ideas about artistic (architectural) practice, rise for a few years, are submerged for centuries, then show up again. This is in keeping with Canto 87 as a whole, which deals with peaks and subsequent declines in cultural traditions: the American "paideuma" of John Adams fading through the nineteenth century; the Chinese culture transmitted to Japan; high points of Roman culture represented by Antoninus and Salmasius; of Greek by Ocellus and Justinian; of mediaeval by Erigena,

213

Richard of Saint Victor, and Dante. Thus, the relation between "monumenta" and "In nature are signatures" is a wry one. The allegedly hollow monumentality of Baroque building is indeed "a monument" to wrong thinking and wrong morality; it reveals, symptomatically, as surely as do vegetable forms, a truth, but an unpalatable one. And the phrase "in nature" is to be understood as sardonically opposed to "in history," which is unstated: in nature the leaf shapes, as Σελλοί (the original inhabitants of Dodona guarding the oracles of Zeus), are oracular, they signify a truth; but a phenomenon such as the Baroque style signifies the truth only by being symptomatic of its perversion.

The objections to Pound the historian remain. One may still refuse to believe that the connection between right ideas about economics and right practice in architecture can be plotted down the centuries, as Pound would have us believe. But at least we perceive that the poet is once again in command of his material, not only keeping a calculated proportion between history-material and myth-material but balancing one against the other artistically, by contriving parallels between them.

As for the altar that is raised in Canto 90, it remains to ask what god it is dedicated to. And the last page of the canto reassuringly reveals, in imagery that has been familiar ever since Canto 2, that the God is Dionysus, patron of the creatures of earth and under-earth. Thus, though Clark Emery is right to say that as we move from the Pisan cantos to *Rock-Drill*, we tend to move from the elements of earth and water into those of air and fire, yet earth and the earthy are not left behind. This is very important, and Canto 91 will explain it.

The myth of Canto 90 is not created *ad hoc* like the mythologies of William Blake. Many another before Pound had envisaged stone prodigiously shaping itself and falling into place at the behest of music. Walter Pater was one, in his "Apollo in Picardy":

Almost suddenly tie-beam and rafter knit themselves together into the stone, and the dark, dry, roomy place was closed in securely to this day. Mere audible music, certainly, had counted for something in the operations of an art, held at its best (as we know) to be a sort of music made visible. That idle singer, one might fancy, by an art beyond art, had attracted beams and stones into their fit places.

And in "Apollo in Picardy" Pater does what in his essay on "Aesthetic Poetry" he had asked modern literature to do and what he had seen William Morris as doing already—that is to say, he makes play with deliberate anachronism, making the figure of Apollo out of ancient Greece reappear disguised in mediaeval France. Pater's idea that archetypal figures and archetypal situations recur in different historical epochs (a perception that in his late essay on Raphael he found embodied by that master in paint) is one that, as has been seen, governs much of Pound's writing in the Cantos, though it has been suggested that he got the idea of it from Laforgue's *Moralités légendaires*. There seems no reason why Pound should not have found it rather in these earlier experiments by Pater, for it is likely that Yeats would have pressed Pater upon his attention.

At any rate, the element of cyclical recurrence and renewal, which governs so many of Pound's ideas about history, governs also his choice of myth and his treatment of myth, in *Rock-Drill* as earlier. It informs also his understanding of science:

> The clover enduring,
> > basalt crumbled with time.
> Are they the same leaves?
> > that was an intelligent question.

Kenner comments very aptly on these lines from Canto 94:

> For one of the purposes of the poem, they are the same leaves; since the form persists, a mode of intelligence in-

forming, as Agassiz would have said, the vegetable order.
The visible is a signature of the invisible....

And undoubtedly John Heydon's doctrine of signatures is one
of the guide lines through these cantos; it explains, for instance,
the birds and beasts reading *virtù* (the "virtue" of the herbal-
ists) out of the signatures of vegetable forms, at the beginning
of Canto 92:

> so will the weasel eat rue,
> and the swallows nip celandine

And this is one example out of many. Yet if we see only the
paradisal element in these cantos, if we see their structure of
values as wholly Platonic (the idea of the leaf persisting behind the metamorphoses of all leafy phenomena), there is the
danger that we shall murmur, "All passion spent," and see
Pound coming to rest in a well-earned quietism. And this is far
from the truth; Pound is as ever, in these late cantos, strenuous,
urgent, and (his own word) "unstill."

The reconciliation is in the idea of "metamorphosis," for this
is the idea that combines similitude in difference with an
absorbed interest in the differences. And accordingly, in Canto
90 as in Canto 2, the pagan authority whom Pound wants to
substitute for the tables of the Old Testament law is Ovid:

> He will ... substitute for the Moses of the Old Testament
> the Ovid of the *Metamorphoses*, with his recognition of
> the vivifying personal immediacy of supernatural forces
> and the constant penetration of the supernatural into the
> natural, producing change; his good sense in maintaining
> a separateness of the empirically knowable from the ex-
> perienced unknowable and in accepting the fact of the
> unknowable instead of speculating upon, generalizing
> from, and dogmatizing in terms of it; and his polytheistic
> tolerance so sharply to be discriminated from the dicta-
> torial nay-saying which Pound finds characteristic of the
> Jewish scripture. (Emery, p. 9.)

216

Hence, in the fifth line of Canto 90, "Baucis, Philemon." As Ovid's case of ideally harmonious human marriage they are an instance of perfect "welding together" ("Beatific spirits welding together"), but also, as some have thought, their story represents the still point in Ovid's poem, the harmony achieved out of its flux of metamorphosis.

Canto 91 is good enough to raise again questions about the assumptions that underlie the procedures of the *Cantos* as a whole, for here many of these procedures are inventive, resourceful, and controlled as at few other places in the whole enormous work. Yvor Winters has challenged the basic assumptions of Pound's method perhaps more justly and searchingly than any other:

> There are a few loosely related themes running through the work, or at least there sometimes appear to be. The structure appears to be that of more or less free association, or progression through reverie. Sensory perception replaces idea. Pound, early in his career, adopted the inversion derived from Locke by the associationists: since all ideas arise from sensory impressions, all ideas can be expressed in terms of sensory impressions. But of course they cannot be: when we attempt this method, what we get is sensory impressions alone, and we have no way of knowing whether we have had any ideas or not.[10]

This is admirably succinct. And it comes as a timely warning against supposing that when we have set Canto 90 against Pound's recorded ideas about the Hellenic and Hebraic components in Christianity, we have as it were broken the code of the poem, which we can now throw aside like so much packaging. Moreover—what is more important—the state, in Winters's words, of not knowing "whether we have had any

[10] *The Function of Criticism* (Denver, 1957), p. 47.

ideas or not" is an accurate description of the state of mind we find ourselves in when we have been reading the *Cantos*.

One may still turn the force of Winters's objection. For this state, of not knowing whether we have had ideas or not, may be precisely the state of mind that Pound aimed to produce—and for good reasons. Perhaps by his arrangements of sensory impressions (that is to say, of images) Pound aimed to express, not "ideas," some of which admittedly cannot be expressed in this way, but rather a state of mind in which ideas as it were tremble on the edge of expression. Indeed, this is what we found him doing in Canto 17, when he re-created the fantasy about the nature of Istrian marble which, arguably, inspired the builders of Venice. "Fantasy," as used by Adrian Stokes in that connection, seemed to mean precisely the state of mind in which ideas tremble on the edge of expression. What we get in Canto 17 is not quite the idea of Venice held in the mind of the Venetian builder before he began to build; rather we have expressed the state of mind in the builder immediately before the idea crystallizes. In fact, the idea crystallizes only in the process of building, and the achieved building is the only crystallization possible.

Something very like this has been claimed for another poem of our time, "Thirteen Ways of Looking at a Blackbird," by Wallace Stevens. This poem, according to Albert William Levi, re-creates "that moment when the resemblances of sense and of feeling are themselves fused in such a way as to point to the resemblances between ideas." [11] And Levi quotes from Stevens himself:

> The truth seems to be that we live in concepts of the imag-
> ination before the reason has established them. If this is
> true, then reason is simply the methodizer of the imagina-
> tion. It may be that the imagination is a miracle of logic
> and that its exquisite divinations are calculations beyond

[11] "A Note on Wallace Stevens and the Poem of Perspective," *Perspective*, VII, 3 (Autumn 1954), 137-46.

analysis, as the conclusions of the reason are calculations wholly within analysis.

This is hardly acceptable as it stands: to call the imagination "a miracle of logic" is to play fast and loose with the word "logic," just as speaking of "concepts of the imagination" is to loosen unmanageably the meaning of concept. Yet Stevens in a blurred and extravagant way is expressing what is reasonable enough: we live (at least some of the time) in arrangements of images which, as mental experiences, have a clear connection with those experiences that the reason is subsequently to establish as concepts. And thus it seems possible that Canto 17 and Canto 91 alike illustrate, as does Stevens's poem according to Levi, "the moment at which the ideas of sensation merge (in most un-Lockian fashion) into the ideas of reflection."

At least twice Pound has tried to re-create such moments in his prose. In his essay on mediaevalism, which was reprinted in *Make It New*, he wrote:

> We appear to have lost the radiant world where one thought cuts through another with clean edge, a world of moving energies *"mezzo oscuro rade," "risplende in se perpetuale effecto,"* magnetisms that take form, that are seen, or that border the visible, the matter of Dante's *Paradiso*, the glass under water, the form that seems a form seen in a mirror....

And the reference to magnetism connects this with a passage from *Guide to Kulchur* (p. 152):

> "I made it out of a mouthful of air," wrote Bill Yeats in his heyday. The *forma*, the immortal *concetto*, the concept, the dynamic form which is like the rose pattern driven into the dead iron-filings by the magnet, not by material contact with the magnet itself, but separate from the magnet. Cut off by the layer of glass, the dust and filings rise and spring into order. Thus the *forma*, the concept rises from death....

Here too "concept" is used loosely. For it is plain that, speaking at all strictly, the *forma* and the concept are distinct. In the first passage, for instance, the *forma* evoked is something common to any number of mediaeval concepts; the one form can be, as it were, separated out into several distinct concepts, some belonging to physics, some to metaphysics, some to psychology, and so on. The one pattern informs all these different manifestations. And the point to be made is that Pound in the *Cantos* characteristically aims at re-creating not the concept, any or all of them, but rather the *forma*, the thing behind them and common to them all. By arranging sensory impressions he aims to state, not ideas, but the form behind and in ideas, the moment before that "fine thing held in the mind" has precipitated out now this idea, now that.

The image of immaculate conception ("I made it out of a mouthful of air"—and the pun on conception is central to Pound's poetry) relates the passage from *Guide to Kulchur* to one from Canto 91, on virgin birth:

> Merlin's fader may no man know
> Merlin's moder is made a nun.
> Lord, thaet scop the dayes lihte,
> all that she knew was a spirit bright,
> A movement that moved in cloth of gold
> into her chamber.

But the images of these passages from the prose—especially those of glass and water, and of glass under water—pervade the whole canto. It begins with two lines of music in archaic notation set to words in Provençal; and continues:

> that the body of light come forth
> from the body of fire
> And that your eyes come to the surface
> from the deep wherein they were sunken,
> Reina—for 300 years,
> and now sunken

That your eyes come forth from their caves
    & light then
        as the holly-leaf
      qui laborat, orat
Thus Undine came to the rock,
                by Circeo
and the stone eyes again looking seaward.

The lines of music make the important if obvious point that at the level of the *forma*, the artists of a period are at one with the conceptual thinkers; the *forma* is behind and in the music of the thirteenth century just as it is behind and in Grosseteste's work on the physics of light. And indeed, when Pound in *Guide to Kulchur* wants to illustrate how "the *forma*, the concept rises from death," his example is from art, from the history of European song. In Canto 91 the example is the same; and even a casual reader of Pound will recognize it as the stock example. The mediaeval *forma* that Pound particularly values is re-created whenever the tradition of song (originating, Pound thinks, in Provence) is momentarily recovered, for instance by Henry Lawes in England in the seventeenth century. It is for this reason that Pound's version of the "Donna mi prega" is dedicated "to Thomas Campion his ghost, and to the ghost of Henry Lawes, as prayer for the revival of music." The whole of Canto 91 is, from one point of view, just that prayer repeated. The "queen," the *forma*, has been lost "for 300 years" —three hundred years since the heyday of Henry Lawes, the cryptic reference thus taking up the archaic music at the head of the page.

But it is important to realize that what is lost, according to Pound, is not just one technique of musical composition nor even one attitude toward such composition; what has gone is not a knack nor an expertise, but a *forma*. It is important to grasp this, because this determines what we mean by saying that it (the *forma*, the tradition) is "lost." Pound has protested indignantly at people who credit him with re-creating a lost sensibility.[12] It is lost in one sense, but in another it never can be lost. In the poem Pound says that it is "sunken"; and this is no mere poeticism, it is more precise than "lost" would be. This is proved by the prose passages we glanced at. The *forma* when it is manifest to thinkers and artists, informing their activities, is like "glass under water"; when we say that it is "lost," we do not mean that it is mislaid (in which case strenuous search would recover it) nor that it is gone for good, but that the glass has sunk back under the water so far that it can no longer be seen. The metaphor is more precise than any formulation in prose. The prayer, accordingly, is for the *forma* to rise through the waves again, not right to the surface but to just under the surface—"Thus Undine came to the rock." At the same time the thinkers and artists must be looking for it; eyes must again look seaward. They are stone eyes because the waiting upon the *forma* must be a ritual ceremonious act, the invocation of a spirit or a god; and the waiting must also be an act of art, because this is the only ceremony that can be trusted—the stone eyes are, for instance, those of the marble goddess replaced on her pedestal at Terracina. The eyes are of stone because they are the eyes of stone statues raised, as by the Greeks, to express man's ceremonious waiting upon the elemental energies of air and water. It may be objected that we are given here not glass under water, but eyes under water; but eyes have most of the properties of glass (a man may for instance see himself mirrored in the pupils of another's eyes), together with an active *virtu* in themselves. The *forma* is an active and activating principle; and eyes under water is therefore a more precise ikon than the glass under water that Pound offered earlier in his prose.

The matters remaining to be explained from these lines are those which most clearly relate Canto 91 to other cantos. Thus, the lines "that the body of light come forth/from the body of fire" take up the imagery of the previous canto; here it is

[12] Introduction to *La Martinelli* (Milan, 1956).

sufficient to note the obvious analogy between light, lambent air, coming clear out of fire, and the eyes coming clear as they rise through the water. More important are the lines "as the holly leaf/qui laborat, orat." Obviously the distinction between the eternal *forma* and its manifestations temporarily in act, concept, and artifact is in many ways like the Platonic distinction between the unchanging Idea of a table and its temporal manifestations in this table and that one. Hence the relevance here of a matter much canvassed in other cantos of this sequence, always in images of foliage; the neo-Platonic doctrine of "signatures," by which every particular holly leaf vouches for an identical *forma* reduplicated endlessly as every holly leaf in its generation grows and withers. The holly leaf, simply by being itself, celebrates a spiritual order, just as, by an old compassionate doctrine, the simple man simply fulfilling his proper vocation makes thereby an act of piety—"qui laborat, orat."

There follow several lines making up one of Pound's characteristic rolls of honor, naming those who seem to him to have stood for this truth or for aspects of it: Apollonius of Tyana, Pythagoras, Ocellus the Pythagorean philosopher, and Justinian the law-giver. An odd name out is that of "Helen of Tyre." The locution links Helen of Troy with that of Eleanor of Castile and other Eleanors of crusading and Provençal times; [13] and we know from the earliest cantos of all that Pound has used the recurrence of this name, and of feminine beauty going along with it, as a witty or fanciful analogy to the great theme of an idea (in the Platonic sense), or a *forma*, fitfully manifested at moments in history. Hence the point of renewed reference to the Platonic signatures, "from brown leaf and twig."

[13] George Dekker, *Sailing After Knowledge* (London, 1963), pp. 200-201, points out that the Provençal line set to archaic music at the head of this Canto "appears to be Pound's own pastiche of lines taken from Bernart de Ventadorn & Guillem de Poitou"; and that it was Eleanor of Aquitaine "to whom Bernart's song was directed across the English Channel."

The poem continues:

> The GREAT CRYSTAL
>
>   doubling the pine, and to cloud.
>   pensar di lieis m'es ripaus
> Miss Tudor moved them with galleons
> from deep eye, versus armada
> from the green deep
>   ·   he saw it,
> in the green deep of an eye:
>   Crystal waves weaving together toward the gt/
>   healing
>
> Light *compenetrans* of the spirits
> The Princess Ra-Set has climbed
>   to the great knees of stone,
> She enters protection,
>   the great cloud is about her,
> She has entered the protection of crystal
>   convien che si mova
>   la mente, amando
>   XXVI, 34
> Light & the flowing crystal
>   never gin in cut glass had such clarity
> That Drake saw the splendour and wreckage
>   in that clarity
> Gods moving in crystal

This writing, unlike the opening passage, is uneven in quality. As against the incomparable compression of "doubling the pine, and to cloud," there is, in "green deep of an eye," an apparently unintended echo of a line from Yeats quoted facetiously in the Pisan sequence, and the remembered facetiousness does harm. However, the meaning continues to be reasonably clear. Water (doubling the pine by reflecting it, and transformed to cloud by evaporation) is now invoked as "the Great Crystal," and the Elizabethan seaman Drake, no less than the queen "Miss Tudor" who protected him, is conceived as entertaining, in his seafaring, some fantasy of this kind, of sea water as the signature of transcendent clarity.

Since a cloud is nothing but sea water moving in the sky, the Princess Ra-Set who climbs into cloud (her hieroglyph is over the page—a barge or gondola on water) is rapt into the clarity just as Drake is when he puts to sea. These illustrations, Drake and Ra-Set, are chosen from a multitude of other possibilities; we should attend, not to seeing how they fit in, but to seeing what they fit into, the re-creation in terms of constellated images of the fantasy held in the mind by any man who wants to act or to speak or to think with clarity. The poet is restoring to life the dead metaphor in the cliché "crystal clear." Working with the three elements of water, air, and fire, he builds up, in each of them and compounded out of all of them, the image of the crystal-clear as the ultimate, or nearly ultimate, good. Pound wants to restore to the expression, "crystal clear," and to the fantasy behind it, the imaginative urgency and power that will inspire men to realize the fantasy in act and artifact.

After a brief snatch of roll-call (Apollonius, Ocellus, John Heydon), comes a passage about "the golden sun-boat." This seems to be a description of Ra-Set's hieroglyph, from which we gather that she was herself a goddess, or more appropriately a priestess, of the sun; the phrase loops over intervening lines to hook on to "Ra-Set over crystal" and her hieroglyph. This sets the key for what is the main business of these lines, the movement from sea water to sun, or rather the extension of the fantasy of the one to unite with the fantasy of the other; if we were to lift the experience from the level of fantasy to the level of concept (a lifting which, as we have seen, it is essential for Pound *not* to make), we could say that the idea of crystal clarity is being brought into harmony with the sun-derived ideas of vigor, fecundity, and ardor. If it is remembered how often Platonic thought has lent itself to strenuous asceticism, and to a crude opposition of supposedly pure spirit to allegedly impure flesh, we shall realize how necessary it is to guard against such misunderstanding by bringing in ideas of fertility and vigor. It is for just this reason that Pound, as in Canto 90, makes the presiding divinity in these matters not Minerva (say) but Zagreus-Dionysus-Bacchus. And this explains why the missing element, earth, had to join in the dance of the other elements at the end of Canto 90.

None of this is at all new. The concluding passage of Canto 90, evoking "the great cats approaching," the leopards attending Dionysus answering the ritual call, is only the latest of many passages in the *Cantos* making the point that any invocation of the spirits of air, of perceptions more than usually delicate and subtle, must also be an invocation of the chthonic powers, the spirits of earth and under-earth. Thus it is that at this stage in Canto 91, when the new context has been prepared for them, we encounter themes long familiar from points earlier in the poem. This continual taking up of certain thematic references, each time seen differently because each time in a new context, is one of the peculiar glories of the *Cantos*, and of the poetic method they exemplify. So here:

> "Tamuz! Tamuz!"
> They set lights now in the sea
> and the sea's claw gathers them outward.
> The peasant wives hide cocoons now
>
> > under their aprons
> > for Tamuz

The cult of Tamuz, especially the local cult that centers upon the ochreous stain appearing at a certain season on a river of the Middle East (the stain on the waters being taken by the worshipper for the blood of Tamuz yearly slain afresh) has been drawn upon repeatedly at earlier stages of the poem, and in words ("the sea's claw gathers them outward") hardly different from the words used here. The watching of the estuary for the fearful sign is plainly related to that watching of the waters already evoked in connection with Undine and with Drake; but since Tamuz is a fertility god, and his cult a fertility cult focussed on the equinox, the one reference makes the necessary bridge from sea to sun, from clarity to fecundity. The cocoons hidden under the aprons to help Tamuz by sympathetic magic have also appeared before, and have been manipulated in several ways. To take one instance, in Canto 77 and elsewhere this has been played off against a sort of parody-ritual in a society based on money values rather than on natural fecundity:

"Trade, trade, trade..." sang Lanier
　　and they say the gold her grandmother carried under
　　her skirts for Jeff Davis
　　　　drowned her when she slipped from the landing boat.

(Whether these lines in isolation are poetry or prose is a pedantic question; the relationship between these lines and others from elsewhere is a poetic relationship.)

At this point in Canto 91, between "hsien" on one side and "tensile" on the other, appears a Chinese character. With these clues to guide us it does not matter if we do not recognize the character; we can realize that Pound is appealing to Confucian authority. And again, whether the appeal can be sustained (we are told that Pound's translations of Chinese are idiosyncratic) does not concern us. We can take Confucius provisionally on Pound's terms, for the sake of Pound's poem; and if we do so, we perceive the same bridge being built from the other end—the sun standing in Confucian sensibility for fertility indeed but also for the clarity of tensile light. Pound would maintain—and this is his justification for printing Chinese characters—that the Chinese ideogram can override unnecessary distinctions in a way our writing cannot. Here, for instance, it is not a case of fertility *but also* clarity; it is on the contrary a matter of fertility and clarity together as two aspects of one thing, which is precisely the notion that Pound wants to establish.

Drake now reappears ("That Drake saw the armada"), and after Ra-Set with her hieroglyph, we continue:

in the Queen's eye the reflection
& sea-wrack—

           green deep of the sea-cave
ne quaesaris.
           He asked not
nor wavered, seeing, nor had fear of the wood-queen, Artemis
                     that is Diana
nor had killed save by the hunting rite,
                                      sanctus.
Thus sang it:
     Leafdi Diana, leove Diana
     Heye Diana, help me to neode
Witte me thurh crafte
     whuder ich maei lidhan
     to wonsom londe.

The Queen of the first line is the "Reina" who was besought
to return at the start of the canto. She stands for the *forma*
that is sunken. But she is also Drake's queen, Miss Tudor, and
it seems that Drake was reintroduced to make this plain. Elizabeth, of course, was celebrated by innumerable poets as Diana.
But in any case Diana, at once the moon goddess of the skies
and the sylvan goddess of the chase, is yet another bridge—
as Tamuz was, and the Chinese character—between the clarity
of light ("the Great Crystal") and "the furry assemblage," the
woodland beasts of the powers of earth. The elements of fire
and water, air and earth have by this stage been drawn together
into "the Great Crystal"; and this means (if once again we
raise to conceptual level what Pound so resolutely keeps below
it) that to attain the ideal clarity in act, thought, or artifact,
makes demands on all men's faculties, the earthiest as well as the
most refined. The archaic language of the renewed invocation
to the lost Queen—this time in her capacity as a goddess of
earth, of woods, and of the chase—looks forward to the only
slightly less archaic language of the lines about the birth of
Merlin, which follow almost immediately. But it has the more
important function of presenting, not as an idea but manifested
concretely in words, that mediaeval sensibility in which the

forma was present and operative as in the modern sensibility it is not.[14]

It follows that such exegesis as has just been attempted is necessarily wide of the mark and wrong-headed, for, since it proceeds by raising to the explicitness of ideas matters that the poet goes to great lengths not to make thus explicit, the reading that exegesis offers is necessarily a travesty of what the poetry means and is. Perhaps this is true of all poetry whatever, but it is true to such a degree of the *Cantos* that Pound seems to have had before him, as one main objective, the baffling and defeating of commentators and exegetes. If so, he has succeeded, for the *Cantos* defeat exegesis merely by inviting it so inexhaustibly. The self-defeating exercise nevertheless may be undertaken to make a point of polemic—in the present case to rebut a case made by Yvor Winters. Winters maintains that Pound's procedure is based on the fallacy that, since all concepts arise from sense impressions, all concepts can be expressed in terms of images. Pound may hold this view, or he may have held it once. But since, in the *Cantos*, he seeks to create or re-create not concepts but the *forma* behind and in concepts (or, in Adrian Stokes's terms, fantasies that precede conceptualizing as they precede artistic endeavor), it follows that the erroneous post-Lockian view, if he holds it or has ever held it, does not damage or invalidate his poem.

When "ideas" do come into this poetry, the poetry immediately goes to pieces around them. This happens in Canto 91 in a passage printed in abusive slang, which is as despicable in diction and style as the despicable ideas it promulgates—"and, in this, their kikery functioned." After this disastrous lurch

[14] Noel Stock, in *Poet in Exile: Ezra Pound* (Manchester, 1964) points out (pp. 25-6) that for Pound religious rites originate with the hunting tribes, worshipping Diana as goddess of the chase, whereas primitive shepherd cultures, fattening for the kill, do not rise to religious perceptions of any fineness.

of tone comes a long passage in which the structure of the images comes close to what Winters describes as "more or less free association, or progression through reverie." It should be clear that the structure of the lines so far considered does not answer to this description. That much of the *Cantos* does answer to it is undeniable. But this looseness of organization over long stretches is deliberate. For only if we are presented with references thus disorganized can we appreciate the drama of their gradual drawing together toward the high points of the poem, where what began as random associations are seen to organize themselves into constellations ever more taut and brilliant, and ultimately into the *forma*. This gradual clarifying and drawing together (which has an analogue in social organizations—see Canto 93, "Swedenborg said 'of societies'/by attraction'") can be seen taking place not just inside a canto but over a sequence of many cantos.

The weight of Winters's objection falls elsewhere, however; and, surprisingly, Pound appears to have foreseen it and guarded against it. In one of his latest pieces of criticism, an introduction to reproductions of paintings by Ceri Martinelli, Pound has censured what he sees as a new orthodoxy derived from misunderstanding of a painter, Percy Wyndham Lewis, whom Pound had championed many years before:

> Lewis said something about art not having any insides, not meaning what several misinterpreters have assumed. I had a word in the early preface to some studies of Cavalcanti. Frate Egidio had already written against those who mistake the eye for the mind.

Mistaking the eye for the mind is precisely what Winters accuses Pound of doing. The early preface to Cavalcanti is presumably the essay on mediaevalism, containing a passage that is indeed, as we have seen and as Pound implies, sufficient of itself to disprove Winters's contention. "Frate Egidio" appears in the notes to Pound's version of "Donna mi prega;" he is Egidio Colonna, an orthodox commentator suspicious of the heterodox Cavalcanti. And he appears also in Canto 94, which starts with several references to John Adams and what followed him in American thought about civics. It continues:

> Beyond civic order:
> > l'AMOR.
> Was it Frate Egidio—"per la mente"
> > looking down and reproving
> "who shd/ mistake the eye for the mind".
> Above prana, the light,
> > > past light, the crystal.
> Above crystal, the jade!

A hierarchy is established among kinds of creditable activity. The setting up and maintaining of civic order, exemplified by John Adams, is one sort of praiseworthy activity. Beyond this comes activity under the aegis of love. Beyond that comes "the light," beyond that "the crystal," beyond that "the jade." What is meant by "the crystal" we have seen from Canto 91; it is the wooing into awareness, and the holding in awareness, of the *forma*. What lies beyond or even above this is "the jade." And a clue to what this may be is provided perhaps by an essay on Brancusi, which dates from as far back as 1921:

> But the contemplation of form or of formal-beauty leading into the infinite must be dissociated from the dazzle of crystal; there is a sort of relation, but there is the more important divergence; with the crystal it is a hypnosis, or a contemplative fixation of thought, or an excitement of the "subconscious" or unconscious (whatever the devil they may be), and with the ideal form in marble it is an approach to the infinite *by form*, by precisely the highest possible degree of consciousness of formal perfection; as free of accident as any of the philosophical demands of a "Paradiso" can make it.[15]

If this indeed is the right gloss on "the jade," it seems that last as first Pound is taking his bearings from the art of sculpture.

[15] *Literary Essays of Ezra Pound*, ed. T.S. Eliot (London, 1954), p. 444.

But it is from sculpture seen in its aspect of carving, as making manifest what is extant. In the Brancusi essay Pound is insistent—what Brancusi gives is "not 'his' world of form, but as much as he has found of 'the' world of form." In the last analysis the art that comes of a marriage between the artist and nature is still, for Pound, superior to the art that comes by immaculate conception, self-generated—"I made it out of a mouthful of air."

XIII

Women of Trachis · Thrones · Conclusion

It has been asserted—in passing, as if it required no argument—
that Pound's mind and temperament have always been fundamentally authoritarian.[1] It would be more plausible to detect
in him from first to last a consistent *gamin* compulsion to cock
a snook at authority. The pained tut-tutting of Chinese pun-
dits over Li Po is echoed for instance in the reactions of some
professional classicists to one of Pound's latest translations, of
the *Trachiniae* of Sophocles.[2] Frederic Peachy, while admiring
much, deplores "occasional orneriness, vulgarity, and desire to
épater, ou plutôt se foutre du bourgeois, et du professeur," and
he objects in particular to "Pound's continuous cheapening,

[1] See Martin Seymour-Smith, letter to Editor, in *The New Statesman*
(London), 31 May 1963.
[2] *Hudson Review*, VI, 4 (1954); and *Women of Trachis* (London, 1956).

through choice of words, of his heroine." For that heroine, Peachy says, "is a lady, something which Pound refuses to comprehend." And Richmond Lattimore concurs: "Deianeira, once the gentle lady though nobody's fool, talks through this version like a brassy, cocksure guttersnipe which, in this version, she seems to be. And all the other characters talk the same way." [3]

Peachy expects his protest—"Deianeira is a lady"—"to provoke an outburst of obscenity from some." It should not, for it honestly brings into the open what for some readers is an insurmountable obstacle between Pound and themselves, while for others it is a positive attraction in him, and for others again it is unimportant one way or the other. This is the tone that Lattimore calls "brassy, cocksure," a tone that is very common in Pound's writing quite apart from *Women of Trachis*, though more prominent later than earlier.

All the same, it is hard to sympathize with Peachy or Lattimore. "Deianeira is a lady"—can we believe this? Can Peachy ask us to believe that Sophocles' idea of regal and matronly dignity in any way comports with what British or American usage of the present day understands as "ladylike"? (Lattimore's expression—"once the gentle lady"—gives us another sort of lady, the *gentildonna* of Cavalcanti perhaps, or of Chaucer; but this is just as incredible, since Sophocles was no more a mediaeval Italian than he was a twentieth-century Briton; and to Pound the mediaevalist *gentildonna* may have presented itself as an attractive gloss which he deserves the more credit for eschewing.) As a matter of fact, Pound does at times come dangerously near presenting Deianeira as Mrs. Miniver:

> Something's gone wrong, my dears, awfully,
> terribly wrong, and I'm scared . . . ;

[3] Both these opinions are cited from *The Pound Newsletter*, 5 (Berkeley, 1955).

and once at least this tone carries over from her to Likhas, who momentarily becames a character from Terence Rattigan or from Eliot's *Cocktail Party:*

> And I was most awfully surprised
> and cheered by it.

It is more understandable to object that Deianeira is too lady-like than that she is not ladylike enough.

The trouble is that "tone," which is an indispensable term of literary criticism, inevitably carries, for some people more than others but for all to some extent, associations of class and social status. This confusion is especially current and damaging in relation to Greek and Latin literature, because in the English-speaking world those literatures have been the basis for the education of a governing elite. This is why it is impossible for some readers to realize that when Pound calls Odysseus a "little runt who finally has to do all the hard work," he is not "cheapening" or debunking him but on the contrary relishing and applauding both the character as created and the art that created him. It is this uneasiness with language, not as literary vehicle but as symptom of social stratification, that leads Lattimore to the extraordinary judgment that Pound's version of Sophoclean dialogue, though "brilliant," is unintentionally comic; for the well-established notion that proletarian idiom can appear only in comedy, and to comic effect, is an obvious overspill from language as a symptom of class into language as literary vehicle. In fact, when Pound goes for cadence and vocabulary to the argot of the proletariat, he means this as a heightening of tone, not as a cheapening; and it is not difficult to see, if only one can forget about language as a badge of class, that in strictly literary terms this indeed is how it works.

The classicists who wrote in *The Pound Newsletter* (to whom, and still more to those who invited their opinions, one must be grateful for this invaluable experiment in audience reaction) differed interestingly about just what language Pound had used for his version. Sir Maurice Bowra spoke of "the colloquial American in which it is written." F.R. Earp, whose opinion Pound is known to value highly, spoke more cautiously of "slang, or what seems so to an Englishman who has not been in the United States since the end of the last century;" and T.S. Eliot, of "English and American slang, some of which is already out of date." On the other hand Sir Maurice Bowra and Professor Earp agree that Sophocles' language is "artificial." And so, it seems, is Pound's; as Richmond Lattimore realizes, it is "a special dialect, part hillbilly, part city-tough, part purely Pound colloquialism. . . ." Thus Eliot's implication that Pound has misjudged—"some of which is already out of date" —is beside the point. Pound is translating Sophocles not into colloquial American, but into a special dialect that corresponds to the special artificial Greek of the original. As in other translations Pound uses archaisms, so here he uses slang. Argument must turn, not on his having put together a special poetic diction, but on whether he has put it together out of the right materials; and there is certainly point to Earp's contention that Pound would have had more excuse for slang in translating either Aeschylus or Euripides than Sophocles.

It had been Aeschylus in fact, rather than Sophocles, who had provoked Pound's interest down the years. And Chapter 12 of *Guide to Kulchur*, telling how Pound tried in vain to render Aeschylus' *Agamemnon*, doubtless gives an accurate idea of how, decades later, he worked at the *Trachiniae:*

> I twisted, turned, tried every ellipsis and elimination. I made the watchman talk nigger, and by the time you had taken out the remplissage, there was no play left on one's page.

The interesting thing is that Pound does not suppose that his and others' failure with Aeschylean language in any way casts doubt on Aeschylean *drama*. Even before he translated the Noh plays, as early as the chapter on Lope de Vega in *The Spirit of Romance* (which incidentally provides some very attractive translation from Lope's Spanish), Pound had shown himself possessed of the Aristotelian insight that in drama language is very much a secondary consideration. For others as well as for Pound this Aristotelian position was restated with singular and valuable intransigence by Cocteau in the 'twenties; and in *Women of Trachis*, as earlier in *Guide to Kulchur*, Pound honors Cocteau both for this theoretical *rappel à l'ordre* and for Cocteau's own versions, which show the theory in practice.[4] One might even square with Aristotle—with his idea of *anagnorisis* or "recognition"—Pound's contention that the art of drama (as of the novel also) is an art of "scenario":

> Neither prose nor drama can attain poetic intensity save by construction, almost by scenario; by so arranging the circumstance that some perfectly simple speech, perception, dogmatic statement appears in abnormal vigour.[5]

It is this that lies behind Pound's isolating of one line of the *Trachiniae*—"What splendour, it all coheres"—as "the key phrase, for which the play exists;" and he deals similarly with Cocteau's *Antigone*.[6]

It follows, in any case, that in drama dialogue matters more than lyric chorus or set speech. And yet, whereas the dialogue of *Women of Trachis* has been appreciated only (very justly) by Denis Donoghue (Ch. 13), the choruses have been generally admired. And it is not hard to see why:

> What mournful case
>   who feared great ills to come,
> New haste in mating threatening her home,
> Who hark'd to reason in a foreign voice

[4] See Francis Fergusson, *The Idea of a Theater* (Princeton, 1949); and Denis Donoghue, *The Third Voice* (Princeton, 1959).
[5] *Make It New*, p. 289.
[6] Pound declares in *The Paris Review*, 28 (Summer-Fall, 1962), p. 26: "The *Trachiniae* came from reading the Fenollosa Noh plays for the new edition, and from wanting to see what would happen to a Greek play, given that same medium and the hope of its being performed by the Minorou company."

Entangling her in ravage out of choice.
Tears green the cheek with bright dews pouring down;
Who mourns apart, alone
Oncoming swiftness in o'erlowering fate
To show what wreck is nested in deceit.

Not only is the level of the diction here proper and acceptable in class terms, but the syntactical ellipses can be decoded easily into orthodox poetical grammar, and—what is more remarkable—the meter is nearer to iambic pentameter than Pound had permitted himself to come in forty years. Moreover, there is rhyme, internal as well as terminal echoes ("case" with "haste"), and sometimes rhyme quite luxuriously intertwined, as at the start of this same chorus:

OYEZ:
Things foretold and forecast:
Toil and moil.
God's Son from turmoil shall
—when twelve seed-crops be past—
be loosed with the last,
                    his own.
Twining together, godword found good,
Spoken of old,
          as the wind blew, truth's in the flood.
We and his brood see in swift combine,
          here and at last that:
Amid the dead is no servitude
          nor do they labour

The "oy" of "oyez" linking on through "toil and moil" with "turmoil," "blew" linked with "truth's" leading to "brood" and chiming into a close on "servitude"—no wonder that Pound, here as elsewhere in the choruses, specifies musical accompaniment: "low cello merely sustaining the voice." Orchestration of this richness cannot, however, be sustained in the normal syntax of modern English, and in this passage there is some very gnomic grammar that might well recall for some readers "The Seafarer" of forty years before. Probably it comes not from Old English but from Old Chinese, for it is in the Confucian Odes, which Pound was translating at the same time as *Women of Trachis*, that we find similar grammatical forms in the service of a similarly intricate harmony of chime and assonance.[7] In the Odes, however, Pound seldom permits himself such bravura pieces as in the Sophoclean choruses.

In 1960 Cantos 96 to 109, which had appeared in ones and twos in the magazines, were published together as *Thrones*.[8] *Thrones* got a good press, and this was surprising since even a loyal reader might feel a sinking of the heart as the *Cantos* moved into their second century. Besides, the *Rock-Drill* cantos had seemed in some ways to be foreshadowing a full close to the whole poem. Insofar as the poem had some sort of affinity with the *Divine Comedy* (as Pound had intimated), it had seemed with the *Rock-Drill* cantos that we were moving at last out of Pound's Purgatorio into his Paradiso, since there were passages and whole cantos of an unprecedented serenity, carried in Dantesque imagery of light and flame and the crystal. And it was true that in some of the new group, notably Cantos 102 and 106, the same paradisal quality was clear and haunting. Also it informed and buoyed the Confucian ethics of Canto 99, where the Confucian tradition was distinguished (yet once more) from those other Oriental traditions, Buddhism and the

[7] See W.A.C.H. Dobson, *Late Archaic Chinese* (Toronto, 1959): "One of the most distinctive linguistic features of L[ate] A[rchaic] C[hinese] ... [is] the non-obligatoriness of the use of many of its grammatical devices. ... Statements are made with the minimum of grammatical indications consistent with clear statement. ... It might seem to those accustomed to the obligatory grammatical indications of Indo-European languages that such selectivity in their use would make for ambiguity or lack of clarity, but in practice this is rarely so...." Quoted by W. McNaughton, *PMLA*, LXXVIII (March 1963), pp. 144-5.

[8] Cf. Pound in an interview in *The Paris Review*, 28 (Summer-Fall, 1962), 49: "The thrones in Dante's *Paradiso* are for the spirits of the people who have been responsible for good government. The thrones in the *Cantos* are an attempt to move out from egoism and to establish some definition of an order possible or at any rate conceivable on earth."

Tao. But Pound much earlier in the poem had jeered at "you who think you will/get through hell in a hurry," and even in *Rock-Drill* it had been clear that the Paradiso was not going to be uniformly paradisal. As for *Thrones*, that title, though it had been foreshadowed in earlier cantos, becomes clearer with Canto 97:

> Mons of Jute should have his name in the record,
> > thrones, courage, Mons should have his name in the record.

And when, six lines later, we hear that "When kings quit, the bankers began again," we know what we are in for: We are still going to hear about the iniquities of high finance, which only a monarch can control. And, in fact, we hear about this, not only in Canto 97, but in 96, which is mostly about the disintegration of Rome and the rise of Byzantium; in 100, which deals with European economic history in the eighteenth and nineteenth centuries; in 101, mostly about the American Civil War; and in 107 to 109, which have to do with English history from the standpoint of the great jurists Littleton and especially Coke. It is this last material, much of it quarried from Catherine Drinker Bowen's *The Lion and the Throne*, which is most disquieting, partly because it seems late in the day to have this wholly new field opened up, but more grievously because some of it is wretchedly written:

> > and that slobbering bugger Jim First
> > > bitched our heritage
> > OBIT, in Stratford 1616, Jacques Père obit,
> > > in 33 years Noll cut down Charlie
> > OBIT Coke 1634 & in '49
> > > > Noll cut down Charlie

Elsewhere the old master is still in evidence: as imagiste ("the sky's glass leaded with elm boughs," Canto 107), as coiner of maxims ("And who try to use the mind for the senses/drive screws with a hammer"), and, supremely perhaps, as the paradisal lyrist of controlled synaesthesia:

                    stone to stone, as a river descending
                the sound a gemmed light,
                        form is from the lute's neck
                              (Canto 100)

But no amount of the old accomplishment can make up for
the insanely pointless jocularity of Jim and Noll and Charlie
for James I, Cromwell, and Charles I, or for the Baconian or
worse bee that is apparently buzzing in Pound's bonnet about
Shakespeare. In fact, one cannot read *Thrones* without remembering that the author had spent twelve years in a hospital for
the insane. The best one can do is to remember Christopher
Smart's *Rejoice in the Lamb*, with which *Thrones* has some
things pathetically in common, as when a cat, because it says
miaow, is said to "talk ... with a greek inflection" (Canto 98).
Rejoice in the Lamb, though plainly the product of a mind un-
hinged, is none the less a work of genius and somehow a great
poem.

In a long and bitter comment of 1945,[9] William Carlos Williams declared of Pound, "He really lived the poet as few of
us had the nerve to live that exalted reality in our time." If
this is true, as it seems to be, the implications are demoralizing.
For if the conception of the poetic vocation, of living the poet,
is indeed an exalted one, it was anything but exalted when the
conception was realized in the life of Pound, at least from
1939 onwards:

> When I think of the callousness of some of his letters dur-
> ing the last six or seven years, blithe comments touching
> "fresh meat on the Russian steppes" or the war in Spain as
> being of "no more importance than the draining of some
> mosquito swamp in deepest Africa," "Hitler the martyr"
> and all that—I want to forget that I ever knew him. His
> vicious anti-semitism and much else have lowered him in

[9] Quoted by Charles Norman, *Ezra Pound* (New York, 1960), pp. 412-14.

> my mind further than I ever thought it possible to lower
> a man whom I once admired. (Williams, quoted by Nor-
> man, pp. 412-14.)

And, from another point of view, what reality is more squalid than that of Pound still mischievously consorting with rabble-rousers, and refusing to withdraw any of his rabble-rousing opinions, while he is haled home to face a charge of treason, found unfit to plead, held in a mental hospital, and mercifully released when the charge against him is dropped? When, in February 1949, the first Bollingen prize for poetry was awarded to *The Pisan Cantos,* and the award was upheld through the storm of protests that followed on the floor of Congress and elsewhere, this was enormously to the credit of American society, but it did nothing to vindicate the exalted reality of living the poet's life. For what it meant in effect was that American society accepted and recognized an absolute discontinuity between the life of the poet and the life of the man. Ever since, in British and American society alike, this absolute distinction has been sustained, and upheld indeed as the basic assumption on which society must proceed in dealing with the artists who live in its midst. Undoubtedly, at the present moment of history it is the most humane, and to that degree the most civilized arrangement possible. Still, the privilege that it extends to the artist is the privilege of the pariah; and it is not at all such a solid or exalted platform as some people thought when from that vantage point they fulminated righteously at Russia over the case of Pasternak's Nobel prize. In Russia the artist was found fit to plead, whereas in Britain and America he is found unfit: which conception of the artist is more exalted? In the event, of course, the Russians, though with a bad grace, decided to agree with the Americans that the artist is, or is likely to be, a political imbecile; whereupon Western observers forgave them for having entertained more exalted ideas of a poet's wisdom and responsibility.

And for much of this Pound is to blame. To be sure, he was

out of his mind. But American society has refused to see him as therefore a special case. Nor is this unjust, for madness is one of the risks that the poet runs:

> We Poets in our youth begin in gladness
> But thereof come in the end despondency and madness.

From now on, the poet may take that risk, but society will not take it for him. To be on the safe side, society will treat him from the first as pathologically irresponsible in everything beyond mere connoisseurship and expertise in his craft. For Giorgio Bocca's question to Pound is unanswerable:

> How is it that you who merited fame as a seer did not see?[10]

Pound has made it impossible for any one any longer to exalt the poet into a seer. This is what Pound has done to the concept of the poetic vocation; and, challenged with it, all he can say is, "I'll split his face with my fists" (Norman, p. 465).

Pound's arrogance ("he always felt himself superior to any one about him and could never brook a rival"[11]) has over-reached itself not only for him but for all poets. Poets can no longer believe what they have believed ever since the romantic movement, that arrogance was not just a privilege of their vocation, but a duty. Charles Olson in the fifth of his *Mayan Letters* declares that Pound's egotism, the fact that Pound recognizes only Confucius and Dante as his betters, "creates the methodology of the Cantos" wherein, "though the material is all time material, he has driven through it so sharply by the beak of his ego, that he has turned time into what we must now have, space and its live air." And so, because Pound's egotism in the *Cantos* "destroys historical time," Olson decides that it is "beautiful." Perhaps not many will find the egotism beautiful, on these or any grounds; and Olson himself sees that, beautiful or not, it is neither useful nor true. For, comparing Pound with his contemporary Edward Dahl-

10 Quoted by Norman, p. 461.
11 Williams, quoted by Norman, pp. 412-14.

berg, Olson points out: "they never speak, in their slash at the State or the Economy, basically, for any one but themselves. And thus, it is Bohemianism," for which it is "much too late." Just so. Bohemia is that privileged pariahs' field from which arrogance may be tolerated precisely because its originating there declares it to be irresponsible, necessarily. And so when Olson further objects to Pound that "the materials of history which he has found useful are not at all of use," he ought to mean that the materials are useless because the stance from which the poet regards them is necessarily distorting and untrustworthy, the stance of the Bohemian. Whatever the original reason for the division between the poet's life and the life of society, whether the blame should rest historically on the poets or on the societies they were born to, the gulf between them is now so wide that, out of the Bohemia he is condemned to, the poet cannot truthfully see or investigate public life at all.

This is what justifies a post-Poundian poet such as Charles Olson in wishing to "destroy historical time" and to rule out of poetry any treatment of "the direct continuum of society as we have had it." Whatever more long-term effect Pound's disastrous career may have on American and British poetry, it seems inevitable that it will rule out (has ruled out already, for serious writers) any idea that poetry can or should operate in the dimension of history, trying to make sense of the recorded past by redressing our historical perspectives. The poet may one day be honored again as a seer. Within the time-span of the individual life, his insights may be considered as not just beautiful but also true; and so they may, when they operate in the eschatological time-span of religion, or even in the millennia of the archaeologist and the geographer. But the poet's vision of the centuries of recorded time has been invalidated by the *Cantos* in a way that invalidates also much writing by Pound's contemporaries. History, from now on, may be transcended in poetry, or it may be evaded there; but poetry is not the place where it may be understood.

Thus it may be true that in the *Cantos*, wherever Pound deals with history successfully, he does so in an elegiac, not an epic, spirit. But it is almost inevitable that it should seem so, for history caught up with Pound and passed him even as he wrote his poem. We no longer hope to understand the past through a poem about it; and so the poem can move us only when, in the course of trying to understand the past, it elegiacally celebrates and mourns it. Moreover, in a paradoxical way the elegiac poet annihilates historical time or at least historical succession. To the elderly prisoner gazing from his cage beside the Viareggio-Pisa highway, the Provence of Bernart de Ventadour was no more remote than the London before 1914 in which he had known W.H. Hudson and Cunningham-Graham, Newbolt and Binyon. Both were equally past and gone, and appear so in the Pisan cantos. This seems to be hardly what Charles Olson had in mind when he praised the *Cantos* for transforming "time material" into "space and its live air," yet it makes sense in those terms. And Pound's ranging of his poetry across as well as down the printed page of the *Cantos*, no less his choosing at times to take his poetic bearings from the spatial art of sculpture—these suggest that to talk of "space," or at least of spaciousness as against sequaciousness, is relevant to what Pound attempted and achieved in the best pages of his poem.

Yet it is unsatisfactory if it is pressed at all far. For a poem's existence in real or imagined space can never be on a par with its existence in time, since a poem's existence in time, which brings poetry near to music, is a fact of another order altogether:

> Ezra Pound is one of the most competent poets in our language, possessed of the most acute ear for metrical sequences, to the point of genius, that we have ever known.[12]

[12] Williams, quoted by Norman, pp. 412-14. Williams goes on: "He is also, it must be confessed, the biggest damn fool and faker in the business."

Despite its incautiousness, this brings us down to earth on the word "sequences." Poetry is an art that works sequentially, by its very nature; therefore, it inhabits the dimension of time quite literally. Charles Olson realizes this, as any one must realize it who praises Pound for the fineness of his ear:

> Let's start from the smallest particle of all, the syllable. It is the king and pin of versification, what rules and holds together the lines, the larger forms, of a poem. I would suggest that verse here and in England dropped this secret from the late Elizabethans to Ezra Pound, lost it, in the sweetness of meter and rime, in a honey-head.

This claim for Pound—that he recovered for English verse something lost to it since Campion or at least since Waller—may get more general agreement than any other. And Olson is surely right to point to this achievement as rooted in something altogether more basic and less conspicuous than, for instance, the luxurious orchestration of the choruses in *Women of Trachis*. It is something that has to do with the reconstituting of the verse-line as the poetic unit, slowing down the surge from one line into the next in such a way that smaller components within the line (down to the very syllables) can recover weight and value. When Pound is writing at his best we seem to have perceptions succeeding one another at unusual speed at the same time as the syllables succeed one another unusually slowly. But succession, in any case, is what is involved—succession, sequaciousness. To slow the pace at which syllables present themselves is not at all to escape from the time dimension; on the contrary, it is to emphasize it in a way we are unused to, for only when the pace is slowed do variations of pace register insistently.

The last quotation was from Charles Olson's manifesto, *Projective Verse*, which is the most ambitious and intelligent attempt by a poet of today to take his bearings, and plot his future course, by his sense of what Pound's achievement amounts to—Pound's and also Williams's. The basic distinction in Olson's essay is between the open or projective verse that he is pledged to, and closed verse. By "closed verse" he means (taking I suspect a leaf from the book of H.M. McLuhan), "that verse which print bred and which is pretty much what we have had in English and American, and have still got, despite the work of Pound and Williams. . . ." We still have it indeed, and in the work of Pound himself. For it appears that the Pound whom Charles Olson honors is the Pound of the *Cantos*, certainly not the Pound of the Confucian Odes, of that "totalitarian" poetry to which he vowed himself in *Guide to Kulchur*. Such at least seems to be the burden of Olson's poem "I, Mencius, Pupil of the Master . . .":

the dross of verse. Rhyme!
when iron (steel)
has expelled Confucius
from China. Pittsburgh!
beware: the Master
bewrays his vertu.
To clank like you do
he brings coolie verse
to teach you equity,
who laid down such rails!

Who doesn't know a whorehouse
from a palace (who doesn't know the Bowery
is still the Bowery, even if it is winos
who look like a cold wind, put out their hands
to keep up their pants

      that the willow or the peach blossom
      . . . Whistler, be with America
      at this hour

      open galleries. And sell
      Chinese prints, at the opening,
      even let the old ladies in—

let decoration thrive, when
clank is let back
into your song
    when voluntarism
abandons
poetic means

Noise! that Confucius himself
should try to alter it, he
who taught us all
that no line must sleep,
that as the line goes so goes
the Nation! that the Master
should now be embraced by the demon
he drove off! O Ruler

    in the time of chow,
    that the Soldier
    should lose the Battle!

    that what the eye sees,
    that in the East the sun untangles itself
    from among branches,
    should be made to sound as though there were still roads
. on which men hustled
    to get to paradise, to get to
    Bremerton
    shipyards!

    II
that the great 'ear
can no longer 'hear!

    o Whitman,
    let us keep our trade with you when
    the Distributor
    who couldn't go beyond wood,
    apparently,
    has gone out of business
    let us not wear shoddy

248

mashed out of
even the Master's
old clothes, let us bite off Father's
where the wool's
got too long (o Solomon Levi

    in your store on Salem Street,
    we'll go there to buy our ulsterettes,
    and everything else that's neat

      III

We'll to these woods
no more, where we were used
to get so much, (Old Bones
do not try to dance

    go still
    now that your legs

      the Charleston
      is still for us

        You can watch

It is too late
to try to teach us
    we are the process
    and our feet

      We do not march

We still look
    And see
      what we see
        We do not see
        ballads
other than our own.

This is a poem like Shelley's "Peter Bell the Third," in which
the pupil (Mencius, Olson) honors his master (Confucius,
Pound) at the same time as he castigates and disowns him.
Rhyme, the poem says, is "the dross of verse," mechanical;
and at the very time when China under Communism has

249

mechanized herself, Pound mechanizes Confucian wisdom into rhyme, to present it to an American metropolis of mechanization, Pittsburgh. The metallic clank of rhyme is wittily exemplified in the comical echo of "vertu" in "you do." "Who doesn't know" may be a rhetorical question, or it may be (in a way familiar from the syntactical ellipses of the *Cantos*) a relative clause qualifying the unstated subject, "Pound." Similarly, "that the willow" may introduce either another object for "doesn't know" or else, in a way again familiar from the *Cantos*, the beginning of a prayer, meaning "Would that...", or "Let...." This dismemberment of the verse-line acts so as to drain away the impetus with which a sentence drives through its verb from subject to object; nevertheless, the impetus is never so sapped that the language acts on us in any way but sequentially, in time. Olson's invocation of Whistler, a mocking invocation, asserts that the Orientalism fostered and catered to by Pound's translation of the Odes is as insignificant as the enthusiasm of half a century ago that produced, in both Britain and America, the vogue for willow-pattern and for *Madame Butterfly*. And the echo of Shakespeare's "Let copulation thrive" says that this is a way of debauching taste. For "Confucius" in what follows we read "Pound," who has (so the poem says) abandoned the cause of open or projective verse at just the time when the battle for it seemed to be won. "What the eye sees," together with the two lines following, is a specific allusion to Fenollosa's essay on the Chinese written character, in which Fenollosa analyses a Chinese ideogram into a picture of the sun tangled among branches; it is alleged that Pound in his translations of Chinese poems has betrayed just that "ideogrammic method" to which his first endeavors with Chinese had led him. And the men who hustle to get to Paradise recall Pound's jeer at those who think they will get through hell in a hurry. In the second section the invocation of Whitman, as another whose cause Pound is said to have betrayed, seems to allude specifically to Pound's "A Pact" from *Lustra*:

I make a pact with you, Walt Whitman—
I have detested you long enough.
I come to you as a grown child
Who has had a pig-headed father;
I am old enough now to make friends.
It was you that broke the new wood,
Now is a time for carving.
We have one sap and one root—
Let there be commerce between us.[13]

In Olson's poem Whitman is associated with wood, whereas the "clank" of rhyme is connected rather with metal, partly because Pound had made the association in this early poem, but partly also because of what Olson says in *Projective Verse* when he recommends what he calls "objectism":

> ... "objectism" a word to be taken to stand for the kind of relation of man to experience which a man might state as the necessity of a line or a work to be as wood is, to be as clean as wood is as it issues from the hand of nature, to be as shaped as wood can be when a man has had his hand to it.

In the third section of Olson's poem, quite apart from the specific borrowing from the Pisan cantos ("we are the process"), the spacing across and down the page, if it is noticeably less resourceful than in the *Cantos*, is plainly derived from there. The poem censures one body of Pound's recent poetry, the translations of the Confucian Odes, in a form which by its own procedures honors other writing by Pound, the writing of the *Cantos*.

Olson's poem, by adopting these procedures, achieves a witty compactness, but it lacks intensity to just the degree

[13] In 1913 the poem read "I make a truce" for "I make a pact." See Roy Harvey Pearce in *The Continuity of American Poetry* (Princeton, 1961), where there is a valuable exegesis of a Whitmanesque passage in the Pisan Canto 82. Pearce's essay is reprinted in *Ezra Pound. A Collection of Critical Essays*, ed. Walter Sutton (Englewood Cliffs, N.J., 1963), pp. 163-77.

that it lacks what its author most values in theory, the weighing of syllables in the line and the leading on of the reader's breath from one syllable to the next. As for the case made against the versions in the *Classic Anthology*—that by using rhyme they align themselves with the closed poetry of print and not with the open poetry of the speaking breath—the obvious retort is that, although in these poems Pound often rhymes, he writes them in free verse, and in a free verse where the syllables are weighed, and the varying pace controlled, as scrupulously as in anything else he has written. The freedom is earned and justified by the poet's acceptance of this responsibility, a responsibility more onerous than any incurred by the writer in regular meter. And the verse is accordingly irregular and gnarled and yet sappy, far more like growing timber than like steel rails. As for the rhyme, these are poems that characteristically celebrate the decorous in private and public life, and the verse must be in keeping; rhyme, when it occurs, is one of several concessions to decorum. But there seems no room for any notion of the decorous in Olson's "objectism," any more than there is room for it in the lawless world of the *Cantos*, or in Pound himself when he is without a master to translate, whose example makes him surpass himself. When we turn from the *Rock-Drill* cantos to the *Classic Anthology*, something is lost but much is gained. And the *Classic Anthology* shows, therefore, that Williams was in the right when, to close his sour and justifiably contemptuous statement of 1945, he wrote:

> When they lock the man up with Jim and John and Henry and Mary and Dolores and Grace—I hope they will give him access to books, with paper enough for him to go on making translations for us from the classics such as we have never seen except at his hands in our language.

Translations of Passages Quoted in French

p. 66. An idea is no more than a sensation that has faded, an image erased.

p. 67. More than one feature characteristic of the Latin poets of Christianity is to be found again in current French poetry, and two are striking: the search for an ideal different from the authorized postulates of the nation summarized in clamor for a comfortable, scientific paganism . . . ; and, for what has to do with the norms of versification, a great disdain.

p. 68. Nothing else, whether we are believers or not, nothing else but mystical literature agrees with our immense fatigue, and so far as we are concerned, we who look forward only to a hereafter of miseries more and more certainly, more and more rapidly realized, we want to limit ourselves to the knowledge of ourselves and of the obscure dreams, divine or diabolical, that come together in our souls from past times.

p. 70. ... there are infinite shadings; but one always has to push a theory to its extreme, if one does not wish to be altogether misunderstood.

p. 71. with Gourmont thought is not at all the result of a struggle, an effort; as others give themselves up to indolence, he gives himself up to thinking and he writes as if he were making sport.

p. 75. Among insects the female is nearly always the superior individual. This is not that marvellous little creature, deviant and infinitesimal king of nature, which we should find if we inspected that worm, the bilharzia, of which the female lives, a mere blade, like a sword in its scabbard, in the hollowed belly of the male.

p. 178. ... that the essential poets [as texts for English poets to study] come down to Gautier, Corbière, Laforgue, Rimbaud. That since Rimbaud no poet in France has invented anything fundamental.

p. 186. I have just given a new version of the *Ta Hio* of Confucius, because I find there some formulations of ideas which seem to me of use for civilizing America.... I revere good sense more than originality....

p. 196. These spirits, however, subtle and imperceptible though they are, manifest themselves in the bodily forms of beings; their essence being a real, true essence, it cannot manifest itself in any one form.

INDEX OF PERSONS

INDEX OF WORKS BY EZRA POUND